Comprehensive Emergency Mental Health Care

Comprehensive Emergency Mental Health Care

Joseph J. Zealberg, M.D.,
and Alberto B. Santos, M.D.,
with Jackie A. Puckett, L.M.S.W.

W. W. Norton & Company, Inc.
New York • London

DRUG DOSAGE
The authors and publisher have exerted every effort to ensure that drug selection and dosage set forth in this text are in accord with current recommendations and practice at the time of publication. However, in view of ongoing research, changes in government regulations, and the constant flow of information relating to drug therapy and drug reactions, the reader is urged to check the package insert for each drug for any change in indications and dosage and for added warnings and precautions. This is particularly important when the recommended agent is a new and/or infrequently used drug.

Library of Congress Cataloging-in-Publication Data

Zealberg, Joseph J.
    Comprehensive emergency mental health care / Joseph J. Zealberg
and Alberto B. Santos ; with Jackie A. Puckett.
        p.   cm.
    "A Norton professional book"—T.p. verso.
    Includes bibliographical references and index.
    ISBN 0-393-70224-3
    1. Mobile emergency mental health services.   2. Psychiatric
emergencies.   I. Santos, Alberto B., 1951- .   II. Puckett, Jackie
A.   III. Title.
    [DNLM: 1. Emergency Services, Psychiatric—organization &
administration—United States.   WM 401 Z41c 1996]
RC480.6.Z43   1996
362.2'04251—dc20
DNLM/DLC
for Library of Congress   96-11915
                                                                          CIP

W.W. Norton & Company, Inc., 500 Fifth Avenue, New York, NY 10110
http://web.wwnorton.com
W.W. Norton & Company Ltd., 10 Coptic Street, London WC1A 1PU

1 2 3 4 5 6 7 8 9 0

To my wife, Angie, and my son, Jason,
and to my parents,
Leo and Sylvia Zealberg,
with love and thanks
J.Z.

CONTENTS

Acknowledgments   ix

Introduction   xiii

Part I *Shifting Paradigms*

1 Taking the Emergency Room to the Patient   3
2 Advantages and Disadvantages of Mobile Mental Health
   Crisis Services   16
3 Establishing Working Alliances with Crisis Patients   24
4 When Must a Patient Be Admitted to a Hospital?   30
5 The Role of Crisis Services within a Community-Based
   System of Care   37

Part II *Nuts and Bolts of Program Operation*

6 Professional Staff Development Issues   49
7 Equipment and Space Requirements   53
8 The Telephone Encounter   60
9 Protocol for Field Work   67
10 Protocol for Collaboration with the Police Department   77
11 Protocol for Emergency Room Work   81
12 Legal and Ethical Considerations   88

Part III *Clinical Management/Special Populations*

13 Managing Violent and Agitated Patients   105
14 Managing the Suicidal Patient   113

15 Managing Special Populations: Children, Adolescents,
and the Elderly   119
16 Managing Other Special Populations: The Homeless,
Prisoners, The Mentally Retarded, Agoraphobics, and
V.I.P. Patients   142
17 Responding to Critical Situations with Law Enforcement   157
18 Responding to Disaster: The Charleston Hurricane
Experience   173

Part IV Crash Course in Medical Psychiatry for the Nonphysician

19 Introduction to the Brain and Nervous System   193
20 The ER Patient: Medical History, Mental Status,
and Laboratory Assessments   199
21 Introduction to the DSM-IV Classification System   218
22 Psychopharmacologic Treatment—An Overview   258

Conclusion: Research and the Future   275

Index   279

ACKNOWLEDGMENTS

MANY PEOPLE HELPED in the development of this volume. Special thanks go to Jackie Puckett, L.M.S.W., Vice President of Social Work for the American Association of Emergency Psychiatry and Program Manager of Charleston's Emergency Psychiatry/Mobile Crisis Program (EPS/MCP). Without Jackie's assistance, dedication, and energy, this book would not be possible.

Some of the finest clinicians in community-based emergency mental health care have contributed to this book. We can only name a few of the many. Maria Durban, M.Ed., and Rebecca Newman, M.S., deserve special recognition for writing substantial portions of the section that deals with adolescent crises. Ryan Finkenbine, M.D., and Scott Christie, M.D., deserve kudos for their contribution to the section on ethics. Scott, and Deborah McAlhany, M.A., contributed greatly to the sections on working with law enforcement. Dona Mc-Bride, R.N., was instrumental in writing the section on protocols for field work. Susan J. Hardesty, M.D., and Nancy Carter, M.S.W., wrote substantial portions of the section on responding to hurricanes and disaster situations. We must also thank Herb Bengelsdorf, M.D., and Diane Alden from Valhalla, New York, for without them, this book would only be a fantasy.

We also wish to thank the staff of the Charleston/Dorchester Community Mental Health Center (CDCMHC) and the Medical University of South Carolina (MUSC) in Charleston, whose ideas and responses shaped this work. Special thanks for criticizing, developing, and expanding specific sections go to Mary Campbell, M.Ed., Richard K. Fisher, D.O., Timothy J. Paolone, M.D., David Todd, M.Ed., and Shannon Tyson, M.D. Appreciation also goes to Mary Hughes, R.N., and Jim Zukauskas, M.A., of our program.

Heartfelt thanks to Thomas G. Hiers, Ph.D., Executive Director of the Charleston/Dorchester Community Mental Health Center, James C. Ballenger, M.D., Chairman of the Department of Psychiatry and Behavioral Sciences at the Medical University of South Carolina, and Joseph J. Bevilacqua, Ph.D., former State Commissioner of the South Carolina Department of Mental Health (SCDMH), for creating and supporting our Emergency Psychiatry Service/Mobile Crisis Program in Charleston. Through that program we have gained the knowledge shared in this book.

Every resident physician and medical student from MUSC who has rotated through the Charleston program since its inception in July, 1987, also deserves credit as a contributor to this book. Thanks must also go to Janis Anderson and Sue Sterling Keck, Administrative Assistants for EPS/MCP, and the full-time clinicians of the EPS/MCP program who have gone on to other professional careers: Vernell Brown, M.Ed., Marsha Crawford, R.N., Joyce Byrum-Crosby, R.N., Laurie Clossey, M.S.W., Connie Strickland, M.Ed., Sharon Cox, M.Ed., and Carol Sloan, R.N. We also wish to acknowledge the work of our young volunteers, Bryant Evans and Mikkel Johansen.

In addition, we also wish to recognize the support of Neil Meisler, M.S.W., Paul Biles, Ph.D., John Connery, M.A., John Morris, M.S.W., Acting Commissioner of SCDMH, Kennerly McLendon, Esq., and Alan Powell, Esq., of SCDMH, and Joseph Good, Esq., of MUSC for legal guidance over the years. Thanks must also go to Dave Shiel, Kirby Bond, Ann Thompson, Steve McLeod-Bryant, Mark Westfall, Rob Wendt, and Lou Muzekari and all our friends at the CDCMHC, SCDMH, and MUSC. In addition, we wish to acknowledge the assistance of Charleston's area law enforcement chiefs and officers, particularly Sheriff Al Cannon, Esq., Chief Reuben Greenberg, Chief Tommy Sexton, Chief Chad Caldwell, Deputy Chief Bob Miller, Sergeants J. D. Williams, Kevin Holden, and Debbie Crocker, and all of the dedicated law enforcement officers of the lowcountry's tri-county area.

Acknowledgment must also go to Charles Gilman, M.D., Ralph Shealy, M.D., James Tolley, M.D., Mary Anderson, R.N., and the clinical and security staff of our local emergency departments. EMS services must also be recognized for their ongoing contributions and special recognition must go to the staff of the tri-county Emergency Preparedness. Reverend Rob Dewey and members of the Coastal Police Chaplaincy have made substantial contributions and provided us with support and guidance in times of great need. We are also grateful to the administration of Charleston Memorial Hospital, particularly

Ms. Agnes Arnold, Director of the hospital. We also appreciate the support of James B. Edwards, President of the Medical University of South Carolina. Thanks must also be given to Mr. Lynn Beasley for his guidance and support.

Special recognition must be given to Sally Hein, Ph.D., and the members of the South Carolina HRD Consortium. Their support for the development of a training curriculum in comprehensive emergency psychiatry allowed ideas to flow from which this book crystallized. That curriculum was developed under contract with the South Carolina Department of Mental Health for the Southern Human Resources Development Consortium for Mental Health. The advice, feedback, and encouragement of Dr. Hein and her group are greatly appreciated.

Judith D. Holz, M.A., edited and coordinated the initial project and draft. She is the gifted, intelligent, and knowledgeable expert who truly allowed the work to take shape and become a book worthy of attention. Words are not sufficient to describe Judy's efficiency, loyalty, intelligence, and creativity. Elaine Henry provided invaluable assistance in editing and reorganizing all subsequent drafts and helped with many last-minute details. Elaine was the voice of calm reason throughout most of the harried times.

Special thanks must also go to Regina Dahlgren Ardini and Susan Munro for their encouragement, wisdom, and attention to detail. They proved that there can be no substitute for skilled editing.

Our greatest thanks to the countless numbers of dedicated physicians who have volunteered their valuable time for our program. Their tireless dedication to the community of Charleston is unparalleled.

We must also thank our wonderful families for their ongoing love, devotion, and extreme patience. Without their support and encouragement, this book would not have come to fruition.

We owe much gratitude to all professionals who have ever been involved in mental health emergency work, and to the American Association of Emergency Psychiatry for its leadership and guidance.

Final recognition must go to the thousands of patients and their families who have suffered from the ravages of mental illness and who have endured through times of severe crisis and psychological trauma. We dedicate this book to them, in hope that their suffering has not been in vain.

> For every atom belonging
> to me as good, belongs to you.
> — *Walt Whitman (Leaves of Grass)*

INTRODUCTION

CURRENT BARRIERS to mental health services mirror many of the difficulties inherent in the U.S. health care system. The United States spends much more than other Western nations on health care, yet millions of American citizens do not have general health insurance coverage.

Currently, approximately seventy cents of every mental health care dollar is spent on inpatient care. Continuity of care between inpatient hospital and outpatient community-based services is lacking in most mental health systems. This gap in continuity fuels the "revolving door" syndrome among the mentally ill, in which patients are shuttled between psychiatric hospitals and outpatient care facilities, most of which operate separately and autonomously from hospital systems.

It is no longer economically feasible to support a mental health care system that relies so heavily on inpatient care, which is now the most costly form of treatment. This is obviously a self-defeating strategy in light of current economic restraints and managed care philosophies. Comprehensive crisis programs offer an opportunity to alleviate some of the burdens of our beleaguered psychiatric care system. Many acutely mentally ill patients can be evaluated, treated, and stabilized by bringing treatment directly to patients in crisis rather than by expecting patients to navigate a discrete maze of service options.

This text outlines a model of effective mobile emergency treatment services to help bridge the gap between inpatient, outpatient, and family-based care. It provides a core of information that encourages seasoned professionals, beginning clinicians, and even students to consider quality mental health crisis services in traditional and nontraditional settings alike. It also demonstrates how to use a comprehensive emergency psychiatric service as a referral center to community-based care, thus emphasizing a systems approach that seeks to use the hospital or emergency department as a last resort. This model of care utilizes mobility within the community, cost-effective and efficient clinical care, continuity of care and follow-up treatment, appropriate assessment and triage of clinical problems, and biopsychosocial interventions involving all facets of the community care network. The importance of teamwork, as well as methods of handling administrative issues that impact upon the clinical care of persons in crisis, is also addressed.

In addition, this volume has been designed as a training manual, and so examples are offered along with selected readings. Medical and physiological information is explained where necessary to illustrate the biological basis of mental illness, and the large pharmacologic armamentarium available to treat these illness is likewise discussed. Those with expertise in the medical field may find the aforementioned medical/pharmacologic information to be useful mainly as a review, as these chapters are directed toward readers who may not have medical training or training in psychiatry. However, many sections, including those that deal with responding to lethal situations or disaster preparedness, will offer a fresh view to even the most experienced clinician. This book is not designed to be a research oriented "data" book. Nor is it meant to be a sophisticated review of comprehensive emergency mental health care. The section references were chosen as only one sample of selected readings; they are not exhaustive in scope.

It is hoped that this volume will help prepare the reader to provide state-of-the-art, community-based, mobile emergency mental health services for now and years beyond.

PART I

SHIFTING PARADIGMS

Chapter 1

TAKING THE EMERGENCY ROOM TO THE PATIENT

> Canst thou not minister to a mind diseas'd,
> Pluck from the memory a rooted sorrow,
> Raze out the written troubles of the brain,
> And with some sweet oblivious antidote
> Cleanse the stuff'd bosom of that perilous stuff
> Which weighs upon the heart?
> — *William Shakespeare (Macbeth)*

TORN BY GUILT, Lady Macbeth suffered an intense emotional breakdown, accompanied by vivid psychotic symptoms. When Macbeth desperately inquired whether his physician could provide a cure, the bold doctor replied, "Therein the patient must minister to himself."

Even in contemporary times, patients (and their families) who experience psychiatric emergencies must all too often fend for themselves. Mental health systems may be inaccessible or intimidating to patients in crisis, and often the responsibility for seeking crisis treatment still rests with the patient, even though he or she may be extremely ill, disorganized in thinking, or too frightened to leave home.

This text will present a different view of psychiatric emergency care, one in which the mental health clinician acts as an advocate for the acutely ill patient, thereby providing efficient, assertive, and effective evaluation and crisis resolution within a proscribed amount of time. Hopefully these methods will help guide the reader so that patients, professionals, and families will no longer feel alone in the midst of the horror of a serious psychiatric emergency. A case illustration using some of these methods follows.

> A distraught mother calls and insists upon your immediate help. Her 30-year-old daughter, Julie, who has bipolar disorder (i.e., manic-depressive illness), was laid off from her job as a stockbroker five weeks ago, and in the previous 24 hours she has begun to experience a recurrence of her manic symptoms. The sobbing mother explains that her daughter has been hospitalized on three previous occasions in local private hospital facilities. Her daughter's thoughts have become quite disorganized, and she has been talking in a nonstop fashion since last night, but now she won't converse and only says "no" to her mother's insistence on going to the hospital emergency room. During the last manic episode, over a year ago, the young woman tried to drown herself in the ocean after cutting off her hair. Her mother fears that this may happen again. The patient has lost all hospitalization insurance benefits as a result of losing her job. While the mother is talking to you, Julie locks herself in the bathroom. This frantic mother, who has suddenly become more frightened, wants to know what can be done to help her and her sick daughter.

Typically, those in the helping professions would see this as a case calling for the immediate involvement of police, emergency medical services (EMS), or the probate court system. From the caller's information, we know that this young woman has a documented history of mental illness, is now acutely manic, and is unwilling to seek help. Her history also suggests a component of danger. Should the police immediately be involved, since she has made a serious suicide attempt in the past? The police may be in the best position to evaluate the situation, especially now that she has locked herself in the bathroom. But will the officers involved know much about serious, acute psychiatric illness? What of the time element? After all, there may be many dangerous and potentially lethal objects and substances in the bathroom where she has taken refuge. Should more questions be asked? Or should 911 be called, thereby passing the responsibility for treatment to EMS or police?

Most commonly, these questions would not even be asked in a traditional psychiatric emergency system; an almost automatic reaction would be to call in the authorities. Law enforcement officials would then go to the house and try to talk the patient into opening the door. If there were no immediate danger to the patient in the bath-room, they might just leave. If the patient appeared to be in imminent danger, the police might break down the door and force her out. Or, if the patient eventually complied and opened the door, she might or might not be taken to a local emergency room (ER) or clinic. In the event that she was taken to an emergency department, she would most likely be hospitalized because of her acute manic symptoms, and would probably be sent (perhaps involuntarily) to a public hospital facility, since she lacked health care insurance. If she were not hospitalized, she might not comply with outpatient care. In all of these different scenarios, the traditional hospital- or clinic-based emergency psychia-try system is relatively inaccessible, and may be unable to assist the patient, her mother, or the police unless the patient is willing to go to an ER. Thus, the burden of care remains on the family, the patient, the law enforcement officials, and possibly the court system.

More than likely, most similar situations would end with the patient being hospitalized, that is, treated in a tertiary mental health care hospital setting that might cost the patient, her family, or taxpayers a large amount of money. She would then be discharged to a system of care that might still be inadequate or inaccessible if a similar crisis reoccurred.

In analyzing such situations from the clinical perspective, the first question to ask is always: What is best for the patient? In modern crisis work, the patient is often not the person asking for help and might not even be the person most in crisis at the time of the call. As in the previous case example, most private citizens and, at times, professional care providers will seek immediate solutions to complex problems, often without a clear concept of what they hope may occur. The mother in this situation feels that her daughter requires immediate hospitalization, a conclusion directly related to her experience with her daughter's previous manic episode. Therefore, the mother may feel that the only possible recourse lies in prompt inpatient treatment. Her hope is that her daughter might be admitted or committed to a hospital and, once there, that she will receive care that will "cure" or "fix" this frightening and overwhelming malady. To the lay person, as well as to the professional, problems associated with an acute illness such as mania can seem almost insurmountable. However, given the current state of psychopharmacological science, effective control and maintenance of such illnesses are often possible at home or within the community-at-large. But to achieve this goal, mental health crisis systems must refocus decades-old ideas and procedures.

In the previous paragraphs we have outlined the actions that frequently occur in response to this type of emergency call. We will now propose another solution, given the resources of an effective, patient-oriented, mobile emergency psychiatry service.

In a more accessible crisis program, a clinician receiving the aforementioned call would begin documentation of relevant information on a structured short form or "log sheet" (see sample log sheet at the end of the chapter). The most necessary data would relate to information that allows the clinician to access the caller in case of a break in the communication system: the name of the caller, the name of the person that the call is about, phone numbers and addresses of both, and a short summary of the presenting problem. Because of the overwhelming anxiety that is part of every crisis, the caller would need guidance throughout this information-gathering procedure. If the form is concise and structured, all relevant information should be accessible in a few minutes. Asking structured questions helps the caller know that an expert is helping on the case, and helps to calm the caller's stress and fear from the outset. The caller may try to insist on a 911-style of response, but without evidence of an *immediate* medical emergency or *imminent* life-threatening condition, a 911-type of immediate response could be inappropriate. If a medical team or the police are truly needed (e.g., if the clinician taking the call learns that the identified patient is currently *attempting* suicide), the clinician should direct the caller to the most appropriate resource and then follow up by also calling 911. If, as in our case, the patient has retreated to an isolated environment, then the approach should be to quickly develop an effective plan to introduce the patient to the help and resources that a mobile crisis response can provide.

After excluding imminent suicidal or homicidal behavior (e.g., by asking the caller if the patient is armed or if the patient has made specific mention of wanting to commit suicide), the clinician would quickly continue to gather clear and current information on the patient's behavior, including medications and dosage that the patient may be taking and any substance such as alcohol, cocaine, or other street drugs that the patient may be using. For safe mobile crisis care delivery in today's environment, perhaps the most essential questions deal with weapons, specifically the presence of firearms in the patient's home or immediate environment. In a great percentage of crisis calls, one or more weapons may be in the patient's residence or may be immediately accessible. The presence of firearms and lethal weapons may make the case more difficult to resolve. Whenever weapons may be present, securing the environment through close collaboration with law enforcement agencies is essential, and callers requesting emergency psychiatric services need to understand the rationale for planning such cooperative interventions.

Fortunately, in the current situation (which is based on an actual case), the patient was unarmed, had no access to weapons, and had come out of the room toward the end of the call. However, since she still refused to leave her home, the crisis team decided to evaluate the patient in her own environment. On arriving at her home, they found her to be rather disorganized in thinking, but willing to accept an intramuscular injection of haloperidol (an antipsychotic medication) after a treatment alliance was formed. The patient's symptoms improved slightly after the medicine was given. Her mother, who was a registered nurse, was instructed to administer more oral haloperidol with some benztropine (a drug to prevent side effects such as muscle stiffness) later that night, and to add lorazepam (a medicine used to diminish anxiety or mania and to induce sleep) at bedtime to her daughter's new medicine regimen. Julie and her family were instructed to call the crisis team anytime if there were any sudden changes in her condition, and a home visit was arranged for the following day. On the next morning's visit, the patient's thoughts were more organized, and the team started her on lithium carbonate. Visited by members of the crisis service on the third day, she continued to show steady improvement in both mood and thought while exhibiting less irritability. Four days after the initial crisis call to the emergency service, Julie went to the unemployment office with a friend and applied for unemployment benefits and a new job. Her entire manic episode had been treated outside the hospital. On the seventh day after the initial call, she began her outpatient appointments with a mental health therapist.

The traditional obstacles outlined in this case mirror many of the difficulties inherent in the current American system of health care. The health care delivery system in the United States is itself in a time of crisis. On the federal level, our government is looking for ways to maximize delivery of health care services in a manner that also maximizes cost effectiveness. America's *mental* health care system is in a parallel state of crisis. For decades, public mental health has focused on deinstitutionalizing the population that has required long-term care (i.e., severely and persistently mentally ill [SPMI] patients who suffer from illnesses such as schizophrenia or severe mood disorders). Emphasis has shifted from the traditional state hospital to a community-based treatment approach. However, little energy has been focused on prevention of serious illness relapse, or on creating systems that take treatment directly to patients and maximize their wellness. Consequently, many misguided efforts have led to a system of mental health care built on an expansion of costly, community-based, *inpatient* services (i.e., hospitals). Yet, it is no longer economically feasible to support a mental health care system that relies so heavily on inpatient management of severe psychiatric disorders. From the offices of the state mental health commissioners to those of community mental health care centers, mental health professionals are under constant siege in their attempts to maintain a balance between delivery of quality clinical services and accountability for public funds. Unfortunately, with the current emphasis on tertiary inpatient care of psychiatric patients, the mental health system is relying on the most costly form of treatment, which seems self-defeating in light of current economic constraints.

Comprehensive crisis programs offer a major way to alleviate numerous burdens upon a beleaguered psychiatric care system. Many acutely mentally ill patients can be evaluated, treated, and stabilized in walk-in crisis clinics or ERs, or by bringing treatment directly to patients in crisis who are unable to come to a treatment center at all. However, current mental health practitioners may not be so eager to embrace what may seem a risky and radical approach to medical, mental health, and psychosocial service delivery. In public mental health care, the thinking for many decades has centered around a system of community mental health clinics backed up by state hospitals and other inpatient resources. In other words, the patient has been expected to come to the centers for outpatient treatment and if the *patient* fails, then hospital facilities become the recipient of this failed endeavor. Usually, the responsibility for this failure is placed squarely on the shoulders of the patient. Terms such as "noncompliant" or "treatment resistant" have often been applied to explain this phenomenon. It is difficult enough for the chronically ill patient to understand

the complicated illness responsible for his or her multiplicity of every-
day problems, much less to be prepared to participate in an equally
complex treatment plan. How many clinicians can truly say that they
completely understand the nature of paranoid schizophrenia or have
successfully devised and managed a comprehensive program of treatment around this devastating illness? Some patients with severe depression find it almost impossible to get out of bed in the morning, yet
their illness may be exacerbated by missed appointments or dropout
from office-based care. Severe depression makes it impossible for some
patients to function, or think, so it is not uncommon for these sick
patients to find clinic-based treatment inaccessible. Well-trained crisis
experts must sometimes spend hours on a phone negotiating an admission for someone who is acutely mentally ill. Imagine what it is like for
a patient in crisis who tries to access the complicated mental health
care system without such advocacy!

What are the expectations of our current system and its demands
on clinicians, patients, families, employers, colleagues, spouses, children, and a multitude of other individuals touched by one person's
psychiatric disorder? As helpers, are our expectations compatible with
the realities that our patients must face 24 hours a day? Can a system
that requires people to access their own care through a maze of limited, expensive, and often inconvenient services really care adequately
for patients with serious syndromes affecting the normality of the
brain? Crisis services must not only provide quality clinical care, but
must also be accessible to the sickest patients in the mental health care
system.

The following example further helps to illustrate the need for nontraditional, creative treatment considerations in developing crisis oriented care.

Sam, a middle-aged man, had been treated by various crisis systems
around the country for two and a half decades. Sam began life with the
proverbial silver spoon firmly secure in his infant mouth. His parents
were both college-educated and financially successful. Indeed, his father
had piloted the family business into a million dollar operation. Sam was
the recipient of much love, attention, and financial security. He had
many friends, was intelligent, hardworking, and enormously talented.
Prior to college, he had been an excellent student and spoke several
languages. His father's business, as well as a large trust fund, secured his
future after graduation. In his personal life, there was a young lady of

equal social standing. He embarked upon a course of study at an ivy league university. The future held great promise.

Unfortunately, schizophrenia entered this ideal picture. To understand its pervasive influence, one only needs to consider the next year of Sam's life. Unable to concentrate on assignments, he failed to turn in required college work. Often confused about time and place, he began to miss class as well as important conferences with advisors and faculty. Unable to understand what was happening, Sam could only trust his own senses, his own understanding of the realities of his situation. He began to feel that others were misunderstanding his position and that people he once trusted were for some reason aligning themselves against him. What other explanation could there be? No one understood what he was saying or the confusion he was feeling. The worse his confusion became, the stronger was his need to make some sense of these events. When he tried to explain to his family that everyone at school seemed bent on destroying him, they seemed to pity him, which only enraged him. He was unable to see why they could not understand. He became angry and rejected what he felt were attempts to mislead him. For some reason, even his family seemed to be part of this plot to bring him down. He began to feel isolated and, even worse, harried. Everyone seemed to misinterpret everything he said. His relationship with his girlfriend ended in anger and accusation. Finally, he was asked to leave school and not return. Desperate to maintain his independence, he enlisted in the United States Army and was promptly sent to the battlefields of Vietnam. After a short and painful tour of duty, he secured a medical discharge because of worsening "nerves" and returned to the United States.

Then began a series of multiple, involuntary hospitalizations in private and university hospitals, during which time he received some of the best care available. However, as his illness worsened, his insurance coverage ran out, and he was hospitalized in numerous publicly funded facilities, including Veterans' Administration and state hospitals. Each time he was discharged, he developed severe extrapyramidal side effects from his medicines (e.g., severe stiffness and restlessness), and because of these side effects he stopped taking his medicines. Then, as the severe paranoia returned, he would not attend outpatient follow-up. At one point, he isolated himself inside a motel room and lived there for a period of several months. Finally, out of desperation, and as a result of his increasing social withdrawal and paranoia, his aunt had him move in with her and her family after his discharge from the state hospital. His psychotic paranoid delusions worsened. Several days after his arrival, a crisis developed. Sam had locked himself in his bedroom, fearing that government surveillance cameras were outside his house. He was no longer taking any oral medicine since he was experiencing severe Parkin-sonian symptoms (i.e., severe tremor and shaking, and rigidity of his body) from his depot antipsychotic drug (i.e., medicine that is given in shot form every few weeks). His aunt did not know what to do. She called the mental health center, which then referred her to the crisis service.

After ascertaining that Sam had no weapons, and after collecting answers to the structured "log sheet" questions, a team of two clinicians was dispatched to the home of Sam's aunt. At first Sam was unrespon-sive to the team's communication attempts and would not unlock his bedroom door or agree to come out. However, the team gently kept up a running dialogue designed to win a therapeutic alliance with him. In-deed, if nothing else had been achieved with this first visit, a simple introduction to the patient and an explanation of the presence of profes-sionals in his home would have been considered a great success.

Building on their presence in the home as a medical team (one of the clinicians was a psychiatrist), the crisis team addressed concerns about the patient's severe extrapyramidal side effects (e.g., stiffness and shak-ing) as reported by the family. No mention was made of any perceived psychiatric problems in this initial introduction. The patient seemed to respond when asked to describe his symptoms through the door. After further questioning and voiced empathy for the patient's obvious pain and suffering, the team convinced the patient that they would be re-sponsive to his need for successful treatment of his symptoms, and he agreed to a physical examination by the team psychiatrist. After 30 min-utes of conversation and much reassurance through Sam's door, Sam allowed the team to come into his bedroom for the examination.

After a discussion in which the physician explained possible treat-ments, and after Sam became convinced that the physician "knew some-thing about muscarinic receptors in the brain," they agreed to a trial of medicine for the aforementioned side effects. Furthermore, after several home visits, Sam was feeling considerably improved and allowed further medication management and ultimate referral to the local mental health center for follow-up treatment. The team made these arrangements for him. When Sam balked on his first follow-up, the team also made several phone calls and another home visit with his newly assigned case manager to insure that Sam did not "fall through the cracks" again.

The cases of Sam and Julie illustrate how to circumvent several pitfalls inherent in traditional emergency mental health treatment. In the first illustration, a bipolar manic patient clearly was in relapse, but refused to go into an institutional setting for treatment. In that case, if mobile crisis services were not available, she might have gone untreated or been brought to a clinic or ER by the police or sheriff and subsequently hospitalized. Mobilization of care allowed the patient to be evaluated and treated within her home. The second case vignette reveals recurrent cycles of crises, interspersed with repeated hospitalizations for a young man with schizophrenia. After years in this type of treatment system, the patient still found traditional care inaccessible to him, especially when in crisis. Home-based crisis services allowed a trust to develop between the patient and the mental health treatment system, thus encouraging the patient to see the system as an ally.

Unfortunately, a great emphasis still remains on treating patients with chronic mental illness in state hospital settings or other inpatient settings. Such a system may help stabilize their acute illness, but does little to help control the patient's symptoms after discharge to the "real world." Upon a predictable relapse, patients with severe and persistent mental illness often will not, or cannot, attend follow-up visits in clinics. Families are then powerless to access care for their loved one, and may need to pursue legal means to have the family member brought in for treatment. After the humiliation of being brought involuntarily to an ER for evaluation, the patient is then frequently "committed" to a tertiary hospital setting, thus perpetuating the cycle. Institution-based inpatient care does little to break this unproductive and expensive pattern. Care that can be taken directly to patients who are in crisis or relapse is often an effective means of breaking the cycle of crisis-rehospitalization-crisis. In addition, this recurrent cycle becomes untenable for concerned family members who may have been living and interacting with the patient and the patient's illness for many years. Families may begin to feel an almost adversarial relationship developing with those commissioned to treat the illness of a family member.

As the aforementioned case examples illustrate, mobile crisis response teams can bring economical, time-efficient, and clinically effective care to patients in need, as well as help to diminish the guilt and anxiety of families directly responsible for the care of their mentally ill family member.

As the era of "managed care" begins to dawn, the use of mobile crisis programs (and other community-based treatments) as a resource in the treatment of the mentally ill begins to make more economic and clinical sense than ever before.

SUGGESTED READINGS

Ellison, J. M., Hughes, D. H., & White, K. A. (1989). An emergency psychiatry update. *Hospital and Community Psychiatry, 40,* 250–260.

Henggeler, S. W., Santos, A. B. (Eds). (in press). *Innovative models of mental health treatment for "difficult to treat" clinical populations.* Washington, DC: American Psychiatric Association.

Puryear, D. A. (1992). Proposed standards in emergency psychiatry. *Hospital and Community Psychiatry 43,* 14–15.

Weissberg, M. (1991). Chained in the emergency department: The new asylum for the poor. *Hospital and Community Psychiatry, 42,* 317–319.

Santos, A. B., Henggeler, S. W., Burns, B. J., Arana, G. W., & Meisler, N. (1995). Research on field-based services: Models for reform in the delivery of mental health care to difficult clinical populations. *The American Journal of Psychiatry, 152*(8), 1111–1123.

CD/CMHC Case #: _____

Caseworker: _____

M.D.: _____

Agency: _____

MOBILE CRISIS LOG SHEET

am

Date: _____ Start Time: _____ pm   Referring Agency: _____

Patient Name: _____   Caller/Contact: _____

(last, first, middle)   Relationship to Patient: _____

Address: _____   Address: _____

_____   Phone: _____ Relationship: ___

Phone: _____ Race/Sex: _____   Insurance: _____

(co. name, address)

Age: _____ DOB: _____ Marital Status: _____

_____

(policy #)

Problem: _____

_____

_____

_____

_____

_____

_____

_____

Is or has patient ever been: (write "no" or specify if present)

Suicidal: _____

_____

_____

Homicidal/Dangerous: _____

_____

_____

Weapons: _____

Psychotic: _____

Hospitalizations/Prior Outpatient Treatment: _____

_____

Abusing ETOH/Drugs: _____

Medications (both medical and psychiatric): _____

_____

_____

Medically Ill: _____

Legal Charges: _____

14

(over)

Problem discussed with therapist and/or supervisor? (If no, why not? If so, why is therapist unable to handle crisis?)_____

_____

Is patient willing to be seen?   Yes ____   No ____   Where: _____
Who will stay with patient until our arrival? _____
Type of Contact: MOBILE / PHONE   (circle one)

Contact Date: _____ Time Out: _____pm Police involved: _____
                                                    am
Assessment: _____

_____

_____

_____

_____

_____

_____

Axis I: _____ Axis I: _____
Axis II: _____ Axis III: _____
DISPOSITION: Admit to: _____ Voluntary / Involuntary   (circle one)
                    Other: _____
Plan: _____

_____

_____

_____

Mobile Crisis Follow-up Plan: _____

_____

_____

                                                              am
Clinician Signature: _____ Time Case Ended: _____pm
M.D. Involved: _____ Clinicians Involved: _____

IMPLEMENTATION OF FOLLOW-UP PLAN

What has been done: _____

_____

_____

Clinician Signature: _____ Date: _____

Chapter 2

ADVANTAGES AND DISADVANTAGES OF MOBILE MENTAL HEALTH CRISIS SERVICES

To see sad sights moves more than to hear them told.
— *William Shakespeare (The Rape of Lucrece)*

WE HAVE ALLUDED to the fact that having a fully mobile psychiatric emergency service can offer many benefits to clinicians, patients, families, and communities. In this chapter we will further explore the advantages of having a completely freestanding, community-based crisis program.

GENERAL BACKGROUND

The concept of treating the psychiatric patient in the community is not a new idea. In a book published in the 1930s, Querido, a Dutch psychiatrist, described the use of home visits in treating mentally ill patients in Amsterdam. In the United States, mobile crisis teams have existed since the 1970s in numerous places such as Peoria, IL, Valhalla, NY, and Madison, WI. There are many advantages to having mobile

---

We thank Richard K. Fisher, D.O., for his contribution to this chapter.

crisis response teams. Psychiatrically ill patients are often too anxious, fearful, agitated, or depressed to come into traditional treatment settings. In addition, ER treatments are expensive and time-consuming, and it is not unusual for patients in crisis to wait for hours before being evaluated and treated. For the patient in great distress, this may be unbearable. Being seen in their own environment makes patients feel more at ease, and helps the crisis professional maximize the patient's home and community resources. Mobile crisis services are often staffed by interdisciplinary teams of psychiatrists, nurses, social workers, psychologists, and counselors. Team members are available 24 hours a day, 365 days a year. Such a model is completely in line with managed care philosophies and the new directions in health care reform, which emphasize efficient, cost-effective, and "user-friendly" treatment services.

PROFESSIONAL TRAINING

Mobile crisis services are excellent training experiences for health care professionals. Many psychiatric emergency services operate inside the walls of a clinic or ER, where the environment is busy and chaotic, yet focused. Evaluations in an ER or clinic can reveal only a small part of a patient's story. Directly witnessing the plight of a homeless man with schizoaffective disorder can educate professionals about the sad realities of people with severe mental illnesses and awaken their zeal and compassion. Mobile crisis work is innately challenging and promotes a wide range of skills, such as systems analysis and problem solving. The professional encounters a wide range of situations and learns to assist patients effectively and efficiently.

Emergency calls requesting outreach services can come from numerous sources within the community, including area emergency rooms and clinics, the police, EMS, the Department of Social Services, local probation and parole boards, probate court, family members, landlords, private individuals, and other health professionals. It is not uncommon for teams to be called to private homes, group homes, shelters for the homeless, hotels, street corners, malls, residential care facilities, public buildings, open recreation areas, or even the back seats of police cars. The entire community serves as the team's "office," and each situation provides an opportunity for creative treatment planning.

There is a certain degree of myopia in simply training a mental health professional or medical professional inside institutional walls. First, it provides the professional in training with a simplistic view of mental illness. Patients come into hospitals, get medical and psychological attention, and then go home. Often, people return again and again. Without the benefit of seeing what goes on in a patient's life outside the hospital, mental health professionals think that a patient might simply be "noncompliant with treatment." However, if a crisis clinician travels through miles of urban streets to the patient's home or over several bridges and islands to the patient's shack or over a mountain to the rural dwelling of a patient where there is no pharmacy or transportation for miles, or witnesses the holes in a patient's roof, the noise of the neighbor's stereo, or the danger from the crack dealer selling his drugs next door, a different view of the patient and his or her life develops.

Professionals need to learn how to treat patients in the least restrictive settings, how to interface with police, EMS, sheriff's departments, child protective services, schools, and job sites. Patients' families need education and guidance. Getting outside "where life exists in its purest form" makes for a meaningful educational experience. Also, if hospitalization can be prevented or admission to an ER can be avoided by making a mobile response, then this is truly the best way to educate professionals to all the concepts of managed care. A mobile response provides care that is user friendly, prevents costly ER or hospital admission, and is the most accessible care option.

PUBLIC EDUCATION

One individual in crisis has an impact on the lives of others in the community, whether they are friends, family, neighbors, coworkers, or passersby. A community-oriented mobile crisis team is able to evaluate those affected and can provide reassurance. Additionally, because of continuing misperceptions about mentally ill persons, those around the patient may become fearful, rejecting, and even hostile to the one who is ill. Addressing these concerns immediately may prevent a lifetime of prejudicial treatment by those whom the patient most desperately needs. Reassurance is most effective when it is delivered at the site of a crisis; such reassurance often prevents rejection of patients by members of their support system, a frequent problem for ERs.

Mobile crisis teams are often highly visible by virtue of their work with patients in crisis in the community. The resultant publicity allows for better public education about mental health issues and resources. A high-profile mobile crisis team can take advantage of every encounter with the media to teach about mental illness and the needs of mentally ill persons, and can inform the public about local mental health resources. The mobile crisis team is obviously better suited to this task than an emergency department.

ACCESS

For many patients with limited finances, a trip to the emergency room or community mental health center is no small undertaking. For patients with severe depression, it may seem impossible to get out of bed and leave the house. Patients in crisis, even if willing to seek help, are often unable to navigate the complexities of coordinating appointments, arranging rides, and obtaining prescribed medication. The situation becomes more complex in areas where public transportation provides sporadic service or is nonexistent. A dedicated team of mental health professionals who are able to assess the patient on site and begin treatment immediately may circumvent this difficulty. This increased accessibility leads to enhanced delivery of services. The team may not necessarily provide transportation to ERs, hospitals, or a shelter if indicated, or all needed services at the scene, but often can operate to facilitate these services.

ACCURACY OF ASSESSMENTS

To be thrust into the controlled chaos of an emergency department when one is already psychologically decompensating may not only worsen the condition but also alter its appearance. For this reason, observing the patient at the site and moment of a crisis allows for the most complete assessment with the least trauma to the patient. Important clues can be found within the patient's crisis environment, such as the presence of suicide notes, empty wine bottles, medication containers, or IV drugs and needles. Often, observations of neighbors, bystanders, or coworkers are lost or delayed when the patient is extracted from the site by law enforcement personnel or family members.

Most people also feel more secure in their own home environment.

A patient may be mildly anxious at home but may become quite agitated in the confines of a busy emergency department or clinic. A home visit can often avoid such behavioral exacerbations and assess how well the patient is functioning in the real world. Mobile emergency services may hear reports that a patient is totally unable to care for herself, but on visiting the patient's home, the clinical team may find a neat, clean house, with the patient preparing a meal. This type of data cannot be ascertained in an ER or clinic setting.

EFFICIENCY AND EFFECTIVENESS

Treatment of patients early in a decompensation may prevent them from needing emergency hospitalization. Many patients are reluctant to go to a mental health center or emergency department early in the course of an exacerbation, often because of unfortunate past experiences, paranoia, or thought disorganization. Patients generally are more receptive to evaluation in their home or on neutral ground. The outreach response of the mobile crisis team allows treatment to be initiated early, reestablishes the patient's connection with the local mental health care system, and reassures the patient, family, or support system, and prevents emergency hospitalization.

COST-EFFECTIVENESS

Mobile crisis teams have the potential to reduce costs in several ways. Mobile visits may circumvent the need for an ER or clinic visit, or even for inpatient hospitalization. This saves significant amounts of health care expenses. Law enforcement personnel are often first responders in crisis calls and are often required to accompany patients waiting in emergency departments. The presence of the mobile crisis team can allow police officers to return to duty more quickly. In some cases, the police do not even need to respond. Other potential savings can be realized through reduced court costs, shorter emergency room and hospital use, and decreased family burden (e.g., a family member may have to take time off from work or borrow transportation to get their relative into a clinic or ER).

Mobile teams have low overhead costs. ER-based programs must contribute to hospital and other operating costs. Inside traditional medical settings, space is a cost factor. Mobile programs need minimal office space as they utilize all the existing space of the community, including homes, shelters, ERs, clinics, waiting rooms, phone booths, restaurants and fast-food places, police stations, schools, retail stores, motels, or private businesses.

LIAISON WITH OTHER AGENCIES

Because of its mobility and visibility, a mobile crisis team can function as a liaison with all public and private community mental health resources, and thus can facilitate appropriate referrals for social, medical, and legal assistance. The team is uniquely equipped to access and initiate referral to community agencies and can provide more effective interventions to people in crisis. A mobile team will often interface with every important community organization. These resources can be used for effective crisis intervention.

DISADVANTAGES AND LIMITATIONS

Although it is a worthy goal to treat patients in their home settings, this is not always feasible or even desirable. For instance, the sudden onset of agitation and visual hallucinations in a 75-year-old woman with no history of psychiatric problems indicates the probable onset of delirium. This can be a complicated syndrome that is basically the central nervous system's way of indicating that a potentially *life-threatening* medical illness is present. Potentially delirious patients require thorough emergency room evaluation and admission to medical units of a hospital. Therefore, a call concerning such a hypothetical case would require that the patient be referred or "triaged" to an ER for continuity of care.

Many situations are dangerous. Strict adherence to safety and security protocols and guidelines insure the safety of crisis clinicians, but anxiety can run high in dealing with barricade situations, jumpers, or the caller who has "a gun in his ear." The management of anticipatory anxiety is important for clinicians.

Sometimes staff are limited in number and unavailable. Like every type of emergency program in existence, requests for assistance need to be triaged so that the most important and urgent ones are handled first. No one likes to wait, especially in a psychiatric emergency. Sometimes people must be triaged to a clinic or ER until the crisis team can be available.

As has been noted, there are real advantages to interfacing with every program in the community; however, because the team doesn't "belong" to an institution per se, they can be seen as "outsiders," which can be stressful for clinical and administrative staff. Regular meetings with referral sources, police, academic departments, ER directors, mental health clinic directors, and others will enhance the working relationships that are so necessary in diminishing any sense of separateness from the clinical care structures.

Another disadvantage may be that constant system tuning and role definition must be attended to. When a clinical service provides assistance to an entire community, and that service is high in quality, the community both wants and expects more. For instance, outlying counties may request assistance, another resource might demand that the program transport a handicapped patient, police officers might not understand why a crisis clinician can't just simply don a Kevlar bulletproof vest, walk up to a man armed with a Sig-Sauer 9 mm handgun, and take the gun away from him. Sometimes people expect magic. Sometimes magic isn't possible. This can lead to disappointment. To underpromise and overdeliver is a fine philosophy for a mobile crisis system. This is not an easy task.

In spite of these examples of difficulties, going to where the patient is still seems the most meaningful approach to rapid crisis intervention. Throughout the following sections, typical interventions will be explored in detail, and suggestions given about how to perform these interventions, under what circumstances, and by which methodology.

SUGGESTED READINGS

Andreoli, A. V., Muehlebach, A., Gognalons, M., et al. (1992). Crisis intervention response and long-term outcome: A pilot study. *Comprehensive Psychiatry*, 33(6), 388–396.

Bengelsdorf, H., & Alden, D. C. (1987). A mobile crisis unit in the psychiatric emergency room. *Hospital and Community Psychiatry*, 38, 662–665.

Chiu, T. L., & Primeau, C. (1991). A psychiatric mobile crisis unit in New York City: Description and assessment, with implications for mental health care in the 1990s. *International Journal of Social Psychiatry*, 37(4), 251–258.

Cohen, N. L. (1990). *Psychiatry takes to the streets*. New York: Guilford.

Crisis in mental health: Issues affecting HHC's psychiatric inpatient and emergency room services: Summary data. (1989, January). New York: New York City Health and Hospitals Corporation, Offices of Mental Hygiene Services and Strategic Planning.

Fisher, W. H., Geller, J. L., & Wirth-Cauchon, J. (1990). Empirically assessing the impact of mobile crisis capacity on state hospital admissions. *Community Mental Health Journal, 26*(3), 245–253.

Gillig, P., Dumaine, M., & Hillard, J. R. (1990). Whom do mobile crisis services serve? *Hospital and Community Psychiatry, 41*(7), 804–805.

Goldberg, H. L. (1973). Home treatment. *Psychiatric Annals, 3*, 6.

Psychiatric house calls routine part of emergency service in Amsterdam. (1991, December 20). *Psychiatric News,* 16–17.

Reynolds, I., Jones, J. E., Berry, D. W., & Hault, J. E. (1990). A crisis team for the mentally ill: The effect on patients, relatives, and admissions. *Medical Journal of Australia, 152,* 646–652.

Tufnell, G., Bouras, N., Watson, J. P., et al. (1985). Home assessment and treatment in a community psychiatric service. *Acta Psychiatrica Scandinavica, 72,* 20–28.

West, D. A., Litwok, E., Oberlander, K., & Martin, D. A. (1980). Emergency psychiatric home visiting: Report of four years experience. *Journal of Clinical Psychiatry, 41*(4), 113–118.

Zealberg, J. J. (1990). Providing psychiatric emergency care during disasters: Hurricane Hugo in Charleston, South Carolina. In N. R. Punukollo (Ed.), *Recent advances in crisis intervention* (Vol. I, pp. 135–143). Huddersfield, UK: International Institute of Crisis Intervention and Community Psychiatry Publications.

Zealberg, J. J., & Puckett, J. (1992). Function of mobile crisis intervention teams after Hurricane Hugo. In L. Austin (Ed.), *Responding to disaster: A guide for mental health professionals* (pp. 185–199). Washington, DC: American Psychiatric Press.

Zealberg, J. J., & Santos, A. B. (1993). Mobile crisis: Comprehensive emergency psychiatry for the future. *The Journal of the South Carolina Medical Association, 89,* 485–489.

Zealberg, J. J., Santos, A. B., & Fisher, R. K. (1993). Benefits of mobile crisis programs. *Hospital and Community Psychiatry, 44*(1), 16–17.

Chapter 3

ESTABLISHING WORKING ALLIANCES WITH CRISIS PATIENTS

Be near me when my light is low.
—Alfred, Lord Tennyson

CLINICIANS MUST DEVELOP and use relationship skills to motivate a patient's and family's interest in obtaining treatment and follow-up care. This is where some "salesmanship" comes into play. Patients come to the attention of crisis services through various routes, including many who do so involuntarily. With patients in crisis it is helpful to use the information uncovered in the interview to gain the patient's interest. Be specific; express professional concern; make the patient become curious about your thoughts; be curious about the patient, not judgmental; help the patient see how motivation for treatment will improve his or her life; help the patient to restore hope; gently point out inconsistencies; don't confront patients directly, but do gently challenge perspectives when necessary. The following examples demonstrate some of these principles.

Bill Bryer is brought into the emergency room by his family (one sister, one brother, and a niece) for symptoms of depression. They've been very concerned about some recent crying spells and vague statements he has made implying that "Life isn't worth it." He is 45 years old, divorced, and works at a local restaurant where he is part owner.

His blood alcohol level is 0.185 (the legal limit of sobriety ends at 0.100), while his drug screen is negative. He has mild high blood pressure (hypertension) but no other health problems.

The ER calls the mobile team. A clinician arrives in the ER, introduces himself, and asks permission to call the patient by his first name. The patient agrees, and says he's been depressed awhile, but not seriously. He talks about how business is bad, how he's been feeling blue, and how no one in his family loves him. They don't approve of the girl he's been seeing; they all think she's trying to take his money. The clinician determines that Bill is not suicidal, homicidal, or psychotic. The formal mental status examination is within normal limits.

Bill waits in the emergency room while his blood alcohol level declines to below 0.800. Then the clinician sees him again. Bill no longer feels depressed and wants to go home. However, the family presses the clinician to put him in the hospital so he can get antidepressant therapy; they think he needs Prozac.

The clinician returns to Bill and asks more about his drinking history. He usually drinks "two beers" a day. In response to further inquiry, he says he actually means two six-packs. He drinks that amount seven days a week, more on the weekend, and he sometimes takes some whiskey or vodka along with the beer. He comes from a "long line of drinking men," and feels this is not important. Yes, he's had the shakes on occasion, particularly in the morning, but they go away when he takes a "small shot" for breakfast. He's not had a long period of sobriety in the last few years. He denies any street drug use.

The clinician's impression is of an alcohol-induced mood disorder. The clinician (C) continues to speak with the patient (P):

C: Mr. Bryer, I'd like to sit down with you and explain what we've found and what we'd like to recommend.
P: Okay.
C: I understand that you've been feeling down in the dumps. I know that you've been sad and depressed.
P: Yeah, that's kinda true.
C: I've gotten to know you pretty well here, in a short period of time. I've also spoken with your family. They've been concerned too.
P: Yeah, they've been bugging me about goin' to see someone for help.
C: Well, I know they've been concerned. Have you been worried about yourself too?
P: Sometimes yes, sometimes no. It depends.
C: But this depression feeling concerns you, does it not?
P: Yeah. But it's no big deal.
C: Well, I see a lot of people who have bad depression here. I know it's one of the most awful feelings that a human being can go through. Would you agree?
P: Yeah.
C: I think I know where a lot of it is coming from. If you'd like,

I'd appreciate being able to share my opinion with you about that.
    [Waits]
P: [After a minute] Okay, go ahead.
C: You know, Bill, . . . may I call you Bill? [Bill nods.] I'm not a family
    member, and I think I can speak to you from an objective position.
    When you first came into the emergency room, you looked quite de-
    pressed and your blood alcohol level was high.
P: Yeah, but the drinkin' doesn't bother me.
C: I understand. But now that your alcohol level is down you're not
    depressed. See, the problem is that the alcohol is probably causing
    most of your depression.
P: Nah, that can't be. I've been drinkin' since I was 23 years old.
C: Well, I can see how that would be confusing. But alcohol is a ner-
    vous system depressant, and when you drink daily, and in significant
    quantity, it can bring you down. Also, you looked and talked fine when
    you first came in. Anyone else would have been quite drunk from the
    amount of alcohol in your bloodstream. You were about twice the
    level of legal intoxication. That suggests that you have a great deal of
    tolerance.
P: So what's all this got to do with depression?
C: I believe alcohol is probably the cause.
P: Can't be.
C: I appreciate that it must be hard to figure this out. But it probably
    is the alcohol, from what you've described. The only sure way to tell
    will be for you to be off the alcohol for several weeks. If the depression
    is still with you, then I agree we need to treat it. But we won't be able
    to treat your depression effectively until all the alcohol has been out of
    your system for awhile.
P: I don't have a problem with alcohol.
C: I respect your opinion on that. But let's reexamine this. You are
    depressed, your alcohol level was over 0.180, almost twice the legal
    limit, and you feel bad in the mornings without an eye opener. We do
    know that heavy alcohol intake frequently causes depressed moods. It
    happens. I'd like to recommend that we begin your treatment there.
    Rather than seeing it as a problem with alcohol, let's focus on how
    sobriety can help alleviate your depression. Then, as I said, if the de-
    pression isn't better, we can consider some therapy and antidepres-
    sants. Would you let me refer you for some alcohol treatment?
P: All right, if you insist. You mean inpatient?
C: What would you like?
P: Definitely outpatient care.

C: I think that will work fine. If you change your mind, I'll give you a few numbers to call about a voluntary admission. Also, I'll give you our 24-hour-a-day phone number in case there are any further developments or emergencies.

The clinician then goes to the family and explains his findings to them. He explains that antidepressants may not even be necessary. He also asks the family to help Bill get to the substance abuse treatment center for outpatient care. Alcoholics Anonymous and Al-Anon are also encouraged. The family agrees with the plan. The clinician shares his findings with the ER attending physician, who also agrees with the plan. A handout is given to the patient with the numbers of the local AA meetings, and the clinician asks Bill if he has any final questions. He does not. The clinician then asks permission to bring in the family. Everyone together reviews the plan. The family then leaves with the patient.

The clinician in this example allied with the patient (and his family), but did not agree with the patient's assessment of his problems. Sometimes patients are accurate in the assessment of their problems. But in this case, it was important to educate the patient and his family. Also, the patient's curiosity was stimulated. Before sharing recommendations with the patient, the clinician asked permission to share his clinical opinion. If the clinician invites a reply, the patient's defensiveness is diminished. He was more receptive to being disagreed with, as he did express desire to hear the clinician's opinion. With substance-abusing patients, the most important goal may be to motivate them toward treatment.

The next example demonstrates some difficulties in the intervention process.

Sandra Shilling is a 26-year-old patient with a previous diagnosis of borderline personality disorder and crack cocaine abuse. She came to the emergency room after superficially scratching her wrist. Her alcohol level is negative. Her urine drug screen is positive for cocaine. The remainder of her physical examination is normal. The scratches on her wrist have been cleaned and bandaged. No sutures were required. The ER doctor wants the mental health clinician to evaluate her for the possibility of hospital admission.

The clinician enters the room to talk to the patient. He has never seen her before, and makes the mistake of addressing her by her first name.

C: Hello Sandra, I'm one of the counselors here.
P: [Looks down: no eye contact, no verbal interchange.]

C: I need to ask you some questions, Sandra. Can you look at me?

P: [Still no eye contact. Sandra's hair has fallen over her face. She is rocking back and forth on her seat.]

C: Sandra, I need to ask you some things. Can you tell me why you cut yourself tonight?

P: Yeah, I wanted to hurt myself, asshole.

C: [The clinician takes this a little personally as he's had a rough day.] Why did you want to hurt yourself, Sandra?

P: I don't know. I'm gonna kill my fucking self tonight and there isn't a goddamn thing you can do about it.

C: Well, that's not true. I can commit you into the hospital if I need to. That is unless you cooperate with me.

P: Stick it up your ass!

C: [The clinician shakes his head and leaves the examination room. He gets a drink of soda. He realizes this is going nowhere at a very quick rate. He realizes he hasn't formed an alliance with the patient. He goes in again.] Ms. Shilling, I'm sorry. I realize that maybe I'm going a little too fast here. I didn't even ask your permission to call you by your first name. Can I offer you anything? Some water or juice perhaps? Have you had anything to eat or drink today?

P: [Turns her head side to side] No.

C: Would you like a cool glass of water?

P: Yeah.

C: Okay. Also, I know you're feeling very tense—can I perhaps find out if the doctors would be willing to give you a little medicine to help you feel better?

P: Like what kind of medicine?

C: Well, I'll ask their advice. Do you have any ideas about what helps you feel better?

P: Yeah. Ativan.

C: Okay. I'll get you some water and ask about the Ativan. Then, maybe when I come back we can talk together.

The clinician leaves, speaks with the ER doctor about the Ativan, and returns with water. The alliance begins with the patient telling her story about feeling all right until she lit up a rock of crack. Soon afterward, she "crashed" and scratched her wrist with a butter knife. After obtaining all necessary information, he asks one final question:

C: Are you still planning on hurting yourself?

P: Maybe yes, maybe no.

C: Okay, I can understand how you'd feel confused about this. If I don't hear from you that you'll be safe, however, we'll need to think about the hospital.

P: I don't know.

C: Well, again, I understand how it's confusing. We can set up a treatment plan for you as an outpatient, but first I need to hear from you whether you'll be safe. We need to decide this now, Sandra.

P: You can't put me in the hospital unless I want to go in.

C: Well, that's not exactly true. I can put you in on an involuntary status if necessary. But we would like for you to be able to choose. What must we do?

P: I'll be okay. I don't feel the need to hurt myself any more.

At this point, there is a reasonable alliance and Ms. Shilling has been direct. She has a family member she can go home with, and is given a follow-up appointment for the next day. She's also given the phone number of the ER and the emergency number of the mental health center. She agrees to call if any more self-destructive impulses recur.

A biopsychosocial approach is necessary for effective crisis resolution. Some patients go into crisis states due to a lack of housing, lack of social group, or relapse with drugs or alcohol, coupled with the resultant shame, humiliation, and guilt they feel. For patients with severe social stressors such as homelessness or job loss, connection with community resources will be essential to effectively resolve the crisis. The best medical and psychological interventions may fall short if the patient does not have a good support system and support plan; therefore, atttention must always be paid to reconnecting a patient to community social supports and resources.

SUGGESTED READING

Slaiken, K. A. (1990). *Crisis intervention: A handbook for practice and research.* Needham Heights, MA: Allyn & Bacon.

Chapter 4

WHEN MUST A PATIENT BE ADMITTED TO A HOSPITAL?

> The mind struggles to establish a connection — a sequence
> of cause and effect — and, being unable to do so,
> suffers a species of temporary paralysis.
> — *Edgar Allen Poe (The Gold Bug)*

ALMOST EVERY PATIENT seen by a psychiatric emergency service has the potential to be hospitalized due to the acute and often severe nature of the symptomatology. Professionals from other disciplines may ask, "How do you know what to do? All psychiatric crisis patients look the same and they all look like they need to be in the hospital, so how do you decide?" This is a question that the crisis clinician may hear from his or her colleagues who are not experts in the mental health field. However, in the era of providing cost-effective treatments, and given the reality of limited hospital resources, it is imperative that the crisis clinician make careful, logical decisions in determining who is truly in need of hospitalization.

INDICATIONS FOR HOSPITALIZATION

Three general questions can guide the clinician with regard to making decisions about whether to hospitalize a patient in crisis:

- Is the patient an imminent danger to self or others?
- Is the patient willing to engage in, and follow, the clinical treatment recommendations?
- Does the patient have a support system or can one be created?

30

All questions must be answered with clinical history and data. For instance, if the answer to the first question is a resounding YES, that would call for hospitalization. On the other hand, the more positively the second and third questions are answered, the more one can move away from hospitalization.

Is the Patient an Imminent Danger to Self or Others?

This must be answered with data and history that reveal the patient's behavior under the following conditions: (a) prior to being evaluated, (b) during the evaluation, and (c) based on predictions of behavior that may occur in the near future.

BEHAVIOR PRIOR TO BEING EVALUATED

- Does the patient have a major mental illness that is out of control? Psychosis, mania, or severe mood disorders will probably worsen if untreated.
- Does the patient have epidemiologic risk factors for suicide (e.g., an elderly white male who is widowed, depressed, isolated, and giving away his valuable possessions)?
- Does the patient have a previous history of suicide or homicide attempts or violence, especially during acute phases of previous mental illnesses which have now recurred (e.g., a patient with paranoid schizophrenia who was so fearful in the past when acutely ill that he barricaded himself in with guns and fired at the police, or a manic woman who believes she's an angel and can fly off buildings during her acute psychotic mania)?
- Is the patient's family history positive for completed suicide or homicide? This could indicate a genetic predisposition to impulsivity, a psychologic modeling for aggression toward the self or others, or a psychological identification with an important relative.
- Did the patient's behavior appear impulsive only in the face of a heated argument or stressor that is now completely resolved? If so, this indicates the patient is *not* in imminent danger.
- Did the patient methodically plan an act of self-harm?
- If the patient made a suicide (or homicide) plan or attempt, how was it discovered? Accidental discoveries imply high lethality.
- Did the patient make attempts to reach out or communicate with anyone, or was she accidentally discovered after the suicide attempt? Attempts to call or tell someone implies lesser lethality.

- What was the lethality of the attempt? Discharged guns, hanging attempts that are accidentally discovered, jumping from significant heights, carbon monoxide poisoning, and overdoses that are accidentally discovered also imply high levels of lethality.
- If the patient had a firearm, did he discharge it while feeling suicidal? If so, hospitalize!!!!
- If the patient hurt himself or took an overdose, did he wish for death as a result? Was the patient aware that the attempt could kill him (e.g., a significant tricyclic antidepressant overdose)?
- If the patient is being treated for a psychiatric illness, is the illness breaking through the medication?
- Is the patient compliant with previous treatments?
- How long has the patient felt hopeless?
- Were there command hallucinations telling her to kill herself or others?
- Did the patient's clues about impending suicide or homicide get anyone's attention, or were they ignored?

BEHAVIOR OBSERVED DURING THE EVALUATION

The following behaviors may imply diminishing levels of dangerousness.

- Is the patient settling down, becoming less anxious, less hopeless, less psychotic, less agitated or violent, more engaged in the process, feeling better or more organized from medications administered in the ER or other setting?
- Is the patient experiencing psychological relief from your intervention and therapeutic interview?
- Is time significantly changing the behavior of the patient in a positive direction? People can feel much better with a dose of medication or once their blood alcohol or intoxication from cocaine clears.
- If the patient attempted suicide, is she glad to be alive? This should be asked directly with every suicide attempt—if the patient answers "No," beware!
- If the patient was intoxicated and is now in a sober state, is he calm, cooperative, and not impulsive?
- Has all suicidal or homicidal ideation disappeared with sobriety? Or is there no change or a worsening in the patient's subjective/objective behavior?

PREDICTIONS OF BEHAVIOR IN THE NEAR FUTURE

- If the patient is suffering from a major mood or psychotic disorder, what is the usual course of that type of illness in the patient?
- How did the patient behave the last time she was manic or psychotic?
- How does the patient respond to vigorous treatment?
- If the patient is at risk for abusing substances after leaving the crisis setting, what will those substances do to his behavior or illness? Will someone be available to monitor the patient? To discard alcohol in the home? To be psychologically available? To call the emergency service if things worsen for the patient?
- Remember that a past history of violence is the best predictor of future violence.

 Is the Patient Willing to Engage In, and Follow, the Clinician's Treatment Recommendations?

You may recognize that the patient must do certain things in order to treat his or her crisis.

- Is the patient willing to comply with your treatment recommendations? It is important to have the patient agree with *your* follow-up treatment plan; patients often think that *they* know what is best for them. DO NOT fall into the trap of letting the patient dictate what is best. If one is in crisis, by definition one is not thinking clearly! You, the clinician, must provide ego structure, logic, and clear objective advice to the patient. Of course, few patients will agree immediately to treatment recommendations. It is the job of the crisis clinician to deal *gently but persistently* with the patient's treatment resistance and to convince her that follow-up with treatment is in her best interest. This might involve some negotiation.

For example, if a clinician recommends follow-up with AA or an appointment for voluntary inpatient detoxification, and the clinician does not believe any other treatment will be helpful, it is not acceptable to have a patient "stop drinking on her own." If a manic patient must immediately begin taking medication for mania, it is not acceptable to let a fully manic patient go home without initiation of medicines to control the mood disorder. It is not an acceptable plan for a dangerously manic or psychotic emergency patient to refuse medicine when it is offered. Do not accept such a patient's reassurance ("Yeah, I'll take some when I get home"), especially if he is refusing your offer of medication at the place of crisis evaluation. It is the patient's right to refuse treatment; however, in an emergency where there is risk of imminent harm to self or others, medication may have to be administered against the patient's wishes.

Is the patient willing to cooperate fully with your examination, and is the information acceptable and valid? Remember that some patients may lie because of fears of legal issues (e.g., patients may not tell about a cocaine addiction since it is illegal and they fear you may "turn them in") or because of shame, guilt, fear, or confusion. If a suicidal patient is lying to you, she is not truly engaged in treatment, and may not be telling you the truth about what she will do for follow-up care. Will the patient call for an appointment in the morning, or agree to contact your crisis service at night, particularly if she reexperiences any crisis symptoms? Will the patient go in for that counseling session or NA meeting? Do you trust the patient? Does your cognitive sense and subjective intuitive sense tell you that you can trust this patient and that you feel comfortable about the treatment plan?

Does the Patient Have a Support System or Can One Be Created?

- Who is available to be with the patient?
- Is there a place the patient can go to for support, such as a shelter, a crisis residence, a family member's home, a friend's place, or to an AA meeting with a sponsor?
- Are the people at that support system friendly and sympathetic or will they make the patient feel worse, guilty, or embarrassed?
- Are the people at the support place reliable?
- Will they watch the patient?
- Are they willing to "suicide proof" their residence by removing or securing guns, rifles, swords, tricyclics, hunting knives, alcohol, etc?
- Will they call the crisis hotline if something happens?
- Is their residence a one-story building, or will the patient need to stay on the eighth floor near an open window? What is the physical environment like?

Again, looking at the above three general categories, the more favorably a clinician can answer those three areas of questions, the more a clinician can move away from acute hospitalization. More negative answers should steer the clinician toward recommending hospitalization.

 ## *ABSOLUTE* INDICATIONS FOR HOSPITALIZATION

In the opinion of many, there *are* some absolutes:

- The suicidal/homicidal patient who has discharged a firearm. This implies the highest impulsivity and lethality.
- The patient whose suicide attempt was accidentally discovered.
- The suicidal/homicidal patient with a plan, means, and intent.
- The patient who jumps from a significant height.
- The patient who barricades him- or herself in and has a standoff with police. When a precipitating argument with others causes such an event, these patients often wish to kill themselves so as to cause guilt and anguish for the ones who remain behind.
- The patient with acute command hallucinations to kill himself or others, especially if these do not respond to vigorous psychopharmacologic intervention in the crisis setting, or if they previously caused the patient to act out the thoughts.
- The patient who is not glad to be alive following a suicide attempt.
- The suicidal patient who will have no support system after leaving the crisis setting.
- The suicidal or dangerous patient who refuses all treatment recommendations.
- The patient with a current and multiple previous lethal suicide or homicide attempts.
- The paranoid patient who, when acutely ill, arms herself due to extreme fear.
- The patient whose history indicates that he becomes dangerous when his mood or psychotic disorder becomes acute. An example would be a patient who, during a previous acute psychotic depression, believed that Satan was inside him, and in response to auditory hallucinations tried to pluck out his eye in an attempt to rid himself of the devil.
- The patient who has previously failed to persist at intensively organized and well-planned outpatient treatment.

- The patient who is delirious. Of course, this patient should be admitted to a medical floor of the hospital. Remember to diagnose delirium by the presence of any of the following: acute onset, visual hallucinations that the patient interacts with, attention deficits, acute disorientation, and waxing and waning sensorium or arousal.

There can be many other indications for hospitalization. The clinician's emotional and cognitive decisions should be congruent; that is, when a decision is made NOT to hospitalize a patient, the clinician's "gut" and "head" should be in agreement about such a decision.

Of course, there are other alternatives to inpatient hospital admissions. For instance, holding beds in emergency settings, crisis residential or foster care beds, or partial hospital programs can be helpful to patients in crisis. Patients who are imminently dangerous should be treated in hospital settings if they meet the above criteria or other criteria as determined by clinicians in different programs with different resources.

SUGGESTED READINGS

Bengelsdorf, H., Levy, L. E., Emerson, R. L., & Barile, F. A. (1984). A crisis triage rating scale: Brief dispositional assessment of patients at risk for hospitalization. *The Journal of Nervous and Mental Disease, 172*(7), 424–430.

Marson, D. C., McGovern, M. P., & Pomp, H. C. (1988). Psychiatric decision making in the emergency room: A research overview. *American Journal of Psychiatry, 145,* 918–925.

Chapter 5

THE ROLE OF CRISIS SERVICES WITHIN A COMMUNITY-BASED SYSTEM OF CARE

Is there no pity sitting in the clouds,
That sees into the bottom of my grief?
—*William Shakespeare* (*Romeo and Juliet*)

ALL PEOPLE GO THROUGH developmental changes in life. Change can be a wonderful part of growth and maturity; change can also be frightening and catastrophic. A job promotion or graduation from college may cause positive change and emotions in an individual. Divorce, loss of a job, or arrest by law enforcement officers may cause negative change and emotions, which when severe enough may lead to a state of crisis in any individual. Crises can arise from internal stress, life change, significant loss (e.g., of a parent, job, home), an overwhelming gain (such as an important job promotion for which one feels unprepared or inadequate, or graduation from college or graduate school), illness, economic strife, family stress, or other factors.

When internal and/or external stresses become so overwhelming that an individual can no longer cope, mild psychiatric symptoms begin to appear, and eventually a crisis develops. If the crisis is severe enough we categorize that phenomenon as a psychiatric emergency.

One of the most common types of psychiatric emergency can be seen in people who have a history of significant mental illness. Like all

37

serious illnesses, psychiatric illnesses can be mild (e.g., someone may have a history of a time-limited "adjustment disorder") or devastating in severity (e.g., onset or worsening of schizophrenia). There are times when such illnesses are stable and quiescent, and other times, especially during periods of stress or due to lack of medication, when the more serious psychiatric illnesses are completely out of control and patients may then become dangerous to themselves or to others. A psychiatric emergency service or program is then called into action to handle these severe crises.

In general, psychiatric emergency programs form an important access point to a community's mental health care system. The role of a psychiatric emergency program should never be viewed as primary, however. Rather, the strength of a crisis or psychiatric emergency system can only be as good as the quality of service offered by a community's mental health care system in general. Mental illness cannot be treated as a series of crises any more than diabetes can be treated as a series of recurrent hospitalizations for a diabetic patient whose blood sugar is out of control. It is the job of medical personnel to prevent a diabetic's illness from getting out of control and resulting in serious illness and costly hospitalization. Similarly, it is the job of a quality mental health care system to prevent psychiatric illness from getting out of control and to treat psychiatric patients in the least restrictive, most cost-effective manner possible to avoid costly hospitalization and clinical relapse.

A community's crisis or psychiatric emergency program should be available when a patient's coping skills are overwhelmed or when a patient's mental illness worsens and begins to manifest dangerous symptoms and signs (a symptom is an uncomfortable feeling of illness that a patient perceives internally; a sign of illness is something that can be observed directly by a clinician). The first goal of crisis intervention with patients who are acutely mentally ill is to attempt to restore their psychologic status toward a state of normalcy. Crisis *prevention* is always the best form of crisis intervention. A high-quality mental health care system will minimize crises by maintaining patients with serious mental illness at levels of optimal stability and function. An emergency psychiatric system will troubleshoot and assist with such endeavors. In order to be effective, a crisis system of care must be an integral part of a larger system of organized mental health care. Without this context, the best crisis intervention therapy or psychiatric emergency care is doomed to fail.

DESIGNING A MODEL OF CRISIS CARE THAT WORKS

There are several qualities an effective emergency psychiatric system must exhibit.

- *Availability*. It has been estimated that perhaps 1 out of every 3 to 5 individuals in the United States will suffer from a major psychiatric disorder during the course of a lifetime (Reiger, 1994). Therefore, it should not be surprising that psychiatric problems are prevalent and indeed commonplace. People who suffer from these illnesses and disorders often experience crises and emergencies and, thus, psychiatric emergency systems of care must be available in every community. Surprisingly, few communities give thought to this problem. Most communities have EMS systems for medical emergencies, but psychiatric emergencies also require sophisticated evaluation and treatment. Well-trained, experienced staff should be available to patients in serious crisis; it is not true that "anybody can do it."
- *Accessibility*. The highest quality clinical programs are virtually useless to patients or their families if they can not access ongoing or acute care. Comprehensive crisis programs must be accessible to patients in distress and should be available to see and treat patients 'round-the-clock. In addition, quality crisis programs should have a mobile outreach component so that patients who are too impaired to seek clinic- or ER-based care can be seen quickly and effectively in their home or community environment. Patients who are delusional and severely paranoid will not come to an institution-based program for care precisely because of their overwhelming fear. Therefore, to truly manage the severe level of crisis in such a patient, the crisis clinic or emergency room must "go to the patient."
- *Integration and systematization*. Crisis systems of care must integrate with all community resources and mental health care systems. Emergency services treat a wide variety of patients with different needs, whether rich, poor, white, African American, Hispanic, Native American, Protestant, Jewish, homeless, etc. In order to resolve an emergency, follow-up and support systems need to be accessed

for patients in distress. The crisis system must be friendly with, and accessible to, every potential community resource available. This will allow the patient to "lock into" ongoing care and support.

- *Multidisciplinary approach.* A bio-psycho-social-spiritual approach is often required to assist a patient who is in crisis. Therefore, to truly resolve a patient's crisis, doctors, psychologists, counselors, social workers, and nurses must work together as a team, bringing expertise and methods from their respective disciplines. There is no one professional that has expertise in every field of human endeavor.
- *Effective communication.* There needs to be effective communication links within a crisis system. The day shift needs to communicate with the evening and night shifts. Duties must be carefully defined and shared. Follow-up communications with patients and therapists or case managers is essential, otherwise the best crisis intervention can fail due to lack of continuity of care. In emergency work, nothing can be assumed unless one witnesses an event or sees it documented. In the field of crisis intervention, all loose ends must be tied up. Careful documentation of records and flow of communication among team members are essential, as is illustrated by the following example:

> Police seek assistance from crisis clinicians to help talk a suicidal man out of his home. He has a shotgun, is intoxicated, and "high" on cocaine. After four hours, he surrenders, and the sheriff's deputies transport him to the ER. The crisis clinicians who helped talk him out assumed that the police would tell the ER staff about the standoff. This was, in fact, not done and the patient neglected to explain this as well. Therefore, he was referred to outpatient treatment and discharged from the ER, which was unacceptable.

FOUNDATIONS OF A SUCCESSFUL CRISIS TEAM

It is important to realize that crisis or emergency mental health programs cannot operate within a vacuum. Mental illness cannot be treated from a crisis standpoint alone. As we have stated, the strength and vitality of a crisis program rests upon its being an integral part of a highly coordinated comprehensive mental health system. Crisis clinicians and professional staff should integrate with all other components of their local mental health care system. Following are several practical and philosophical characteristics that are important in the development of a high-quality system of care.

- *Belief in a shared mission to treat people in local settings.* Crisis clinicians and mental health specialists should be committed to the idea that patients must be treated in their own communities. The advantage of this is that care can be coordinated between hospitals and clinics, families can become involved in the patient's treatment, and patients can be involved in appropriate psychosocial support groups (e.g., Narcotics Anonymous, AA). Communities should never rely on sending mentally ill people away from the community to isolated state hospitals, where follow-up is nearly impossible.
- *Complete training and ongoing education.* Professionals must be fully trained in the use of biopsychosocial techniques and should receive ongoing continuing education in order to become familiar with the rapidly changing neurosciences and clinical psychiatric knowledge base. Clinicians should keep abreast of new medications, scientific theories, medical information, and the latest techniques of psychosocial therapies and resource management.
- *Effective communication between programs and agencies.* Patient care must flow smoothly in order to maintain patients at their maximum state of wellness. Inaccessibility of mental health systems can contribute to patient relapse. Crisis professionals can often identify the cracks in the system and should alert their administrative leaders to these weaknesses. Appropriate agreements between crisis programs and community agencies must be worked out so that patients can be referred to comprehensive treatment resources. Crisis programs should also set up liaisons with hospitals to coordinate follow-up and assist in making outpatient referral more efficient. This can be done by delivering chart documents, sharing information on medication regimens, and coordinating between doctors and case managers. Memoranda of agreement (MOAs) with police, hospitals, or substance abuse treatment centers will insure smooth communication, and ongoing meetings with program directors should be encouraged so that suggestions can be followed up with appropriate administrative changes.
- *Accessibility to community-based intensive care settings.* The best crisis programs, even if mobile, will never replace the need for inpatient beds, crisis beds, and emergency room facilities. Sometimes

these resources are needed for clinical management due to unacceptable levels of risk or for treatment of patients who are too ill to
be managed in a noninstitutional setting.

- *Clear program goals and desired outcomes.* In traditional mental
  health centers, it is often unclear what is expected in terms of productivity, that is, how many patients should be seen, how often,
  how quickly, and where. Clarifying these expectations can enhance
  morale and productivity and can diminish work-related anxieties
  and conflicts. Program and agency directors must define their opera-
  tional expectations and monitor the outcomes. They must define
  what is truly essential: client satisfaction? time between consultation
  request and seeing the patient? return of patients to the ER? diminished state hospital commitment rates? Different programs must
  define these goals differently.
- *Field work.* In order to adequately serve the community's needs,
  clinicians cannot stay in their office and wait for patients to come to
  them. By going to the patient, case managers and therapists can
  avoid crisis situations and patient decompensation. This idea is often anxiety-provoking to clinicians at first, but once a system is used
  to provide community outreach treatment, it often becomes the
  preferred mode of patient-therapist interaction.
- *Frequent meetings of team supervisors.* Mental health care systems
  require ongoing "tuning" in order to keep operations working effectively. Crisis programs that interface with an entire mental health
  system will often be able to experience some of the issues that
  interfere with system accessibility. Therefore, regular meetings of
  team supervisors should be encouraged. Job functions should be
  fluid and change should be welcome.
- *Flexible staff scheduling.* Mental health crises and patients' needs do
  not occur between 9 and 5. Therefore, a mental health system
  should have clinical staff working beyond the confines of the traditional eight-hour day.
- *Supportive management that fixes administrative conflicts.* All mental
  health professionals get paid to take care of patients. Therefore,
  administrators should take a proactive approach in supporting clinicians' needs. Administrators must empower clinicians to do their
  jobs.
- *Financing.* No public mental health system can survive without generating revenue. Patients who require entitlements such as Medic-
  aid need to be assisted through the administrative procedures in-

volved to obtain their benefits. Mental health programs should enlist the assistance of entitlement workers when necessary.

- *Liaison with jails.* It has been estimated that 7% of the jail population suffers from chronic mental illness. In addition, it is common for people to claim they are suicidal after being arrested. In order to treat these patients within the community, jail outreach is advisable. Crisis programs should provide back-up and emergency coverage for ongoing mental health clinical support in the jail.

- *Working with families.* Patients do not live in a vacuum. Family-oriented therapies and treatments provide extra support to patients and often diminish the likelihood of relapse. For instance, British researchers have gathered data that indicate that patients with schizophrenia in families who exhibit so-called "high expressed emotion" have a greater likelihood of relapse. Diminishing stress in such families, or in a patient's support system, can often end a crisis.

  Family education may also prevent a crisis from developing. For example, a patient with a psychotic mood disorder may show rapid improvement in a few weeks after beginning medication. Crisis clinicians must anticipate the natural response of patients or their families to assume that medicine treatment is no longer necessary once the patient feels completely normal. Educating families to encourage the patient to continue medications can help avoid a relapse.

- *Supportive management and supervision.* Working with severely mentally ill people is a very difficult job. Clinicians require ongoing supervision, support, guidance, and assistance in processing their own feelings and reactions toward patients. Without such supervision, stress can build up within teams and lead to "infighting." Good supervisors will nurture their staff while providing realistic administrative policies and thorough leadership. Administrators should take an active approach in supporting clinicians' needs and should never involve them in administrative conflicts. Clinicians should be instructed to take care of patients' needs and allow the administration to solve any administrative conflicts.

INTEGRATING EMERGENCY SERVICES INTO LARGER SYSTEMS OF MENTAL HEALTH CARE

Like patients, psychiatric emergency services do not operate in a vacuum. It is important, even essential, to integrate crisis services into ongoing clinical care programs so that patients can be quickly stabilized and transferred to more definitive follow-up treatment. Although it is important for a good crisis service to stabilize patients until the crisis phase has passed, it is not possible or advisable for patients to be case managed by an emergency program; the crisis system will become "bogged down" in patient case management issues and long-term care, which could slow the overall emergency system and response time and make it less accessible. Therefore, members of a comprehensive emergency service should make powerful alliances and liaisons with other treatment resources. All available community resources (shelters for homeless or battered or abused women and children, residential care facilities, emergency rooms, substance abuse treatment centers, mental health clinics, and private psychiatric practitioners, among many others) need to be contacted and introduced to the emergency service's availability and mission. Once the emergency service is seen as an important and integral part of the community's resource base, the crisis service can utilize the vast array of systemic resources available in the community.

Creating Professional and Administrative Alliances

Successful crisis programs quickly gain a "magical" reputation. Everyone in the community will want a piece of ownership and expect instant help from an excellent emergency service. Unfortunately, magical expectations cannot be met, and promises that cannot be kept should never be made. The directors of a comprehensive crisis delivery system must have a clear idea of what they will, can, and cannot do. This should be stated clearly and succinctly. In fact, the directors are often the *only* ones in the community who know exactly what it is they do. A good rule of thumb is to always "underpromise and overdeliver."

It is important to make friends with emergency room directors and the chiefs of local law enforcement agencies. Sheriff's and police departments are often involved in commitment of patients, and are very knowledgeable about the community's mental health care needs. When developing mobile crisis services, it is critical to meet with local law enforcement to explain the crisis service's mission, to establish communication protocols, and to define the "do's and don'ts." For example, police department personnel will almost always express the hope that new mobile crisis programs will handle domestic disputes.

Police will need to know when and when not to call upon the mobile team. Some programs will respond to domestic disputes; others, only if the domestic dispute involves someone psychotic, suicidal, or mentally ill.

Roles should also be defined with ER directors. Crisis programs should ideally have a medical director who can set up professional relationships with area ER directors. Physician-to-physician communication is essential. What is expected? How is "medical clearance" defined? Does everyone require a drug screen or physical examination? When are these mandatory? When are these completely unnecessary? What about connections to clinics and hospitals? What are the admission criteria? What outpatient resources are available?

Crisis program directors should also know the directors of their community's clinics. What resources are available for nonfunded (i.e., indigent) patients? What is the waiting period for an outpatient appointment? Can this be expedited? Meetings with executive directors and with clinical program directors of mental health resources are critical. Reciprocity is very important: Crisis programs need referral networks; hospitals, practitioners, and clinics need patient referrals.

Directors and clinicians should meet with as many people in the human services network as possible. The Department of Social Services (DSS), hotline telephone services, child protective services, and workers at other community agencies need to know about available crisis services. What constitutes a bona fide crisis? How is the crisis program accessed? Where are patients seen? What time of day? For how many visits? Will the program cover "on call" responsibilities for private hospitals and psychiatrists? What if someone is simply intoxicated? Will they be seen? Does the program transport patients? There are a number of clinical/administrative questions that need to be defined, addressed, and then explained to the community at large. It is advisable to meet with probate judges and the sheriff's group of deputies who transport mentally ill patients. It is also good to know the community's police hostage negotiators and to cross-train whenever possible.

In summary, a beginning crisis program must be set up to integrate with a community's entire array of resources. An effective program will rapidly gain acceptance; a poorly organized crisis program will quickly cause havoc and antagonize professionals, patients, and families alike.

SUGGESTED READINGS

Henggeler, S. W., Schoenwald, S. K., Pickrel, S. G., Rowland, M. D., Santos, A. B. (1994). The contribution of treatment research to the reform of children's mental health services: Multisystemic family preservation as an example. *Journal of Mental Health Administration, 21*(3), 229–239.

Henggeler, S. W., Santos, A. B. (Eds). (in press). *Innovative models of mental health treatment for difficult to treat clinical populations.* Washington, DC: American Psychiatric Press.

Hillard, J. R. (1994). The past and future of psychiatric emergency services in the U.S. *Hospital and Community Psychiatry, 45,* 541–543.

Meisler, N. (1991). State mental health agency responsibility for outreach. In N. L. Cohen (Ed.), *Psychiatric outreach to the mentally ill.* San Francisco: Jossey-Bass.

Reiger, D. A. (1994). ECA contributions to national policy and further research: A ten-year retrospective on the NIMH epidemiologic catchment area program [Special issue]. *International Journal of Methods in Psychiatric Research, 4*(2), 73–80.

Santos, A. B., Ballenger, J. C., Bevilacqua, J. J., Zealberg, J. J., Hiers, T. G., McLeod-Bryant, S., Deci, P. A., & Rames, L. J. (1994). A community-based public-academic liaison program. *American Journal of Psychiatry, 151*(8), 1181–1187.

Stein, L. I. (1992). Crisis stabilization services for persons with psychotic illnesses. In J. B. van Luyn, et al. (Eds.), *Emergency psychiatry today* (pp. 25–28). New York: Elsevier Science.

Stein, L. I., et al. (1990). A system approach to the care of persons with schizophrenia. In M. I. Herz, et al. (Eds.) *Handbook of schizophrenia: Vol. 4. Psychosocial treatment of schizophrenia* (pp. 213–246). New York: Elsevier Science.

Stroul, B. A. (1991). *Profiles of psychiatric crisis response systems.* Rockville, MD: National Institute of Mental Health.

PART II

NUTS AND BOLTS OF
PROGRAM OPERATION

Chapter 6

PROFESSIONAL STAFF DEVELOPMENT ISSUES

A chain is no stronger than its weakest link.
— *English Proverb*

AN EXTENSIVE KNOWLEDGE base must be mastered if one wishes to become an expert in the field of psychiatric emergency care. In this chapter, we will explore some general personal qualities that are necessary for the professional development of a crisis clinician. We will also outline some general philosophic ideas for supervision of crisis clinicians. When personal qualities of clinicians mesh well with the supervisory philosophy of a crisis program, optimal results can be obtained.

PERSONAL QUALITIES OF THE EXPERT CRISIS CLINICIAN

One might ask how crisis professionals can prevent themselves from completely "burning out." The best answer to that question is: "Know thyself." Many enter the mental health field to combat their own "internal demons," their own intrapsychic experiences, life experiences, psychological traumas, and needs. All human beings experience hurt, disappointment, and other painful feelings. These experiences and unconscious motives often lead people into the mental health profession. To be an effective crisis professional, a person must know his or her own internal motivations and conflicts and be able to accept supervision around issues of patient care and clinical management.

Every potential crisis clinician should understand him- or herself, have some appropriate methods for managing stress, have a good understanding of the potential countertransference issues that may arise in clinical interactions with patients, and be open to ongoing supervision and feedback about his or her personal performance.

An excellent crisis clinician might have the following traits:

- *Empathy.* The crisis clinician must be able to place himself in another's plight.
- *Honesty.* The truth must be delivered to patients in a caring, gentle way, without challenging her integrity.
- *Toughness.* Severe mental illness can wreak havoc on a human being. Crisis work is not for the faint-hearted! Also, firm limits must be set at times. Self-assertion is a must.
- *Compassion.* People in crisis are often at their worst and may feel hopeless. A clinician must see the good in the suffering patient.
- *Resourcefulness.* Often, real-world solutions, such as help with transportation or housing, are necessary to resolve a patient's emergency. The crisis clinician must be able to access the necessary resources.
- *Creativity.* A crisis clinician must synthesize and organize a great deal of information and develop rapid plans for treatment. Each situation involves individualized treatment planning.
- *Tolerance.* Sometimes a clinician must manage three phone calls at once or triage five different emergencies. He must tolerate irate patients, impatient professionals, and internal anxiety.
- *Humor.* The clinician must be in tune with the "cosmic joke" — the tragic-comic side of life; she must be able to laugh at herself.
- *Tenacity.* A good crisis clinician will always search for another option to serve the patient's needs.
- *Intrepidity.* A crisis clinician must often be brave, that is, he often must take action in the face of fear. However, he must never endanger himself, his colleagues, or his patients.

TEAMBUILDING

As much as possible, emergency services staff should be team-oriented. Teambuilding does not come easily and requires ongoing supervision and collaboration. If the biopsychosocial model is used, then it is important to have staff with backgrounds and expertise in the areas of medicine, nursing, psychology, counseling, and social work. Teamwork is critical in bringing the necessary resources to the patient in crisis. Staff should know who is in charge and be able to approach senior staff and supervisors with clinical problems and thorny administrative issues. Communication is a must. If 24-hour-a-day services are provided, one shift must communicate with the next. Open communication must be encouraged and everyone involved in crisis work must be provided with constructive criticism. It is critical that a crisis team communicate *all* information relevant to cases at hand. Skills and qualities necessary to foster a sense of effective clinical teamwork include active listening, conflict management, negotiation and mediation skills, an understanding of group dynamics, and psychologic reflection and introspection.

Crisis clinicians must also see themselves as part of a broader team, that of the mental health care system of a state or community, and therefore to avoid language and situations that foster an "us versus them" mentality. The emergency psychiatry service is part of the community's helping professions in general—a partnership with police, EMS, and social services, and part of the larger system of psychiatric and medical care in a community. It is this broad sense of teamwork that makes for a real sense of community and professional involvement.

GENERAL GOALS FOR STAFF SUPERVISORS

Emergency mental health requires extraordinary patience, maturity, insight, and cleverness. It is taxing, difficult, overwhelming, and challenging. Crisis clinicians must understand the meaning of their work in a broad context. A good supervisor and leader of a crisis team will concentrate on meaningful, philosophical, and very practical supervisory issues such as the following:

- Provide a long-range vision for the future.
- Emphasize that treating severely and chronically mentally ill patients is rewarding.
- Expose staff to the larger picture of administrative systems and processes. Teach how their crisis work fits into the overall scheme of clinical care for the mentally ill.

- Help staff understand the importance of continuity of care for patients and their families.
- Emphasize a model of care that teaches rehabilitation as well as short- and long-term treatment.
- Help nurture a sense of social conscience.
- Work to obtain assistance from psychiatrists who are compassionate, energetic, and knowledgeable about clinical, research, and administrative issues. Enlist the assistance of psychiatrists who are available for didactic and clinical teaching and supervision.
- Orient staff to as many components as possible of the mental health care system and its resources.
- Encourage networking and fostering of relationships with fellow professionals.
- Define mutual goals among collaborators.
- Develop flexibility—if supervisory feedback is poor, the leadership will be responsive.
- Provide optimistic leadership and role modeling. Quality leadership will model a "Let's do this" rather than a "You do this" approach.
- Model an "It can work" approach to problem solving.
- Teach the philosophy that treatment utilizing local community resources is almost always preferable for patients. Hospitalization of patients at sites distant from a their home or family (i.e., some state hospitals) is less than ideal.
- Use consistent high standards of clinical care.

SUGGESTED READINGS

Fichtner, C. G., Flaherty, J. A. (1993). Emergency psychiatry training and the decision to hospitalize. *Academic Psychiatry, 17*, 130–137.

Hillard, J. R., Zitek, B., Thienhaus, O. J. (1993). Residency training in emergency psychiatry. *Academic Psychiatry, 17*, 125–129.

McPherson, D. E. (1984). Teaching and research in emergency psychiatry. *Canadian Journal of Psychiatry, 29*, 50–54.

Chapter 7

EQUIPMENT AND SPACE REQUIREMENTS

You can't make bricks without straw.
—*English Proverb*

WHAT DOES A comprehensive emergency program need? As with any specialized job, professionals who perform their duties in a high quality crisis or emergency mental health system require specific tools as well as specialized training. Patients who are suffering from severe psychiatric disorders require specialized interventions and treatments and effective, efficient resources. Professionals who wish to provide the highest quality of care to crisis patients should consider the following space and equipment requirements.

SPACE REQUIREMENTS

Mobile Programs

Little actual space may be required for clinical operations within a mobile crisis program (i.e., patients are not seen on-site). Mobile programs encourage clinicians to see the patient out in the community and actually discourage clinicians from remaining in offices, clinics, or ERs. In such programs, however, space is required for staff communications and administrative functions, for team meetings and "rounds," and possibly for sleeping quarters if staff are staying the night on-call. Additional space is important for storing documents, supplies, equipment, and vehicles that may be needed for mobile calls.

Office- or Clinic-Based Programs

Some crisis programs will see patients in an office or clinic. Staff will require at least one or more "safe" rooms for seeing acutely ill patients. It is important to minimize the number of extraneous items in such rooms so that agitated patients will not harm themselves or others. For example, a nail file, scissors, or staple gun can be used as a weapon. Offices or clinic rooms should be painted cool, neutral colors, and care should be taken to make the environment attractive, yet not overstimulating. The office setting should be one in which patients feel comfortable and safe, and one that they may easily exit if feeling paranoid or extremely agitated. It may be a good idea to have panic buttons installed in discreet places or to have a clear procedure for getting police help if needed for agitated or threatening patients.

Emergency Room Programs

Emergency rooms are often filled with busy personnel, unstable sick patients, screaming children, and victims of trauma, and thus may be very intimidating to psychiatric patients. ER chaos may make a person in crisis feel all the more vulnerable and upset. Also, examining rooms in emergency departments are often filled with potentially dangerous items, such as needles, scalpel blades, and other medical equipment. If crisis patients are to be seen in an ER setting, it is useful to coordinate with the ER staff and director so that a "user-friendly" and safe area can be created for patients and professionals.

Depending on the work load, at least one room should be designated and equipped for psychiatric interviews. A room should also be available with the appropriate equipment for secluding or restraining agitated patients if necessary. Ideally, the seclusion room should be separate from the interview room. The following general considerations should be addressed for each psychiatry work space.

- A video camera placed in a protective housing may be installed to monitor patients continuously; it is too easy for psychotic or agitated patients to attempt to hurt themselves in poorly monitored seclusion rooms.
- Walls must be solidly constructed, since patients can very easily break through plywood and drywall.

- Electrical outlets must be covered and ceilings and light fixtures must be "break-proof."
- A locked, secure door to the room is also desirable.
- Doors should always swing out so that patients cannot barricade themselves in a room by piling up furniture or other large items behind the door. Glass should never be used in such a door; a polymer plastic (e.g., Lexan) is preferred.
- Heavy grade, plastic, spill-resistant furniture can be ordered for a comfortable interview environment. This type of furniture may be least attractive, but it works best.
- A heavy bed bolted to the floor can be safely used if an emergency patient requires restraint. Otherwise, solidly constructed stretchers with low centers of gravity should be available. Beds or stretchers used for restraint must be equipped with heavy-duty, well-padded straps.

Emergency rooms are probably the best places to assess and treat severely agitated or combative persons (if indeed seclusion or restraint is indicated), provided that the ER environment has been adequately designed for both the patient's and staff's safety. JCAHO (hospital accreditation) guidelines for patient safety are quite specific about the procedures that should be implemented for use in conjunction with appropriate equipment. Space for psychiatric emergency patients must be well-maintained and cleaned on a 'round-the-clock basis. Frequent repairs to the area are often necessary, due to patients' agitation and fear. Mental health emergency specialists should assist their medical colleagues in formulating procedures and policies on dealing with dangerous patients, and should also be involved in the training of ER and hospital security staff in the prevention and management of aggressive behavior.

TECHNICAL EQUIPMENT

Identification

Clear identification of clinical staff is a must. All clinicians should have easily visible photo identification badges, and procedures must be in place to update these regularly. Coordination in advance with police and other emergency responders will ensure that crisis personnel are readily identifiable at emergency scenes.

Communication

- *Telephones.* Many people will be calling the crisis service, so high-quality telephones with hold buttons, redial and speaker features, and "emergency trace" capabilities are preferred. (Although helpful, many programs do just fine without the ability to trace a call, and in some locales call tracing is impossible.) The phone set should reveal the caller's number along a display screen (helpful with abusive callers or suicide calls). In addition, phone repair service should be available within a few hours. If a professional answering service is used, the crisis program's administrators should train all operators in how to answer the phones and how to forward messages to clinical staff. Answering service staff frequently "turn over" so periodic training updates are essential. A TDX model phone should be available for hearing impaired callers.
- *Pagers.* All clinicians should carry pagers. Pager models that digitally display messages are ideal. Pager service should be adequate to cover the entire geographic range of the emergency service.
- *Cellular telephones.* Cellular telephones are also a must if a program plans to work in the community using mobile crisis interventions. Portable cellular phones are ideal, since they can be used in a car and taken into clinical sites. Cellular phones and pagers allow for easy design and use of call-back security check-up systems. Clinicians in the community can call back to their office for a "safety check" at designated intervals. The combination of both communication tools (i.e., phones and pagers) increases the reliability of safety checks, which are important to assure the safety of crisis clinicians in the community. This also allows for an expansion of the geographic range of contact (e.g., to a rural area without regular telephone availability), as well as call-back supervision on issues of patient care.
- *Fax machines.* Fax machines are essential. Clinical information must be sent and received from hospitals, clinics, private therapists, and administrative offices. For mobile crisis programs, cellular car phone/fax machines are ideal to send and receive information while in the field. Attention must always be paid to procedures for securing approval for information transfer; patient confidentiality must be protected, and patient consent for information exchange is *always* desirable. Memoranda of agreement between cooperating institutions are very helpful.

- *Computers.* A computer is needed, and an integrated software system or database can make statistical and clinical information easy to store, update, organize, and retrieve. It is important to be able to access data efficiently and rapidly for generating statistical reports, clinical data profiles, and patient information if needed for police emergency calls from the community. During a life and death emergency, you do not want to have to search by hand through hundreds of unorganized forms. For most programs, funds are budgeted for computer hardware and software. However, if necessary, information can still be organized "the old-fashioned way," by alphabetical order, code number, or date of last clinical interaction. Staff should also be able to access paper or microfiche copies of clinical data, since computers do break down at times.
- *Transportation.* Whenever possible, personal vehicles should not be used for mobile crisis work. Vehicles should be unobtrusive, yet plainly marked for identification by police with small decals on the back and/or side of the vehicle (e.g., M-1 or PES, or something that symbolizes a program's name but does not advertise it to the public at large). Unmarked police-type vehicles are not desirable, since clinicians do not want to be mistaken for undercover police (especially in high drug traffic areas). Mobile crisis vehicles should probably not have emergency lights unless the clinicians receive driver's training in advance from the police; if police request immediate assistance and the clinical staff are needed in a hurry, clinicians may ask for a police escort or ride inside police vehicles. Raincoats, boots, flashlights, maps, and jumper cables should be kept in the vehicle. Log sheets, clinical data sheets, commitment papers, etc., should be stocked in the vehicle as well (table 7.1 lists other supplies that should be kept in the vehicle.) If the program is located in an area where periodic floods occur, near rough or mountainous terrain, or in areas of heavy snow, consideration should be given to purchasing 4-wheel-drive vehicles.

PSYCHOPHARMACOLOGIC SUPPLIES

In emergency departments, it is important to have access to appropriate resources for patients who will require physical examination, laboratory screening, and alcohol/drug assays. ERs should have floor stock medications suitable for rapid control of the agitated or psychotic

Table 7.1

Necessary Equipment to Stock in a Mobile Crisis Vehicle

1 medicine box stocked with:
- psychotropic medications
- syringes
- alcohol pads
- band-aids
- needles
- sterile and unsterile 4 × 4 and 2 × 2 gauze pads
- equipment for drawing blood
- PO and IM (oral and injectable) neuroleptics and antidepressants
- PO and IM Benadryl
- PO and IM Cogentin
- lithium and Tegretol
- Depakote

A separate bag of sample medicines.

A doctor's bag containing:
- stethoscope
- disposable thermometers
- Rx pad
- alcohol pads
- rubber gloves
- sphygmomanometer (blood pressure cuff)
- tongue blades

A box or bag containing:
- clean-up supplies
- hand-washing supplies
- rubber gloves
- flashlights
- 1–2 blankets
- comfort items for clients, such as cigarettes
- ASA, Motrin, Tylenol, and Maalox

patient, including haloperidol (Haldol, an antipsychotic drug), fluphenazine hydrochloride (Prolixin HCl, another short-acting antipsychotic drug), lorazepam (Ativan, an antianxiety drug, also called an anxiolytic or sedative drug), and droperidol (Inapsine, a sedating antipsychotic drug), which is useful for extremely violent, agitated patients. Benztropine (Cogentin) and diphenhydramine (Benadryl) should be available to treat any side effects (such as extreme muscle stiffness and tightening) caused by the antipsychotic drugs. All medications should be available in both oral and injectable forms. These agents should also be available to clinic-based or mobile programs, although some of these agents may not be available outside of the hospital setting (e.g., lorazepam, which is a controlled substance). A fishing tackle box is a handy device for carrying medicine samples into the field.

SUGGESTED READING

Barton, G. M., & Friedman, R. S. (Eds.). (1986). *Handbook of emergency psychiatry for clinical administrators.* New York: Haworth.

Chapter 8

THE TELEPHONE ENCOUNTER

Learn calm to face what's pressing.
— *Horace (Odes)*

TELEPHONE CRISIS INTERVENTION may be the most anxiety-provoking aspect of emergency mental health work. In crisis clinics, hotline programs, psychiatric emergency departments, or mobile crisis settings, clinicians sometimes feel a great deal of anxiety about what will happen on the phone. When will it ring? Who will be calling? Will it be a routine message, a simple need for information and referral, or a distraught teenager with a loaded gun to his head? The anxiety can be overwhelming. Sometimes it's difficult for crisis clinicians to leave an office, for fear that they will miss "that one important suicidal call" and a life may end. At other times it's anxiety provoking for a crisis clinician to answer a phone. No matter what the situation, it is ALWAYS important for a crisis clinician to remember one idea. The caller is *always* calling for help — your help! If the caller did not want help, he or she would not have called!!!

INTRODUCTION TO TELEPHONE RESPONSE: GUIDELINES FOR CLINICIANS

The telephone call is often the means for a patient's first encounter with a community's emergency mental health system. This initial contact must be friendly, courteous, helpful, and succinct. Crisis clinicians must focus on problem solving. The telephone must not be used as an

60

opportunity for long, rambling discussions of issues, but rather as the first instrument to be used to assess and treat a potential mental health emergency.

General Principles

- The MOST important principle for dealing with an emergency phone call is to remain CALM!
- Assume that the caller wants your help, even if he is angry or hostile. If your help was not desired, the caller would not be wasting his time.
- Identify yourself or the program you are with, for example, "Hello, this is Dr. Branton with Mobile Crisis. How may I help you?" A friendly tone and positive beginning will often help to put "the brakes" on the crisis and the patient's anxiety.
- Develop an immediate alliance with the caller by listening actively. Remember, he cannot see you. You must use audible cues to develop rapport, such as "hmmm-hmmm" or "I see" or "I think I understand" or "Tell me more, please." Occasionally callers will become more agitated or angry if the clinician says, "I understand how you feel"; the better phrase would be, "I respect how you feel about this" or "I can see why you feel the way you do." No matter how experienced you are as a mental health clinician, you can never truly tell another human being that you "understand how you feel."
- Help the caller focus on the current, main problem. Use a semistructured set of questions for obtaining and gathering information (discussed below). Asking questions after an alliance is formed will instill confidence in the caller and help to diminish his anxiety. He will realize that he is talking with an expert. After establishing an alliance and getting general information for assessment, help the caller by offering resources, assisting with problem solving, or by providing necessary and realistic reassurance. Since the caller is in crisis, active problem solving is often called for.
- Remember, even if a person is calling about someone else, the caller will also be in crisis by definition. Assume that anyone who is aware of the crisis situation will also be in crisis. Make this assumption no matter how skilled the involved parties are.
- Many callers will express suicidal thoughts, however, few of the callers will be in imminent danger.

The Truly Suicidal Caller

- Remain calm. This is often very difficult initially, since the person calling often must project his or her anxiety and dysphoria onto the crisis clinician. Understand that by feeling a degree of helplessness or anxiety, you are actually allowing the patient to rid herself of uncomfortable feeling and, thus, you are providing relief to the patient.
- Use audible cues to gain a rapid alliance and to show patience, empathy, and caring. To establish an alliance, personalize the call as quickly as possible. Ask permission to address the caller on a first-name basis.
- Remember that the caller is ambivalent. He or she called for *your* help. If she desired to die immediately, she would not have called. Never believe that the caller is "crying wolf." Take every threat of suicide seriously!
- Be confident. Believe you can help the person through the crisis.
- As soon as possible, find out:
  1. the caller's full name, location, and phone number. If the caller gives only her name or phone number, and is actively suicidal, enlist the help of another staff member to use any available data to find an address or background information on the patient. Having a telephone system that displays a caller's telephone number can be very helpful. Most communities publish telephone books where phone numbers can be traced to corresponding addresses. Sometimes traces can be accomplished through telephone company supervisors, if necessary.
  2. specifics about her ideation, means, plan, intent, and whether she has already harmed herself.
  3. if the caller has harmed herself; if she has:
     a) keep her on the line. Reassure her that you want to help.
     b) don't hang up, even if she does.
     c) call EMS and police through 911. With a serious attempt (e.g., a serious tricyclic antidepressant overdose), seconds count!
     d) again, NEVER assume that the patient is faking or minimizing. Don't fall into the "crying wolf" trap.
  4. if the caller has intent; if she does, consider a mobile response, if available, or tell her to go to the ER. A truly suicidal patient should come to a clinic or ER only if accompanied by a responsi-

ble party. If a caller's suicide intent is serious and the caller refuses these options, call police or EMS.

- If, through interaction with the clinician, the caller feels better and can truly say that she has no intention to harm herself, arrange a follow-up plan — for example, a visit to the patient's home or location, an evaluation in the closest ER or walk-in clinic, or some other less emergent treatment.
- Rule out homicidal ideation in the suicidal caller. Severe stress or depression can lead to both suicidal and homicidal thinking.
- If the caller cannot guarantee her safety over the telephone, assume she must be seen for evaluation. If the caller refuses, police or EMS should be called.

The Chronic or Manipulative Caller

Chronic and manipulative callers are some of the most difficult patients. Many have an axis II personality disorder or a comorbid axis I disorder (see chapter 21). Crisis programs alone cannot treat these patients. They must be engaged in ongoing treatment with a therapist or case manager, who must develop a personalized cohesive treatment plan. The crisis service must play a significant role, however, in providing acute intervention with these patients. Crisis programs should always be involved in the development of a clinical management plan, since chronic or manipulative patients will always "test" the limits of any cohesive approach to their treatment. Often, such patients will use the telephone for such limit testing. Because they cannot tolerate their unbearable anxiety and dysphoria (psychologic discomfort) they must often "unload" or project these feelings onto others. The clinician must be empathic, firm, and communicative.

- Realize that the person is often *projecting* psychologically painful thoughts and feelings onto you.
- Because you are the recipient of such dysphoric feeling states, you may become anxious and frustrated (and even hostile at times) with this type of caller; use this understanding to empathize with the patient's feelings, then set limits. Once you are experiencing the *same* feelings the patient has projected onto you, then you can truly feel how frustrated the patient must be. This again is your conduit to forming an empathic connection with the caller.

- Limit setting may include telling the caller that:
  1. he needs to refer to his therapist for ongoing, definitive treatment.
  2. phone "treatment" is not effective.
  3. if he is too out of control, he must go to the emergency room (mobile responses for these patients are often less helpful, as they may escalate the undesired behaviors).
  4. if he threatens to harm himself, you'll call the police or EMS.
  5. if the caller is in treatment, he must discuss these feelings with his therapist.
  6. he should call a friend, AA, hotline, etc.
- Follow the treatment plan outline. Again, treatment plans should come from a patient's therapist and not from an emergency service. The emergency mental health system should be a consultant to these difficult patients and to their therapists. Crisis services should enforce treatment plans in order to prevent splitting (i.e., the patient seeing the crisis clinicians as helpful, but his therapist as singularly unhelpful). The crisis program should be involved in the planning phase of such a treatment plan. Sometimes, in the treatment of a borderline patient, a therapist or case manager may suggest that the patient call the crisis line for two 15-minute periods over a weekend. Such a plan, when structured and approved by all parties, can benefit both patients and therapists alike. Once agreed upon by the therapist, the patient, and crisis programs, an emergency service should ideally have copies of relevant treatment plans and must enforce the plan to the letter.
- Realize that patients who have difficult personality disorders may not be happy with the recommended outcome. Often (particularly with patients who have little self-esteem), the patient may have to devalue the crisis clinician in order to feel better (i.e., by putting you "down" he will feel better, as this makes him feel relatively "superior" or "up").
- Be a gentle, repetitive, yet firm "voice of reality" with such a caller. Limit setting is a *must*.
- Supervision is often required around dealing with such difficult patients. The crisis clinician must always ask for supervision, so that countertransference feelings do not lead him or her to become overly involved, aggressive, seductive, or intimidated by the psychopathology of these patients.

Summary of Telephone Response

- It will be a *rare* occurrence for a caller to kill himself while on the telephone. If it happens, it is *not* your fault.
- Occasionally, even the best crisis clinicians feel unsure of what they are doing with a particularly difficult caller. *After you have established an alliance with the patient,* you may put someone on hold or call him or her back if you are in a crisis panic (but only if you have the caller's name and phone number). Say something like, "Fred, I have to deal with another emergency temporarily—I need to put you on hold—please give me your number in case you are accidentally disconnected." Then get quick consultation from your back-up staff or supervisor.
- Be confident. You will know how to handle almost every crisis call you receive. You will rarely, if ever, not be able to resolve a call positively.

SPECIFIC INFORMATION THAT MUST BE OBTAINED FROM THE BEGINNING OF A CRISIS TELEPHONE CALL

"The horror of that moment," the King went on,
"I shall never, *never* forget!"
"You will, though," the Queen said,
"if you don't make a memorandum of it."
—*Lewis Carroll (Alice's Adventures in Wonderland)*

Emergency mental health programs should always fill out a "log sheet" for every clinical interaction (including patient evaluations, patient phone calls, alerts from the treatment community, etc.), for several reasons:

- This will afford a significant data base for the program, which can be used for clinical and statistical purposes.
- It fulfills an important communication link (e.g., day shift personnel must know what happened during the night shift).
- It provides documentation for medical/legal issues.
- If a mobile response to a patient is to be considered, "the homework" needs to be done so that all information pertaining to the patient's security and the safety of the clinical staff can be addressed. Each

phone call should be logged in and referenced to the crisis program's data bank (files, computer database, etc.).

In order to standardize practice, it is recommended that each program design its own log sheet (see sample log sheet at the end of chapter 1) to include data the clinician should obtain with each telephone encounter.

SUGGESTED READING

Echterling, L. G., & Hartsough, D. M., (1989). Phases of helping in successful crisis telephone calls. *Journal of Community Psychology, 17,* 249–257.

Chapter 9

PROTOCOL FOR FIELD WORK

I was sick, and ye visited me.
—*Matthew (25:36)*

THE PREMISE OF THIS BOOK is that a truly responsive psychiatric emergency service will be accessible to the patient in need, regardless of where the patient is. A mobile response into the community is perhaps the least costly, most efficient and cost-effective manner of handling a patient's crisis. However, for clinicians who have not gone on house calls or into the community at large, it may at first be an intimidating idea, but with practice and experience, mobile responses quickly become the preferred mechanism for providing effective crisis intervention.

Whenever a mobile response is planned, it must be thought out carefully and clearly delineated. This chapter will review some of the ideas behind safe and meaningful mobile crisis responses.

GOALS OF A MOBILE VISIT

Clinicians must ask, "What is this visit supposed to accomplish?" Some answers may be:

- To assist or respond to the patient's immediate dilemma.
- To provide support and structure in an unstable situation.
- To assess the client and the situation. Be aware that in a relatively

We thank Dona McBride, R.N., Mary Hughes, R.N., and Mary Campbell, M.Ed., for their contributions to this chapter.

less emergent call there may be time for more in-depth assessment and planning.

· To initiate a treatment alliance. (Some patients will need medication, but it may take more than one visit. Can anyone really imagine taking a medicine prescribed by strangers who show up at your door?)

The following factors also influence the goals of the visit:

· The mission of the particular mobile crisis program.
· Educational, research, and clinical components of the program.
· State Department of Mental Health policies and procedures.
· Dangerousness of situation.

BEFORE THE MOBILE VISIT

Initial Phone Contact

The mental health professional must be aware of, and deal with, the strong pressure and anxiety that a crisis creates. Remember that anyone involved in a psychiatric crisis or emergency will also be in crisis themselves, due to the overwhelming nature of the anxiety, fear, or trepidation experienced. Thus, all professionals, family members, or mental health clinicians who refer an emergency or crisis situation to a mental health program can exhibit crisis-related behaviors. Most people will not be aware of these feelings, but one can see them break through in atypical behaviors such as annoyance, a sense of entitlement, or an aggressive, demanding attitude.

Careful preparation is the key. All calls should be carefully screened by clinicians, who are expected to employ a highly facilitative "How can I help you?" approach from the first moment of telephone contact with a caller. There should be no cumbersome intake or appointment procedure, but clinicians should ask a series of structured questions before agreeing to respond to a request for mobile emergency services. As described in chapter 8, rapid use of an organized information sheet is helpful for the initial assessment. Such questioning helps diminish the caller's anxiety and gathers critical data quickly and thoroughly. If time allows, collecting further in-depth data is helpful, but in a life-or-death emergency (e.g., a call for assistance from police concerning someone about to jump off a building) it is best to use cellular car phones en route to the location. (When police call to request assistance in life-or-death situations, the team can often respond immediately without gathering much phone data, as security is often already on site—see chapter 17 for further discussion.)

Many calls to a mobile emergency psychiatry program do not require a mobile response or face-to-face visit. Often, people call for phone counseling or information about referral to community resources, such as battered women's shelters, hospice programs, AIDS support groups. However, if a patient's psychiatric distress requires that he or she be seen immediately—if the patient is extremely dysphoric, depressed, suicidal, homicidal, or psychotic—this is sufficient indication for a mobile response.

The clinician should then determine the optimal environment for the mobile response. More information will help to answer this question. For instance, if the patient has hurt himself or has taken a serious drug overdose, the patient must be triaged to an ER setting (by police or EMS), and the mobile response should be directed to that ER after the patient has been medically evaluated and stabilized. On the other hand, if the patient is severely depressed, but guarantees that he won't harm himself, then a visit to the patient's location is probably in order.

Prior to a mobile response, clinicians should attempt to determine if the patient is suffering from a medical or neurologic emergency, or whether the identified patient is willing to be seen by members of a crisis team (since unwilling patients may pose greater safety risks to staff). Such determinations will indicate different actions. For example, if a patient calls after having taken 2000 mg of imipramine (Tofranil, a classical tricyclic antidepressant that can be fatal if 1000 mg or more is taken), a mobile crisis clinician must find out the exact location of the caller and have EMS immediately dispatched there to transport the patient to an ER. A mobile response from mental health clinicians would only delay potentially life-saving treatments. When the patient is medically stable, he or she can be evaluated by crisis professionals.

In the majority of requests for mobile assistance, clinicians are at little, if any, risk. If, however, a situation is potentially dangerous (e.g., an assaultive patient or a suicidal or homicidal person in possession of a loaded gun), the team members should attempt to calm and support the person over the phone before or during their ride to the patient's location. If a patient is armed, or potentially dangerous due to a past history of violence or current state of agitation, police should AL-

WAYS be asked to accompany the crisis clinicians to the patient's location. The patient should be informed that the police are coming too, and any resistance from the patient should be dealt with in a therapeutic manner prior to seeing the patient face-to-face. Often, reassuring the patient that the police can leave once everything is under good control (of course, this could even mean *after* the patient is brought into a hospital) will help the patient agree to let law enforcement officers contain and secure the situation. When a mobile team is responding to a police request for assistance, clinicians should maintain cellular phone communication with a distraught patient or with the officer in charge while en route as it may help to decrease the danger. Such communication will minimize everyone's anxiety and thus decrease the likelihood of harmful actions.

Whenever mobile crisis clinicians request police support, clinicians should meet police at a remote spot away from the patient. Police must be informed about the situation, why a mobile call is necessary, what the goals of the call are, and what is needed from them. The team should be open to suggestions by the police, who have clear expertise in security and safety issues. (See chapter 17 on working with police.)

Security Policies and Procedures

Policies and procedures provide a framework for mobile visits. Most procedures are designed for the safety of clinical staff, patients, and others involved. For example, when leaving on a call, the team writes down on an erasable board the time they leave, who is going, the vehicle used, and the destination; later, someone at the office will log in callbacks when the team checks in with staff. A callback system should be developed whereby clinicians call their office upon arrival at a site, within a specified period of time after entering a scene, and at its conclusion. If a clinician does not call the office within a specified amount of time (e.g., 30 minutes), the person who is tracking the team in the field should contact them by phone or beeper; no response should then be an indication for police to check on the safety of the team. A large wall map keyed into a street listing and directory is essential to locate a street quickly, cross-reference it, and then locate it on the marked grids of the wall map; thus, the team's destination can be found immediately.

Team members should work closely with the area's police and sheriff departments and must have specific communication protocols with law enforcement dispatchers. Working relationships, role definition, and protocols for working together must all be worked out and defined prior to beginning mobile responses to the community (see chapter 10). The team should, at the very least, always alert police dispatchers of their destination via cellular telephone so that officers can reach them rapidly if needed. Standard procedure is always to contact the police department that has jurisdiction where the mobile visit is to occur. The mobile team can determine if police should be present during the visit or if they need only be "on standby."

In the majority of crisis cases, police do not need to be called to the scene. If there appears to be a medical emergency, EMS is dispatched to the scene (if unclear, the team should respond with EMS and/or police). If the client is in current treatment with a mental health professional, information from the therapist can be invaluable and should be accessed if possible.

If there is no security risk, the team may choose to respond alone without the police. In fact, a mobile response may be the preferred method of contact in as many cases as possible. Again, one *absolute* rule is that a crisis team should never visit an armed suicidal or homicidal patient without the police. The likelihood of injury in such cases is just too great. Caution is the first rule, especially when dealing with agitated or potentially dangerous patients.

The field team should always consist of at least two individuals. For supervision, the team may contact a senior supervisor via beeper or cellular phone to review the case and develop treatment and disposition plans.

DURING THE MOBILE VISIT

Arriving at the Scene

Mobile emergency mental health services can perform evaluations in car dealerships, stores, restaurants, funeral homes, churches, parking lots, night clubs, and cemeteries, as well as bridges, interstate highways, and roofs of buildings. In fact, there is no place in the community that is immune from a crisis. Wherever the location, here are some tips for initial evaluation of such situations:

1. Survey the location.
   - What is taking place?
   - Who is there?
2. Survey the patient's behavior.
   - Watch for clues that the patient may be violent (e.g., yelling, loud voice, presence of alcohol or drugs, opening and closing of fists, paranoid staring, agitation and pacing, hitting things, etc).
   - Does the patient have access to potential weapons (sticks, rocks, bottles, knives, guns, etc.)?
   - Does the patient know that clinical staff are coming? Is he or she willing to meet and talk with a staff member? If the patient is unaware that the team is coming, then the risks of the visit are obviously greater. No one likes being surprised, especially by strangers. Whenever possible, a patient should be informed by a friend or family member of a mobile visit.

   Note: Clinical staff cannot enter a patient's home or apartment unless invited by the patient or someone in co-ownership (e.g., family members) of the residence. Otherwise, clinicians may be sued or arrested and charged with trespassing (see chapter 12).
3. Check the physical setting.
   - Are walkways and entrances lighted?
   - Where are exit doors?
   - Are there people close by to assist if necessary?
   - Can staff get to the car quickly?
   - Are there any barking dogs that may be dangerous or trained to attack?
   - What is the hygienic condition of the place? Is urine or feces present? Foul odors? Soiled furniture? Unkempt pets? Unbathed client or family members? Insects? Spoiled food? Substandard housing? Does the patient have adequate heat?

   Note: If the client could have an infectious disease such as TB or hepatitis, use universal precautions and aseptic techniques. Most patients are understanding about professional job requirements and rules. If rubber gloves are worn, explain to the patient that this is a rule you must follow.

Entering the Scene: Introductions

1. *Always* stand to the side of a front door when you first knock.
2. When someone comes to the door, introduce yourself using the

patient's/family member's formal name (Mr., Mrs., Ms.) unless otherwise instructed by a family member, or unless a first-name-basis relationship already exists.

Showing proper respect helps to increase trust and rapport. But most of all, it's just a humane way to conduct oneself. There may be a time when clinical staff need to make a special request, such as turning down a TV set or stereo, or to set limits, and this must also be done in a respectful way. Conversely, shouting out or demanding orders will tend to escalate a situation. If a staff member is perceived as aggressive or controlling, rapport may be undermined. (Of course certain patients with personality disorders may perceive clinicians as controlling or aggressive even when none of these behaviors is actually present.)

3. Address the client and the family in a warm, cordial way. Ask permission to enter. Show appropriate IDs as necessary. During introductions, team members should identify themselves, state what agency they are with, and how they were referred:

"Hello, Mrs. Smith, I'm Dona McBride and this is Dr. Christie. We're from the Mobile Crisis Program. Your sister called us needing some assistance. May we come in?"

Danger Signs

Observe the environment for safety. If weapons are near (even scissors), offer an excuse to leave the room and ask the police to secure the weapon. If the client is agitated, see if he responds to gentle direction to "please sit down." If the patient is incapable of calming down, beware! The patient is communicating to staff that he is having great difficulty controlling himself. Staff may need to leave and ask police to transport the patient to a safer place. Do not be shy about telling a patient that he or she scares you. Sometimes, if patients are severely mentally ill, they do not have the insight required to recognize escalating emotion and agitation.

Sometimes patients are offended that family members "think I'm crazy" or are embarrassed that family members have called a mobile crisis program. One way to respond is to say, "Your sister (or other person) is worried; she cares about you" or "Your sister asked us to look you up; she was concerned about your well-being."

Tips on Interviewing

It is good practice to ask the patient for permission to talk with him or her. Give as much control to the patient as possible, keeping safety issues foremost in mind. Asking him or her about medical problems or stressors is a good "ice breaker." The questions to be asked in taking a history are discussed fully in chapter 20.

In every patient interaction, no matter what the setting, it is most important for the clinician to develop a strong therapeutic alliance with the patient. If a patient is suspicious of crisis staff, sometimes it helps to make "small talk," perhaps asking about a particular object in the room (e.g., a photograph), or commenting on the loveliness of the patient's home. This also assists in discovering whether the patient can pay attention and comprehend the conversation. If the patient is psychotic, he or she may make bizarre statements. For example, one patient thought that her kitchen was a TV studio with bugging devices and microphones.

Take into consideration what is needed. If the client is psychotic or too agitated, it may be best to obtain most of the history from a family member or close friend. Sometimes asking the patient to answer questions regarding his medical, psychiatric, or social history can reveal his level of agitation. After a few questions, he may be too agitated, hostile, or psychotic to continue.

If possible, interview the client in a quiet, private place. One way to open is: "May I ask you some questions about your health history?" or "Can you tell me about . . . ?" Very often, rapport and trust are forged during the history taking. The crisis professional should employ good listening techniques and empathy. Avoid power struggles and disputes. Obtain information as efficiently as possible but try not to be abrupt or to appear condescending toward the client or others involved. Make a great effort to be nonjudgmental about the environment. Ask about the current status of the client, the onset of the problem, and precipitating events. If time permits, ask questions pertaining to the client's health history, chronic medical problems, current medications (ask the patient to show you his medication bottles), past and present psychiatric treatment, alcohol and drug use, family and social history, and a brief mental status assessment. Gathering the above information helps to assess the patient and present an appropriate treatment plan.

Most of the time, it is helpful to interview the client and/or family in separate rooms if possible. This helps to decrease argument or competition for attention. This also allows for more confidentiality, and for the family or caretakers to feel more supported by the clinical team. If family members begin to argue, always separate them.

No set order exists for establishing a rapport with a patient experiencing a psychiatric emergency. The crisis clinician has to arrange the interview creatively and intuitively to build an alliance with the patient.

Showing Respect and Cultural Sensitivity

- Address persons as Mr., Ms., Mrs.; speak about them to others as "this gentleman," "the lady." Do not use terms such as "a drunk" when speaking to others about the patient.
- Bear in mind that people from different cultures may have different expectations for eye contact, appropriate physical distance between people, etc.
- People may have culturally differing ideas of the etiology and treatment of illness (e.g., belief that depression/psychosis is caused by devil, spirits, evil root, etc.).

ENDING THE MOBILE VISIT

- If another emergency intervenes, quickly terminate by making plans for the client. If the client needs hospitalization, set these arrangements in motion. If the client needs other resources, provide names and telephone numbers and be sure to follow-up with the client later.
- If you are at a patient's home and he or she refuses to be seen, be aware of trespassing laws. It may be possible to ask a family member to let staff in, but unless the situation is a life-threatening emergency, be wary of trespassing. Above all, be respectful of the fact that this is, after all, the patient's home.

AFTER THE MOBILE VISIT: FOLLOW-UP

When necessary, the team should be able to visit patients several times until a crisis is resolved. At other times, it may be necessary to follow up an initial visit with periodic telephone calls to the patient. If a person requires hospitalization and no local beds are available, the team may provide more intensive services to manage patients in the community until a local bed becomes available. Intensive outreach services often alleviate the need for hospitalization. Finally, in order to support issues of continuity of care, patients' therapists should always be contacted by the emergency team in an attempt to ensure linkage to long-term mental health care providers. If appointments are not kept, the team may need to follow up with additional mobile responses.

Chapter 10

PROTOCOL FOR COLLABORATION WITH THE POLICE DEPARTMENT

Out of this nettle, danger, we pluck this flower, safety.
— *William Shakespeare (King Henry IV)*

THE POLICE ARE a vital link in psychiatric emergency systems, but they may lack specialized training in responding to *psychiatric* emergencies. The police are frequently the first responders to crisis calls from homes or other community sites. They must often provide emergency assessment of family crises, violence, substance abuse, unusual behavior, or altered mental status. Police also apprehend or transport mentally ill persons.

A close liaison between emergency psychiatry or mobile crisis programs and local police departments is mutually beneficial and leads to an improvement of care for psychiatric patients in crisis. If a psychiatric emergency program is to provide care for patients in a community-based fashion, that is, by going to the patient in crisis, then it is *essential* to have a close working relationship with the police department. This type of relationship will allow the clinicians to work in a safe environment, and will allow the police to most effectively use their expertise. Clinical staff may act as consultants to the police in some

We thank Maria Durban, M.Ed., Deborah McAlhany, M.A., Susan J. Hardesty, M.D., and Shannon Tyson, M.D., for their contributions to this chapter.

situations, providing negotiation skills and expertise in mental illness and substance abuse. In other situations, the police provide security and advice to clinicians in dangerous situations. Police can also be used to check on patients who may be suicidal but unreachable by phone, or as part of a patient's treatment plan in order to set appropriate limits or to prevent suicidal acts. For example, if a borderline patient cannot guarantee that she won't harm herself, yet refuses all attempts at intervention, the police may have to be called to check on her.

If a psychiatric emergency service is visible in the community, then police feel more receptive to being involved in matters of patient care. A camaraderie develops between both professional disciplines. If police are always being asked by institution-based programs to "check out" their patients, they can often feel that they are being inappropriately utilized. Working together "on the streets" quickly changes this perception and brings a new sense of validity to mental health in the eyes of the police department.

DEVELOPING THE COLLABORATION

If a program model is assembled for reaching out to wherever the crisis patient is, the emergency mental health team will need to define its working relationship with the police department. There are several administrative and practical steps in this initial process:

1. Hold initial meetings with the police department to discuss mutual goals openly and to negotiate circumstances and procedures for collaboration. Explain why the program is being developed, the goals and funding of the program, and how it can help patrol officers. For instance, if a crisis clinician goes to a suicidal person's home, it will save an officer from needing to respond.

    It is also important for directors of crisis programs and clinicians to meet with the chiefs of police departments in the community. Police departments are hierarchical, that is, the chief tells his commanders what to do and they in turn direct the line officers. Therefore, it is important for any director of a crisis program to know the police departments' chiefs and to form an alliance with them.
2. Visit as many police precincts as possible.
    • Meet with the field officers during their "roll calls." Explain your operating procedures in detail. Tell them under what circum-

stances you will call upon their services and how you can consult together in the field. Let them know of your working schedule, call availability (24 hours a day, evenings only, etc.), and geographic catchment area. Explain when and how you might call upon them for assistance.

· Meet with dispatch operators to review protocols for check-in with police and for back-up support from police.

3. Define operating procedures in detail.

· Policy decisions regarding personal exposure to harm, the issues of wearing body armor, etc., should all be worked out in advance. Otherwise, false expectations may be created, which can lead to a sense of frustration or bad feelings. It is recommended that crisis clinicians *never* allow themselves to be placed in harm's way.

· Many programs do not allow clinical staff to enter any direct line of fire or danger, or to wear body armor (which may give a clinician a false sense of security). The directors of a crisis program must explain their working procedures in explicit detail. Crisis clinicians must be carefully informed of these procedures, and must follow them to the letter.

· Crisis clinicians must understand that in a critical situation in the community, they are consultants to the police, and all activities and major decisions at the scene of an incident must be coordinated through the commanding officer.

4. Realize that training of all parties will take several months and that police departments, like *all* agencies, "turn over" staff. New officers and commanders may be constantly coming into or leaving the police system. Therefore, periodic inservice programs and updates of new information will need to be offered. From time to time, training programs should be held for new officers and other interested persons in the community. Mental health and psychiatry are fields of rapid change. Keep the police department up to date and interested by sharing new and exciting treatment and research information. Get involved in officer education.

5. Maintain the collaboration with periodic meetings with the police to reclarify mutual responsibilities and goals and review critical situations.

6. Debrief police when they are involved in critical incidents, act as informal consultants, and provide referrals for police personnel who may need mental health treatment.

7. Some communities have police chaplaincy programs that interface daily with law enforcement departments. Get to know the chaplains and discuss how a crisis program can interface with them.

MOBILE CRISIS AND LAW ENFORCEMENT
IN CRITICAL SITUATIONS

Collaboration between police officers and mental health personnel can allow both sides to complement each other in resolving acute emergencies, such as "critical incidents." In such situations, a person may be locked in a room threatening suicide or homicide, standing with a knife held to his chest or neck or a gun to the head, or threatening to jump from a bridge or rooftop. Such critical incidents involve physical or emotional barricades that present enormous challenges to the police and crisis workers trying to resolve them. Much of the success of a collaborative approach lies in ongoing, open communication between an area's police department and the psychiatric emergency team well in advance of the actual crisis situation. This exciting and difficult topic will be discussed further in chapter 17.

The bottom line is this: In a community-based, fully mobile psychiatric emergency program, police and mental health must be best friends! Otherwise, the job cannot be done.

Chapter 11

PROTOCOL FOR EMERGENCY ROOM WORK

Many shall run to and fro,
and knowledge shall be increased.
—*Daniel (7:13)*

MOBILE CRISIS PROGRAMS respond to psychiatric emergencies wherever they occur, that is, in patients' homes, places of business, schools, bus stops, shopping malls, motels, or practically anywhere in a community. Frequently, it will be necessary to evaluate and treat psychiatric patients who present to ERs. Thus, it is important for clinicians to be familiar with the general working environment of an ER and to understand the personnel who work there. This chapter will provide an introduction to the ER environment and the key personnel who work there.*

In many parts of the country, patients in crisis must be prescreened by mental health clinicians prior to hospitalization, especially prior to hospitalization in a state psychiatric facility. Such policies make sense; psychiatric hospitals are often overcrowded and should therefore take only those patients in urgent need of hospital care. Because the sickest psychiatric patients are often brought to medical ERs and then sent to state hospitals for admission, emergency mental health professionals

---

*Some crisis professionals work in psychiatric emergency rooms and will therefore be familiar with emergency departments and their staff. This chapter will review the personnel who work in an ER from the point of view of someone who is not familiar with this acute care environment.

81

should be available to see patients in community ERs. Some mental health programs are completely ER-based. In most communities, crisis clinicians will need to see patients in an emergency room setting from time to time. This chapter will therefore also discus some of the issues and dynamics a crisis professional should be aware of.

ER PERSONNEL: WHO ARE THEY?

It is often necessary to involve medical staff in the emergency evaluation of a crisis patient. Psychiatric patients may frequently present special problems for ERs and ER physicians. For instance, crisis patients take a great deal of patience and time and often require special intervention techniques, which simply may not be possible for an ER doctor who might have to see 20 or 30 patients in an hour. Therefore, crisis professionals must explain their goals and procedures to the ER personnel to insure maximal cooperation and sharing of treatment goals for patients.

In an ER, the most important individual is the *ER director*. He or she is the "captain of the ship" and sets policy, hires physician staff, creates treatment protocols, and makes life easy or difficult for mental health patients and staff. If mental health clinicians are to intervene in the treatment of psychiatric patients in emergency rooms, it is important to have a series of regular meetings with the ER director. At such meetings, mental health experts should ask about the needs and expectations of the medical and nursing staff. It is important to state that mental health experts can bring diagnostic and treatment expertise to the ER environment and as consultants to the ER can assist in making better clinical decisions. Expert consultation also diminishes overall medical/legal liability for ER physicians. It is important to develop memoranda of agreement (MOAs) so that mental health care professionals are appropriately covered for official privileging and credentialing within the ER. Also, ER directors must understand the degree of clinical supervision in a crisis program, so that they and their physician staff can develop a sense of trust in the clinical decisions which are made.

In exchange for the support of the ER staff, crisis clinicians might offer training for both physicians and staff. The presence of crisis clinicians often has a calming effect on a busy or tense ER milieu, and crisis clinicians will often be in an excellent position for informal "debriefing" of ER personnel (who dislike formal counseling but thrive on informal conversation about stressful subjects). It is important for mental health clinicians to remember that everything they do should be approved by the ER *attending physician*, who is ultimately responsible for patient care and issues of liability. Good ER physicians wish to clear the ER of patients by the arrival of the next shift. This should be kept in mind by crisis clinicians, as psychiatric evaluations are often time consuming and mysterious to ER personnel.

The *nurse manager* leads the nursing staff, who do much of the important clinical care of ER patients and is therefore also an important person to get to know. The nurse manager is also involved in policy development and will want to know your opinions about such policies as seclusion and restraints, searching patients, emergency medication administration, clinical record keeping, and other matters of importance. Crisis clinicians should be aware of all policies and procedures by which an ER operates.

EMS officials and paramedics are often encountered in the ER setting. Their job is frenetic and difficult. They are a high-energy group and often exhibit bravado and irreverent humor, which are necessary ego defense mechanisms for this group of brave and skilled professionals. Crisis workers should get to know EMS professionals since these are the people who are often responsible for saving the lives of suicidal patients.

Police and security personnel are other important professionals who appear in the emergency setting. Uniformed officers are most interested in getting back out on the street as soon as possible. Whenever feasible, ER protocols should be developed to accomplish this goal. Police often have essential information and should be consulted whenever they bring a patient in for treatment. Because the police are so busy, it is not uncommon for them to bring in a patient in crisis and immediately return to duty out on the street. If the officers have critical information that is necessary for the emergency evaluation and treatment of the patient, police dispatch may be used to contact the appropriate officers for more information. Sheriff's deputies often bring in patients under civil detention orders for evaluation and possible involuntary hospital admission. Again, it is important to speak to these officers to obtain critical information and history, and to enlist them as valuable members of the ER mental health team. Further-more, in most ERs hospital security guards are available to assist with patients or visitors who may be out of control. Clinicians should get to know these security guards on a first-name basis. They will protect not only patients' welfare, but also the welfare and safety of all staff.

The ER requires rapid evaluation and treatment, but a thorough evaluation of a patient in crisis, including a good interview and appro-priate treatment recommendations, may actually take longer. ER per-sonnel should be warned about this longer time frame in advance, and that thoroughness, although time-consuming, will ultimately lead to improved patient care and diminished legal liability. In addition, fol-low-up and continuity linkages must be provided for patients, espe-cially if they are not hospitalized. The crisis clinician's provision of such continuity of care will give ER physicians and staff extra reassur-ance and make them more comfortable in trying alternatives to tradi-tional hospital admission.

GOALS AND TECHNIQUES OF AN EFFECTIVE ER CONSULTATION

ER professionals are often uncomfortable around crisis patients. It can, therefore, be helpful for the mental health professional to take a moment upon entering the ER to assess the tension/anxiety level. At times, the atmosphere may be friendly and relaxed and at other times, tense and chaotic with hostile overtones. In the latter case it is impor-tant to develop a dialogue with the ER physician about the patient. In this way, the crisis clinician may be able to reduce the tension level and effect a better outcome for the patient, who will then be treated by a more relaxed and friendly health care provider. For instance, don't ask an ER doctor, "Is the patient medically cleared?" This can mean different things to different doctors and in different patient situations. In a patient who presents with depression due to a failing grade in school, a medical clearance may simply involve recording the patient's vital signs (i.e., taking his or her temperature, pulse, respiration rate, and blood pressure). On the other hand, a healthy 70-year-old woman with no psychiatric history who presents with sudden confusion and hallucinations will not be medically cleared until she is thoroughly examined, including careful laboratory analysis of her body's functions. Therefore, when talking to an ER doctor or nurse, it is more important to develop a dialogue by asking, "Can you tell me about the patient?" This question will allow a discussion so that all parties know what the patient requires. In addition, the ER attending physician will need to be kept abreast of the developments that occur during the (sometimes time-consuming) patient's evaluation. This will help to keep the attending involved, and will also diminish that physician's anxiety level.

ER staff often want mental health clinicians to assume total care for the psychiatric emergency patient. While clinicians may assume some responsibility, the psychiatric patient is always the responsibility of the ER attending physician. The consultative process is one of mutual cooperation.

After the evaluation, the mental health clinician should present his findings to the ER physician in charge of the patient's care. A discussion should ensue around the mental health clinician's recommendations. In most cases, the ER staff will agree with the findings of the clinician. However, in cases where there are serious disagreements, the mental health clinician should discuss the situation and his findings with his own supervisory staff. The supervisor may address any remaining concerns with the ER physician and clinical staff.

Following is an example of a good ER consultation.

EMS brings in a 23-year-old woman who has taken a small number of Tylenol pills after an argument with her boyfriend. Her Tylenol level is nontoxic (less than 140 at four hours after the overdose), so she will not need medical antidote treatment. She appears physically stable and can go home if she is psychiatrically stable. Dr. Simpson, an ER physician, is worried about her and wants to know if she should be sent to a state hospital. He pages Carl Young, the mental health crisis clinician on call for the ER.

Dr. S: Hi, this is Dr. Simpson in the emergency room at Hope Hospital.
Mr. Y: Hi, Carl Young here. I'm the crisis clinician on tonight. How can I help you?
Dr. S: I've got this lady I'd like for you to see. She took a Tylenol OD but she's fine now.
Mr. Y: Okay. Can you tell me her name? [Writes it down] Has she ever done anything like this before?
Dr. S: No, this is the first time.
Mr. Y: Anything bring it on?
Dr. S: Some kind of fight with her boyfriend.
Mr. Y: Okay. Is the boyfriend with her?

Dr. S: Yeah, he's in the waiting room. I'll ask him to stay.

Mr. Y: Yes, that will be helpful. Was her Tylenol level in the toxic range?

Dr. S: No. It was 32 at four hours.

Mr. Y: Any other medical problems?

Dr. S: No, she's healthy.

Mr. Y: Okay, I'll be there as soon as possible. Thanks very much.

Mr. Young arrives at the ER 15 minutes later. He says hello to Dr. Simpson, the charge nurse, and the ER security guard. He reviews the ER chart, tells the patient's boyfriend that he'd like to speak to him in a little while, and then sees the patient. She is much calmer, did not show any signs of suicidality prior to the quarrel, and regrets having taken an overdose. She agrees to outpatient care, is glad to be alive, and will call the 24-hour hotline number if she feels worse. Her boyfriend is quite concerned. Mr. Young counsels them both together, and feels secure that the danger has passed. It is now time for him to speak with Dr. Simpson.

Mr. Y: Dr. Simpson. Do you have one minute for me to talk with you regarding our patient? [Notice he uses the word "our," suggesting a sense of shared responsibility.]

Dr. S: Sure. What do you think?

Mr. Y: Well, I feel this was truly an impulsive thing. She has no history of previous suicide behaviors and she is glad to be alive. She has had no neurovegetative signs of depression or any other psychiatric disturbance and her family history is negative for completed suicide. She is willing to go into treatment as an outpatient and she and her boyfriend are back on good terms. She agrees to call our 24-hour hotline if she feels impulsive. I'm going to help her get an appointment for some short-term counseling in our clinic. I think it's okay to let her go.

Dr. S: Okay. She has all the phone numbers and knows who to get in touch with?

Mr. Y: She sure does! May I tell her you'll be discharging her?

Dr. S: Okay. Sounds appropriate.

Mr. Young then speaks to the patient and writes down the plan for her and gives her a sheet with emergency phone numbers to be used if needed. He then fills out the one-page ER consultation report and puts it on the patient's chart. (Table 11.1 lists information required in an ER consultation report. Even the best consultation is useless if it cannot be articulated in writing.)

Carl Young then says goodbye to Dr. Simpson and other staff.

Table 11.1
Sections of a Brief ER Consultation Report

Patient's sex, race, age, marital status, date of birth (identifying data)

Patient's reason for presentation (chief complaint)

History of recent problem (history of present illness)

Concise summary of any previous problems

Mental status report

Impression or assessment (diagnosis)

Treatment plan or recommendation

Professional signature and date

In summary, we have introduced the reader to the world of the ER. Emergency rooms are busy, sometimes scary, and intimidating to patients and even, at times, to mental health clinicians. By understanding the needs of the professionals who work in ERs, and by providing expert consultation to those individuals, a spirit of colleagueship and fun will develop over time.

SUGGESTED READING

Weissberg, M. (1990). The meagerness of physicians' training in emergency psychiatric intervention. *Academic Medicine, 65,* 747–750.

Chapter 12

LEGAL AND ETHICAL CONSIDERATIONS

With malice toward none; with charity for all;
with firmness in the right.
— *Abraham Lincoln*

MANY FORCES CREATE a need for ethical and legal guidelines in the practice of mental health care: advances in science, the civil rights and consumer movements, increased public education, and the cultural and religious complexity of modern American society. These guidelines provide a foundation for complex and often difficult decisions.

Dilemmas arise when community, professional, or personal values are in conflict. Since values differ within society and among individuals, it is often difficult to arrive at a satisfactory choice in many situations. Frequently, consensual values will lead to specific principles of conduct, codes, and laws upon which clinicians may rely. However, when no consensus exists or when professional codes or laws change or are ambiguous, clinicians are faced with a difficult decision-making task.

ETHICAL THEORIES AND PRINCIPLES

- *Autonomy* relies on the "moral autonomy" of rational adults, so that patients have the ability and the right to make health-care decisions; the patient is self-governing. Autonomy is usually employed in conjunction with the principle of respect.

We thank Ryan Finkenbine, M.D., and Scott Christie, M.D., for their contributions to this chapter.

- *Respect* is a fundamental principle that demands compassionate care for all persons, although there may be individual differences in race, religion, abilities, or character. This includes efforts to restore or maximize the patient's competence or other capacities.
- *Utilitarianism* is based on the fundamental obligation of making a decision that tries to produce the greatest possible happiness for the greatest number of people. No fundamental right to truth, informed consent, or confidentiality is recognized unless they result in maximizing pleasure and minimizing pain. This is often invoked as moral support for the use of paternalism in patient care.
- *Paternalism* occurs when the state or an individual acts in what is believed to be another person's best interest without that person's consent. State paternalism includes the requirement that patients go to licensed practitioners for treatment and that only certain drugs be prescribed. This treatment may be justified when patients lack the capacity to make reasonable relevant decisions, for example, young children, mentally retarded persons, and some psychotic persons.
- *Justice* is the fair distribution and application of psychiatric services. Fair procedures are especially relevant to involuntary hospitalization situations. This is the principle underlying the issue of whether health care is a right to which all are equally entitled or a privilege that must be purchased.

ETHICAL ISSUES

Despite an awareness of ethical theories and principles, human behavior seldom lends itself to clear-cut, black-and-white standards, and conflicts between values and different principles may arise. Furthermore, the very nature of emergency psychiatric interventions often means that a life-or-death situation will be involved, that an urgent time factor will be operating, or that a patient may be mentally incapable of decision making on a temporary basis (alcohol intoxication or manic episode) or as part of a chronic problem (paranoid schizophrenia or mental retardation). Below are several issues that often cause problems in the emergency psychiatry setting.

- *Confidentiality,* which is based on respect for an individual's right to privacy, is the professional obligation to hold secret all information given by a patient. Legally, confidentiality *must* be breached in the following two circumstances:

1. Emergencies: The patient is acutely suicidal or homicidal, or is threatening serious bodily harm to self or others.
2. Mandated reporting: Clinicians are required by law to report child abuse and neglect.

- *Informed consent,* founded on the principles of autonomy and respect, and refers to the broad interaction between clinician and patient that allows for individual decision making. Informed consent relies on the forthrightness of truth-telling and disclosure and assumes that patients have the capacity for reasonable decision making. The patient has the right to refuse treatment or to agree voluntarily to treatment procedures.
- *Involuntary treatment* refers to interventions that are felt to be in the best interest of a patient or others, but which are performed without the patient's consent. These interventions are often based in utilitarian theory, and may be considered a form of paternalism. Involuntary treatment is invoked when patients lack the capacity for decision making or when they pose a risk of harm to themselves or others. Patients may not be hospitalized indefinitely without judicial review of their commitment. Sedation, seclusion, or restraint may be unavoidable for reasons of safety, but behavior control *alone* is not a sufficient goal of ethical psychiatric care. The least restrictive alternative of outpatient care is preferable to inpatient care; similarly, treating a patient on an open ward is preferable to seclusion.
- *Cultural differences* may involve any or all ethical values and may pose barriers to effective psychiatric care. Psychiatrists must take care to make assessments and offer treatments that are in accordance with the mandates of Western medicine, but which consider the individual patient's cultural background as well. Keep in mind that language barriers may prevent effective communication of important ethical aspects of care such as obtaining informed consent.
- *Sexual relations with patients/clients* are seen as an abuse of power and a breach of trust by the therapist, and a lack of respect for the patient and his or her autonomy. Ethical and legal sanctions exist against such behavior.

The following cases illustrate some of the ethical problems commonly faced by the emergency psychiatric clinician.

A patient is seen in the emergency room. He is angry and agitated, but not manic, psychotic, or intoxicated. The patient claims to have been "framed" by one of his coworkers, Mr. Jackson, and has subsequently lost his job. He tells the clinician, "I'm not crazy" and "As soon as I get out of here, I'm going to bust ol' Jackson's head in." He says he's never been violent in the past. Despite the patient's protests, the clinician orders that the patient be held while the police are notified.

Is the clinician's action ethically justified?

The above case highlights the issues of confidentiality and involuntary treatment. With regard to the latter, holding the patient against his will in this case serves the best interest of society. He should be kept in the least restrictive setting until further information is available or action is taken. The right to confidentiality of this specific patient *must* be breached under the "duty to warn" (see also legal section below).

The conditions under which courts have supported breaking confidentiality to protect a potential victim are:

* when violence is foreseeable
* when the therapist has enough control over the patient to prevent the violence.

Foreseeability is determined by three factors:

* a threat to a named or clearly identified victim
* a plausible motive
* a history of violence

The presence of two of these factors is usually sufficient to allow foreseeability. In the above case, therefore, the clinician acted ethically.

A mobile crisis psychiatric unit arrives at the house of a young Caucasian male at the request of his mother, who talked with her son earlier in the day and is "worried." The patient is familiar to the psychiatric team and has previously been diagnosed with schizophrenia. When the team arrives, he is found to be disheveled, dirty, and foul-smelling. He is nonviolent and claims to have been reading the Bible for the past several days. He displays some looseness of association, but is without auditory or visual hallucinations or frank delusions. He states that he has been taking his antipsychotic, haloperidol, "almost every day," but a pill count reveals only 50% compliance. He agrees to come to the hospital for a brief inpatient admission, but refuses to take anymore haloperidol because he believes "I've just had too much in my life." The clinician decides to give a small intramuscular injection of haloperidol to help clear the patient's thoughts.

Has the clinician acted ethically?

This case involves issues of paternalism and informed consent. There are four elements of informed consent:

- truthful disclosure of information
- assurance of comprehension by the patient
- voluntary decision making by the patient
- capacity

Capacity refers to an individual's ability to make decisions about specific aspects of their own care, even while other reasoning ability may be absent or distorted.

In this case, the clinician may be acting in what he feels is the patient's best interest (paternalism), but he apparently makes little effort to determine capacity or to provide information, thus rendering comprehension and voluntary consent inapplicable. Without informed consent, the clinician has relied on involuntary treatment without ethical justification to administer a medication.

A 54-year-old woman presents to her oncologist's office. The patient has been in treatment for the last year for breast cancer and she has been feeling well until recently. Now she comes in and tells her oncologist that she can't take any more, she's tired, and she wants to kill herself. She bought a gun this morning and plans to use it on herself when she returns home. Two weeks ago an x-ray revealed that she had metastatic cancer throughout her body. She is afraid of suffering. She does not want to die alone, but she is too afraid to go on with life.

The oncologist calls the crisis service and a crisis clinician comes to his office. The patient cries easily while she tells her story. Her daughter, who is 20 years old, overhears her mother's crying and takes the patient home before anyone knows of her intention. She mistakenly believes that the crisis clinician has upset her mother. The daughter does not know about her mother's suicidal ideation and intent.

The crisis clinician confers with the oncologist. The oncologist says, "I'm sorry, I can't do anything." The crisis clinician believes that the patient is suffering from a significant major depressive disorder. The crisis clinician recommends that involuntary papers be filled out so the patient can be placed in the hospital for treatment of her depression. The oncologist replies, "I'm sorry, but it's her right to kill herself. She is terminally ill. She has little time left to live anyway, a few months at the most."

What would you do?

LEGAL ISSUES

Since psychiatric emergencies often involve involuntary, incompetent, or dangerous patients, concerns are often raised on one hand about the patients' rights and on the other about the safety of those potentially in danger from violent individuals. Below we describe the legal aspects of caring for these patients.

Confidentiality

> All that may come to my knowledge in the exercise of my
> profession or in daily commerce with men, which ought not to
> be spread abroad, I will keep secret and will never reveal.
> —*from the Hippocratic Oath*

Confidentiality may be defined as the professional obligation to hold secret all information given by a patient. However, in certain situations, confidentiality can and *must* be set aside. This is usually the case when the psychiatric patient is acutely suicidal or homicidal or is threatening serious bodily harm to self or others. In general, where imminent danger is concerned, it is better for emergency clinicians to seek assistance. If a patient is harboring an imminent suicide or homicide plan, it is important not to collude with the patient in keeping this a secret. In emergency situations, information can be divulged or gathered if it is in the interest of resolving the severe emergency and if it is on behalf of the patient's protection. For example, telling a family member of the importance of getting rid of all alcohol in the household is appropriate if the patient deliberately cut his wrist while under the influence of heavy alcohol abuse. On the other hand, in a nonsuicidal patient, a clinician would not want to tell a patient's boss of the patient's substance abuse just because it is bad for the patient to be drinking. In general, then, it is wise for a crisis clinician to act if anyone's life is in imminent danger. When in doubt, the clinician should discuss any setting aside of confidentiality with his or her supervisor. Always act in the best interest of the patient to protect life; breach confidence only when it resolves an emergency issue.

A famous court case, Tarasoff v. Regents of University of California, 1976, dealt with a student who was a voluntary outpatient at the mental health clinic of the University of California; he told his therapist that he intended to kill a student identified as Tatiana Tarasoff. The therapist realized the seriousness of the intention and after conferring with a colleague decided that he should be committed for observation under a 72-hour emergency psychiatric detention provision of the California commitment law. The therapist notified the campus police both orally and in writing that he was dangerous and should be committed.

The therapist's supervisor, however, was concerned about the breach of confidentiality, vetoed the recommendation to commit him, and ordered all records pertaining to him be destroyed. Meanwhile, the campus police detained him but then released him on his promise that he would stay away from Tatiana Tarasoff. Two months later, he killed Tatiana as he had previously announced he would do. Her parents then sued the university for negligence.

The California Supreme Court deliberated the case for 14 months and finally ruled that a physician or psychotherapist who has reason to believe that a patient may injure or kill someone must notify the potential victim, the victim's relatives, or the authorities. The ruling does not require a clinician to report fantasies; instead, it requires a therapist to report an intended homicide. It is the clinician's duty to exercise good judgment. The court concluded that the client's right to confidentiality was overridden by the clinician's duty to warn potential victims.

After the initial Tarasoff decision, the American Psychiatric Association was concerned that the ruling would have adverse effects on clinician-patient confidentiality and thus interfere with successful therapy. The California Supreme Court agreed to rehear the case. In this second decision, the court held an even more stringent requirement: that the duty was to *protect*, rather than to warn, the intended victim. This duty might be accomplished by warning the victim, calling the police, or by conventional clinical interventions such as hospitalization or civil commitment of the patient.

Must a clinician exercise the "duty to protect" with any patient who voices homicidal ideation? The answer is no. Many patients in crisis will voice angry statements or ideas when initially presenting. Like suicidal ideation, it is important to understand whether the patient has any serious intent to carry out such an idea. If, upon further examination, the patient says, "No, I was just letting off some steam" or "I'd never hurt anyone, I was just angry, that's all" or "I felt like hurting him for a moment but that's past now" and can guarantee that he or she has no plan or intent to hurt anyone and the clinician believes this in good clinical faith, then Tarasoff-type interventions are not necessary. On the other hand, if the patient says, "I'm going to kill John Smith, and you can't stop me" or "I'm gonna beat the crap out of the next two people who cross that street corner" and the patient continues to have intent, then the duty to protect should be invoked. Again, this may require hospitalization of the patient and warning of the intended victims. If the intent is acute and serious, such that serious harm is imminent, the potential victim should be directly warned. If the clinician cannot reach the potential victim, then police should be used to contact the person. It is not always enough just to hospitalize a homicidal patient. If the potential victim is not warned and the patient escapes from the hospital, a catastrophe may result. In cases where a clinician invokes the Tarasoff rule, the clinician must carefully document all information.

The clinician is also required by law to report child abuse and neglect. Generally, clinicians are also expected to report gunshot wounds, as well as abuse of the elderly or of inmates in institutions.

In some states, mental health agencies are allowed to cooperate with law enforcement in ongoing criminal investigations. Supervision should be sought prior to contacting law enforcement agencies, especially when imminent danger is not present.

Civil Commitment

The laws governing involuntary hospitalization of the mentally ill are generally called civil commitment laws (i.e., no crime has been committed and the patient is not under arrest). It is important to remember that each of the 50 states has its own laws regarding psychiatric hospitalization; clinicians should be familiar with the laws in their own state.

Increasingly restrictive guidelines that focus primarily on the criterion of dangerousness have limited the power of emergency services to impose treatment on nondangerous but severely impaired individuals, such as those incapable of looking after their own needs for safety or shelter. An important trend is the effort to obtain legislation that recognizes the need to commit patients who are not likely to cause physical harm but are so severely ill that they are incapable of making an informed decision about treatment. Some of the legal issues involved in the commitment process include:

- *Parens patriae.* This phrase comes from the time of feudal English kings, who acted as fathers to their subjects and presumably in their subjects' best interests. This doctrine allows the state to intervene and act as a surrogate parent for those who can't care for themselves or for those who may harm themselves (including the mentally ill and minors).
- *State police power.* States have the right to protect the safety of society. This right is limited by Minimum standard of the 14th Amendment, which guarantees due process.
- *Standard of proof.* "Clear and convincing evidence" is the standard by which a judge finds a person committable. In contrast, "beyond a reasonable doubt" is the standard a judge uses to find someone guilty of a major crime.
- *Personal evaluation.* The evaluation of a patient is necessary by a psychiatrist or doctor prior to involuntary hospitalization. If there is no standard evaluation according to peer practice, a clinician can be sued through false imprisonment litigation. Crisis patients must receive standard clinical evaluation and treatment. They cannot be hospitalized on an involuntary basis if they've not been personally examined, nor can they be sent against their will to hospitals by merely examining them through windows, closed doors, or by heresay.
- *Right to refuse treatment.* Even if committed, stable patients still maintain the right to refuse medication treatment. However, in an emergency situation, treatment can be administered by a physician against the patient's wishes. State laws vary. Involuntary use of medication is permissible in cases of threatened violence in an emergency.

The case of *McCabe v. the City of Lynn (1995)* is particularly relevant to mobile emergency mental health services. Rose Zinger, a 64-year-old woman who lived in Lynn, Massachusetts, suffered from physical and emotional difficulties. She spoke and understood limited English. She was apparently a holocaust survivor during World War II. A physician signed an order of involuntary commitment. The police had been advised that she would not cooperate and that Ms. Zinger might become agitated. Police forced their way in, a struggle ensued, and an ambulance was called to transport the patient to the mental health facility. She became more excited. Because of her large size, they could not carry her downstairs on a stretcher. She was forced to go down each step on her buttocks. She was placed face down on a stretcher and handcuffed behind her back. Ms. Zinger then had a cardiopulmonary arrest and died in spite of CPR. The administratrix of her estate, Mary McCabe, filed suit. The decision was found for the plaintiff; her Fourth Amendment rights had been violated (i.e., her right to be free from unreasonable search and seizure) since no "exigent circumstances" (emergencies) were initially apparent.

This case is particularly important, since mobile crisis services are often requested to assist at the eviction of someone who could be potentially "mentally ill." The McCabe case would argue against facilitating in such procedures. If no emergency situation exists, then a psychiatric team should not be infringing on the rights of privacy of an individual. In addition, if a situation does occur where a crisis develops (e.g., the person barricades himself in or takes a hostage), a crisis team will not have credibility to negotiate with a patient if they are part of an "eviction team." In addition, violation of Federal law is not covered by professional malpractice insurance, so monetary damages are not covered! The police should obtain a search warrant in the absence of exigent circumstances. Crisis professionals beware!

Documentation of Clinical Data

Written documentation of clinical data is an absolute necessity in crisis intervention work. Documentation facilitates better follow-up care and affords legal protection. Each patient record should document:

- presenting problem(s)
- demographic information (age, date of birth, sex, race, marital status, address, and phone contact for follow-up care)
- previous psychiatric history
- significant life events

- relevant habits (e.g., drinks a six-pack of beer a day)
- medications
- family history
- medical issues
- mental status examination findings
- differential diagnosis
- a clear picture of the care provided (what actually was done, by whom, and when)
- plans for disposition/follow-up
- involvement of patient and family in evaluation and treatment procedures
- disposition planning and instructions to patient
- provision for and sensitivity to continuity of care. Where and when can the patient or responsible party be reached? Will another member of the emergency team or another mental health professional be able to gather all the necessary information from the record?
- the referring source
- next-of-kin or responsible party information
- legal status of patient, if appropriate

Patient consent and confidentiality should be considered in accessing different health care systems. Careful documentation of follow-up plans and the implementation of these plans must be made.

Documentation of suicidality and homicidality is critical. If a patient has neither of these ideas, the clinician must record this as "No suicidal/homicidal ideation." If ideation is present (or assumed because its absence is not documented), then there must be a statement regarding a patient's suicidal and/or homicidal plan, means, and intent. If a crisis clinician documents an absence of suicidal/homicidal ideation, plan, means, or intent, *and* the patient attempts or completes suicide, a therapist would probably not be found liable in a lawsuit, since therapists are expected to provide the usual standard of clinical care, and are not expected to be able to predict perfectly. On the other hand, if a patient commits suicide after seeing a clinician, and there is no documentation about that patient's suicidal behavior, a good prosecuting attorney will convince a court that the patient was never asked about suicidal ideation.

Remember: In medico-legal matters, if it wasn't documented, it was never done!

Memoranda of Agreement

Liaison with community resources facilitates disposition planning. Formal, written agreements with facilities and providers are best with:

- inpatient units
- outpatient services
- residential facilities
- child services
- adolescent services
- chemical dependency services
- geriatric options
- services for the mentally retarded
- forensic services
- mental health care providers
- social services
- the fire department
- the police department
- ambulance services

Informal agreements are often sufficient with:

- clergy
- lawyers
- local physicians
- local health officials
- shelters for abused spouses, temporary housing
- self-help organizations, such as AA

It is important to:

- identify one person in each community resource with whom emergency staff can work and communicate to facilitate disposition linkage.
- clarify the quality and extent of service the particular agency can routinely provide.
- keep an up-to-date resource file and make it accessible to emergency staff.
- Document MOAs for each resource and file them for easy access at both the emergency and the community resource.

- Offer joint education programs for community resource staffs to enhance collaboration and sense of unity of purpose.

Managed Care and Hospitalization

In situations in which managed care patients (i.e., those people who belong to managed care health insurance plans) need hospitalization, there usually is no difficulty in obtaining approval in emergency situations. However, there could be situations where initial denial does occur. If the indications that have been outlined in this book are followed, then every attempt would have been made to treat the person in the least restrictive, most cost-effective fashion. However, if the clinician does encounter difficulty, then he or she should formally appeal the managed care agent's denial and ask to speak with supervisors "on up the scale" if necessary. In the final analysis, if a clinician believes a patient must be hospitalized because of dangerousness, then the patient should always be admitted to the hospital. The following recent cases may have bearing on these issues:

- *Wickline v. State of California (1986)*. This ruling stated that a clinician who complies without protest with limitations imposed by a third party payer, when his medical judgement dictates otherwise, cannot avoid his ultimate responsibility for the patient's care. This ruling involved a obstetrician-gynecologist, but it is easy to see how the law can be interpreted for mental health.
- *Wilson v. Blue Cross of California (1990)*. In this situation, there was harm caused by a violent patient who was refused admission to a hospital. The responsibility rested with the managed care corporation for refusing to grant hospitalization approval. A caveat to clinicians: In a case where suit was brought against a managed health care plan (Corcoran v. United Healthcare [1992]) the managed care group was found exempt from liability because the insurer was covered by ERISA, the Federal Employee Retirement Security Act, which is exempt from lawsuit.

In summary, mental health law involving emergency psychiatric patients can be boiled down to one idea: If a true emergency situation exists, ALWAYS ACT to prevent imminent harm to the patient and others and do everything possible to resolve the emergency. If your actions are performed in the service of resolving a psychiatric emergency, you should feel comfortable that you are doing the correct action. If sharing of critical information or providing action is not a necessary step in resolving an emergency situation, then always err on maintaining a patient's confidentiality. When in doubt, always turn to your senior colleagues or legal representative for clarification and supervision. Finally, document everything that you do. Again, in the legal world, if there is no documentation, it was never done!

SUGGESTED READINGS

Armitage, D. T., & Townsend, G. M. (1993). Emergency medicine, psychiatry, and the law. *Emergency Medicine Clinics of North America, 11,* 869–888.

Bentham, J., & Mill, J. S. (1973). *The utilitarians: An introduction to the principles of morals and legislation, and utilitarianism.* Garden City, NY: Anchor Press.

Fletcher, J., et al. (1994). *Introduction to clinical ethics.* University of Virginia: Center for Biomedical Ethics.

McNiel, D. E., & Binder, R. L. (1987). Predictive validity of judgments of dangerousness in emergency civil commitment. *American Journal of Psychiatry, 144,* 97–200.

Segal, S. P., Watson, M. A., & Goldfinger, S. M. (1988). Civil commitment in the psychiatric emergency room. Part I: The assessment of dangerousness by emergency room clinicians. *Archives of General Psychiatry, 45,* 748–752.

Segal, S. P., Watson, M. A., Goldfinger, S. M., & Averbuck, D. S. (1988). Civil commitment in the psychiatric emergency room. Part II: Mental disorder indicators and three dangerousness criteria. *Archives of General Psychiatry, 45,* 753–758.

Segal, S. P., Watson, M. A., Goldfinger, S. M., & Averbuck, D. S. (1988). Civil commitment in the psychiatric emergency room. Part III: Disposition as a function of mental disorder and dangerousness indicators. *Archives of General Psychiatry, 45,* 759–763.

PART III

CLINICAL MANAGEMENT/ SPECIAL POPULATIONS

Chapter 13

MANAGING VIOLENT AND AGITATED PATIENTS

Can a man take fire in his bosom, and his clothes not be burned?
Can one go upon hot coals, and his feet not be burned?
—*Proverbs (10:24)*

SOME PSYCHIATRIC EMERGENCY patients may be potentially violent. Psychotic and mood disorders, drugs or alcohol, dementia and delirium, domestic violence, personality disorders, and other stress-related phenomena may cause violent, agitated, and assaultive reactions in patients. The astute crisis clinician will be knowledgeable about signs of impending violence, and will be acquainted with the techniques for limiting the potential for danger.

When a call for a mobile response into the community (e.g., a house visit) suggests *any* possibility of undue agitation, aggression, or violence by the patient, the clinicians who venture out should always involve the police in their response (see chapters 10 and 17). Sometimes patients may be so violent that police should secure them first and then call in a mobile response. When a patient is not manageable in a community setting, it will be necessary to "triage" him or her to the ER where there are facilities and safety techniques necessary to contain a violent or agitated patient. Since the majority of truly assaultive patients will be seen in ER settings, this section will focus on such interventions.

HOW TO APPROACH AGITATED PATIENTS
IN THE EMERGENCY ROOM SETTING: CAT

If you've ever taken a course in life-saving CPR (cardiopulmonary resuscitation) techniques, you will have learned about the ABCs of this technique: airway, breathing, and circulation. These are the most important principles necessary to save the life of an individual who may have suffered a cardiac or respiratory arrest. Similarly, there is a mnemonic device that helps the crisis clinician deal with potentially violent patients in the ER setting: Crisis clinicians need to have nine lives like a cat, and the CAT approach is recommended. CAT stands for control, assess, treat. So, in approaching a violent or potentially violent patient in the emergency department, one should:

1. Control behavior
2. Assess quickly
3. Treat specifically

The astute clinician might ask, "Why not just treat someone immediately? We have powerful medications that can sedate the most violent patients. Why go through the other steps first?" Because a number of conditions may cause severe agitation. One must first exclude a potentially life-threatening medical problem as the cause of a patient's agitation. This is illustrated in the following vignette:

A 40-year-old man was picked up by the police at 11:15 a.m. for violent behavior. He was breaking windows with a tennis racket, yelling, cursing, and kicking and biting the police who had brought him into the ER. He arrives in the ER in restraints and is still screaming and cursing. He is wearing a tennis outfit. Immediately, an intramuscular injection of 5 mg of the high potency antipsychotic drug haloperidol (Haldol) is given to the patient. About five minutes later a nurse notices the Med-Alert bracelet on the patient's wrist. The bracelet indicates that the patient has diabetes. Immediately a blood glucose (sugar) is checked and run "stat" to the hospital laboratory. His glucose is 23 (normal glucose levels should be 60–120). A 50% dextrose solution is injected into the patient's vein, and he immediately stops his violent outbursts. He is calm, polite, and a little confused, but the confusion almost immediately subsides. Five minutes later he falls asleep for three hours because of the sedating effects of Haldol. If his diabetes had not been discovered, he might have suffered irreversible brain damage after 90 minutes of profound hypoglycemia.

This clinical vignette illustrates how violence can be caused by a multitude of problems. The ER staff were very anxious because of the patient's loud, frightening behavior. Once his behavior was controlled, they needed to assess him briefly yet thoroughly. Controlling a patient's behavior allows the clinician time to think in a state of less anxiety. The initial assessment can then proceed in a logical manner. We shall now discuss these techniques in more detail. Some of the following techniques may be applicable to seeing patients in the ER setting and in many cases, outside of the ER or clinic. Attempts should first be made to control a patient's agitation.

CONTROL BEHAVIOR

It is most important to control a patient's behavior; techniques range from the least to the most restrictive alternative. The clinical staff must use the least confining approach with patients, but also must maximize safety for all.

Nonphysical Means

- Attempt to establish a rapid alliance by talking with the patient. Use the power of speech. Use simple, ordinary language. Do not assume that the patient understands why he or she is in the emergency room. Some patients believe that the ER staff will harm them. Provide continuous reassurance, if necessary.
- Be calm and observant as you approach a patient. If the patient is visibly upset and agitated, it is advisable not to wear any items that could be used for potential harm, for example, remove ties, necklaces, watches, or pens and pencils. Keep an appropriate distance when you approach; stop about six feet away. Watch the patient for any sudden moves.
- Make sure you are not alone at this stage with a potentially violent patient, especially in a closed-in area.
- Introduce yourself, and address the patient by his or her last name. Use formal etiquette at first. Ask permission to address the patient by first name or a nickname; continue to address the patient for-

mally if he or she prefers. Never address the patient by first name without asking permission; patients in crisis often lack self-esteem and respect will bolster their ego strength. Ask the patient what he prefers to be called, for example, Mr. Richard Marx may want to be called Mr. Marx, Richard, Dick, Rich, or by another nickname. Find out.

- If you do not feel endangered at this point, ask whether it is permissible to shake hands with the patient. If he accepts a handshake, then this is a sign that the patient can form a trusting relationship and is not too angry or paranoid. On the other hand, if he refuses permission to shake hands after the initial introduction, be particularly vigilant (if you are not feeling safe approaching a patient, always ask for assistance from security).
- Explain procedures using simple language. "We need to check your pulse and blood pressure." *Do not use jargon,* such as, "We need to take your vital signs." The term vital signs may imply to a paranoid patient that you wish to drain out his blood or cut out a vital organ. Such confusion may precipitate violence. Explain procedures, limits, and clinical processes in simple yet reassuring language.
- Keep a soft voice, a relaxed posture.
- Use water, food, or juice to judiciously foster an alliance with the patient. Remember, however, that if the patient is too out of control he or she may throw these items at staff. In general, an offer of nourishment implies that you want to nurture the patient, which diminishes both the patient's anxiety and the likelihood of violent behavior.
- Give the patient feedback in a gentle, concerned way. If a patient is acutely ill (psychotic, labile, manic, etc.), he may not know that he is within your interpersonal space (e.g., if his face is directly against yours) or he may not be able to recognize that his voice is loud and angry. Acute brain dysfunction will impair a patient's ability to recognize his or her own behavioral patterns.
- Never turn your back on an angry patient. When leaving an agitated patient in a seclusion room, keep talking to him or her as you leave.

Physical Means

If verbal intervention does not calm a violent patient, it may then become necessary to use physical restraint or seclusion. The behavioral control may actually comfort a patient who feels psychotic or completely out of control. The following issues must be kept in mind:

- Familiarize yourself with the seclusion and restraint policy in the ER and use the security team. A clinician should never try to restrain a patient alone and, ideally, should allow experts in security to handle the physical interventions. If a patient tries to run out of the ER past the crisis clinician, the clinician should immediately ask for security assistance; the clinician should never get in the patient's way. It is always preferable to have security personnel in the ER or hospital carry out procedures for physical restraint; they are trained in physical intervention techniques and have superior expertise in these matters.
- Most ERs have seclusion rooms. If a patient appears agitated in a seclusion room or is looking out of a window in the door, DO NOT OPEN THE DOOR! First, ask the patient to move back, away from the door, before opening it. If the patient listens to your commands and appears calm, he or she probably has some degree of control. Otherwise, ask for assistance from security. Never be shy about asking security to stay with you in a patient's room if you are scared or if you believe the patient wants to harm you. Patients will occasionally tell you that they want to hurt you or that you should leave their presence. Listen carefully to these warning signs.
- Don't ignore secluded or restrained patients. Explain the procedures for seclusion and restraint to patients, and reassure them that you and other staff will regularly check on them.
- Explain that seclusion/restraint is temporary until they can show control. NEVER take patients out of restraints until they have proven by their behavior that they are completely back in control.
- Patients in seclusion or restraints must be searched. ERs should have policies regarding this procedure. Usually nurses or security will search the patient to insure that he doesn't have any weapons that could be used to hurt himself or a clinician. Shoestrings, pointed shoes, boots, belts, and any metal items that may be used for harm should be taken from him. Always verify that the patient has been searched.
- When releasing restraints, start with the patient's weak area, most commonly the left arm. Then wait at least 10–15 minutes. If the patient is still calm, take out the opposite leg. If the patient is calm

after 15–20 more minutes, he or she may be ready to come out of restraints. This procedure should always be discussed with the doctors and nurses in charge of the patient's ER care. Remember: Restrained patients are completely helpless and totally vulnerable, so if they are taken out prematurely they may act violently due to their absolute fear and vulnerability.

ASSESS QUICKLY

In an ER setting, it should be up to the medical staff to quickly evaluate the assaultive or violent psychiatric patient who requires immediate seclusion and/or restraint in order to rule out a potentially life-threatening process that could be causing the patient's psychiatric symptoms and signs. Clinicians should know the following medical guidelines:

- With the acutely violent, agitated patient, rule out hypoglycemia, head injury, neurological illness, or life-threatening physical disease. Quickly look for signs of injury (e.g., bruises on the head, especially around the eyes or behind the ears, or blood coming out of the patient's ear—all these may signify skull fractures), Med-Alert bracelets, and vital sign abnormalities, such as fever, hypertension (high blood pressure), rapid irregular heartbeat, etc.
- Take a quick history from the patient and reliable historians who can corroborate the patient's story (e.g., family, police, EMS, the patient's doctor, old ER records, etc.). Make sure the patient does not suffer from a significant medical illness.
- Obtain vital signs, for reasons noted above.
- Quickly obtain a brief physical, attending to any acute problem.
- When indicated, check lab tests to rule out delirium, alcohol, and drugs. These results will help with the diagnosis. Again, diagnosis will determine the kind of treatment the patient will require.

TREAT SPECIFICALLY

Psychotic and agitated behavior must be treated vigorously. Appropriate medications will achieve rapid tranquilization and reduction of violent symptoms. Psychopharmacologic agents should be used aggressively with acutely agitated patients, as these medications work effectively and rapidly reduce the danger to patients and staff. They also bring about a great deal of symptomatic relief to patients. These issues will be discussed in chapter 22.

An entire history, interview, and mental status examination need not be completed before offering an agitated patient some medicine. It is often prudent to address a patient's discomfort directly, and to offer medical treatment that can soothe the patient, reduce tension, or diminish frightening or uncomfortable feelings and thoughts.

CONCLUDING RECOMMENDATIONS FOR MANAGING VIOLENT PATIENTS IN THE ER

- Monitor adverse incidents.
- Help ER staff maintain a professional approach.
- Don't take nervous system dysfunction personally. Teach others not to do so either.
- Debrief any personnel with even a minor injury caused by a patient.
- Never deny potential danger! Denial of potential violence appears to be the number one reason that health care professionals are injured.
- Remember that past behavior is the best predictor of future behavior. If a patient has a history of past violence, he or she may be violent some time in the future.

In conclusion, there is one caveat that needs to be addressed. The model that has been outlined in this section is an ideal, that is, in the best of all circumstances the patient's violent behaviors should first be controlled, then assessed, and finally treated. However, in the "real world" of the ER, patients are often severely psychotic, combative, and dangerous when their psychiatric disorders are out of control. Therefore, in times of great risk, the patient may need to be immediately restrained and given an injection of a sedating medicine in order to calm him or her and to prevent serious harm to others. Sometimes patients are so violent that they may break through thick leather restraints and try to hurt themselves thereafter. Even in these circumstances, however, the astute clinician should be highly suspicious of the possibility of an underlying medical illnesses.

SUGGESTED READINGS

Beck, J. C., White, K. A., & Gage, B. (1991). Emergency psychiatric assessment of violence. *American Journal of Psychiatry, 148,* 1562–1565.

Fava, M., Rosenbaum, J. F., Pava, J. A., et al. (1991). Anger attacks in unipolar depression, Part I: Clinical correlates and response to fluoxetine treatment. *American Journal of Psychiatry, 150,* 1158–1163.

Soloff, P. H. (1987). Emergency management of violent patients. In R. E. Hales, & A. J. Frances (Eds.), *American Psychiatric Association annual review* (Vol. 6, pp. 510–536). New York: American Psychiatric Association.

Torrey, E. F. (1994). Violent behavior by individuals with serious mental illness. *Hospital and Community Psychiatry, 45,* 653–662.

Chapter 14

MANAGING THE
SUICIDAL PATIENT

To be or not to be: that is the question.
—William Shakespeare (Hamlet)

SUICIDE IS A VEXING PROBLEM for crisis clinicians. Statistical and epidemiological data helps clinicians understand the risk factors critical in identifying the prototype of a patient who may be at risk for completed suicide. This profile may be helpful with a large number of patients on a statistical basis, and may be predictive if one examines the risks of thousands of people. However, statistics may not always help the crisis clinician with an *individual* emergency patient. Crisis clinicians must understand the patient's individual risks, as well as how that individual may fit into the prototypical suicidal profile.

Emergency clinicians need to understand and use statistical, epidemiologic information, but they must also use their "emotional sensors," that is, their so-called "gut feelings," as well as their data gathering and informational skills. Patients will often give clues to their suicidal ideation by making vague references to ending life, giving away valuable possessions, or making out a will. Sometimes even families and friends are unaware of the person's suicidal thoughts. The clinician should always assume that a suicidal person is serious, and must thoroughly evaluate any mention of suicidality.

SUICIDE EVALUATION

There are approximately 30,000 suicides per year in the United States, a rate of approximately 12/100,000 persons (Robins & Kulbok, 1988;

Blumenthal & Kupfer, 1990). Epidemiologic and other factors for suicide completion include:

- Gender: Although 4 males to every 1 female complete suicide, females have more suicide *attempts* than males.
- Race: Whites are at greater risk than Native Americans, who in turn are at greater risk than African-Americans; Hispanic Americans are at even lower risk.
- Age: Adolescent rates have tripled in the past 30 years, but overall completion is still lower than for the elderly.
- Risk of individuals with mental disorders:
    1. Mood disorders: About 15% of people with mood disorders (e.g., depression and bipolar disorder) commit suicide.
    2. Schizophrenia: 10% of people with schizophrenia die by suicide.
    3. Substance abuse: Alcohol and cocaine are *frequently* involved in suicide completion.
    4. Panic disorder: Several studies imply that panic may be predictive for suicide completion in patients with depression.
    5. Comorbid axis I and personality disorders: Patients with borderline personality disorders and concomitant major depressive episodes may be at very high risk.
- Isolated people, those without support systems, are at risk.
- Individuals who are recently unemployed, especially those fired or laid off, are at risk.
- Recent loss of a significant relationship is a factor. For example, depressed alcoholics who have lost their "last important relationship" or who have "burned their last bridge" in the previous two months may be at high risk for suicide completion.
- Individuals who are divorced, widowed, or separated are at greater risk than those who are married.
- Past significant attempts, if continued, may predict completion.
- Positive family history of completed suicide may predict behavior modeling or indicate a genetic propensity toward suicidal behaviors.

ASSESSMENT OF RISK

After a patient attempts suicide, or when the patient presents with suicidal ideation, the crisis clinician must ask the following questions in order to further assess the patient's risk and need for hospitalization:

- Under what circumstances was the patient's suicide attempt discovered? If the patient made earnest attempts to reach out to someone (i.e., the patient called a friend, family member, therapist, EMS, police, hotline, etc.), this might indicate ambivalence and a wish to live. Use great caution if the patient was *accidentally discovered* by someone. This implies an extremely high degree of lethality and inpatient treatment will *always* be indicated.
- Is the patient in a high or low risk demographic group?
- Does the patient have a major axis I and/or axis II disorder? (chapter 21)
- Does the patient have not only suicidal ideation but also a plan, means, and intent? The more specific the plan, means, or intent, the higher the risk. Has the patient made attempts before?
- Was the attempt lethal? Was the attempt to harm self made by using a gun, by hanging, by carbon monoxide poisoning, or by an overdose with a tricyclic antidepressant (TCA)?
- Does the patient feel hopeless, no better after clinical intervention?
- Does the patient give a positive or negative response to the question "How do you feel about not having died?" A wish for death following an attempt is a true lethal wish and hospitalization is indicated.
- Does the patient have "command hallucinations" that order her to harm herself? If she always hears command hallucinations (and some patients with schizophrenia do), have these changed and become more acute and threatening?
- Is the behavior different from the so-called deliberate self-harm syndrome or "parasuicidal behavior"? Some patients, particularly borderline patients, have a need to cut or bang on themselves when they feel more dysphoric or upset. At times such behaviors can actually bring a sense of relief and diminished tension to these patients. Sometimes these patients just wish to feel pain. At other times these patients also wish to die. The clinician must explore this behavior carefully.
- Does the patient have dramatically failing health or a severe chronic illness such as emphysema or kidney disease?
- Is there a family history of completed suicide, which may indicate behavioral modeling or a genetic predisposition to suicide or impulsivity?
- Has the patient been significantly embarrassed or humiliated due to arrest or public exposure of illegal or immoral activity? Such intense humiliation and shame may lead to a suicide attempt.

There is good news for the crisis clinician:

- Only 1% of all patients who attempt suicide will complete it within the next year.
- 99% will not.

TREATMENT OF THE SUICIDAL PATIENT

In general, if the patient is able to guarantee or verbally contract for his or her safety, you have reviewed the aforementioned assessment factors, and you deem the patient to be of low lethal potential based on history and examination, you can treat him or her as an outpatient. However, it is important to make certain that the patient has a support system available and agrees to stay in touch with the emergency clinical service. The patient must also agree to all recommended follow-up procedures, such as scheduling and attending an outpatient appointment or agreeing to a follow-up mobile visit to the home, taking medicine, and getting rid of firearms.

Many patients will feel unsafe if they leave the ER or clinic because of persistent suicidal ideas. Similarly, if a mobile response team leaves after a visit, the patient may not be able to guarantee his physical safety because of ongoing impulsivity. It may then be necessary to hospitalize these patients or provide them with a crisis residential setting or holding bed, where they can be safely monitored by professional staff. Clinicians should admit a patient to an appropriate secure setting if the patient

- has a lethal plan or was only accidentally discovered after an attempt.
- hears acute command hallucinations to kill himself.
- cannot assure his safety.
- has no support system to return to, or one cannot be created (family, clergy, friends, etc).
- doesn't feel any sense of psychological relief after intervention.
- has not been truthful.
- will not agree to treatment recommendations for immediate or follow-up care (e.g., patient refuses to take medicine, to continue treatment as an outpatient, or refuses to call if thoughts of harming self recur).

• has medical complications or problems warranting hospitalization.
• has fired a gun in the attempt.

Patients may experience transient suicidal ideation due to personality disorders or relationship difficulties. Often, empathic interviewing and arrangements for support will ameliorate the crisis and diminish the patient's suicidal thinking. For extreme dysphoria, however, the crisis clinician should ask a physician or psychiatrist to administer an anxiolytic or sedative drug such as lorazepam (usually 2 mg by mouth for mild agitation, by intramuscular injection for extreme agitation) to relieve the patient's discomfort. If the patient remains agitated, in denial, or is still dysphoric, hospitalization is strongly recommended.

EVALUATION OF THE ALCOHOL-INTOXICATED PATIENT WITH SUICIDAL IDEATION

It is not unusual for intoxicated patients to present with acute suicidal ideation. For the most part, the risk of suicidal behavior is short-lived and is limited by the degree of intoxication the patient experiences. In general, it is not possible to do a complete and effective psychiatric or clinical evaluation with an intoxicated patient. It is important to have a temporary holding facility where suicidal intoxicated patients can be kept safely until the acute effects of the intoxicating substance wear off. More than 90% of patients who present to the emergency room setting with acute suicidal ideation while intoxicated will no longer be suicidal upon reaching sobriety. A good general rule with this type of patient is to get the patient to a secure area, such as an ER setting, and have him observed until he is sober (or at least until his alcohol [ETOH] level is below 0.100).

Because of the acute effects of alcohol on the central nervous system (CNS), patients with chronic alcohol dependence or acute high alcohol levels will feel very depressed. Upon reaching sobriety, or upon going through a detoxification program, the majority of these patients will no longer be depressed or suicidal. However, a small percentage of these patients will have comorbid axis I disorders, such as major depression, schizophrenia, or bipolar disorder, and will need inpatient admission for treatment of these disorders. The alcoholic patient who continues to have strong suicidal ideation with plan and intent should be hospitalized if these thoughts continue in spite of reaching sobriety. Transient suicidal ideation that clears with sobriety can often be dealt with on an outpatient basis if the patient agrees to follow up recommendations and has a support available (e.g., shelter, home, AA sponsor).

A note of caution. Clinicians should always inquire whether the suicidal patient owns any firearms. If they are present in the patient's home, emergency clinicians should make every attempt to have these weapons secured by relatives or close friends. If there are no reliable supports, then the police can be used, who are often willing to secure and hold the weapons of someone who is potentially harmful to self or others.

SUGGESTED READINGS

Blumenthal, S. J., & Kupfer, D. J. (Eds). (1990). *Suicide over the life cycle: Risk factors, assessment, and treatment of suicidal patients.* Washington, DC: American Psychiatric Press.

Fawcett, J., Scheftner, W. A., Fogg, L., Clark, D. C., Young, M. A., Hedeker, D., & Gibbons, R. (1990). Time-related predictors of suicide in major affective disorder. *American Journal of Psychiatry, 147,* 1189–1194.

Kellerman, A. L., Rivara, F. P., Soures, G., et al. (1992). Suicide in the home in relation to gun ownership. *New England Journal of Medicine, 327,* 467–472.

Robins, L. N., & Kulbok, P. A. (1988). Epidemiologic studies in suicide. In A. J. Francis, & R. E. Hales (Eds.), *American Psychiatric Press review of psychiatry* (Vol. 7). Washington, DC: American Psychiatric Press.

Shader, R. I., & Greenblatt, D. J. (1992, April). Neurobiology and pharmacotherapy of suicidal behavior (from expanded and updated papers presented at the Fifth World Congress of Biological Psychiatry in a satellite symposium, June 10, 1991, in Florence, Italy). *Journal of Clinical Psychopharmacology, 12*(2)(Suppl.).

Stanford, E. J., Goetz, R. R., & Bloom, J. D. (1994). The no-harm contract in the emergency assessment of suicidal risk. *Journal of Clinical Psychiatry, 55,* 344–348.

Weissman, M. M., Klerman, G. I., Markowitz, J. S., et al. (1989). Suicidal ideation and suicide attempts in panic disorder and attacks. *New England Journal of Medicine, 321,* 1209–1214.

Chapter 15

MANAGING SPECIAL POPULATIONS: CHILDREN, ADOLESCENTS, AND THE ELDERLY

Age, I do abhor thee, Youth, I do adore thee.
— *William Shakespeare*

OBVIOUSLY, THIS TEXT is geared toward the treatment of adults who experience crisis or psychiatric emergency situations. However, a significant number of children, adolescents, and elderly patients seek assistance from crisis services, and their presenting problems seem to be growing in complexity. This chapter will overview some ideas that every crisis clinician must bear in mind when evaluating and treating these patients.

The psychiatric treatment of the child or adolescent in crisis differs inherently from the treatment of the adult psychiatric patient. In dealing with the adult patient in crisis, the main question generally is whether or not to hospitalize; often families are not involved. With the child or adolescent in crisis, however, it is imperative to treat the entire system involved with the patient. Acting-out behavior rarely occurs in a vacuum; rather, it is the product of multiple dynamics operating

We thank Rebecca Newman, M.S., and Maria Durban, M.Ed., for their contributions to this chapter.

within a system and encompassing the entire system. Sometimes the negative behaviors of a youth can be interpreted as the outlet for all pressures bearing down on the system, with the child or teenager as bearer of the illness permeating the system (i.e., the young person becomes the "identified patient"). From this standpoint, the direction of treatment may focus on facilitating a stabilization of that system as a whole. This process provides each member of such a system the opportunity to return to a state of normalcy, thus "cooling the crisis" and therefore diminishing the potential for acting-out behaviors.

Elderly patients are often unable to leave their environment because of poor health, fears of community violence, or due to cognitive difficulty. Their psychosocial needs may be overwhelming, due to their needs for shelter, caregiving, medical care, or due to the fact that they are widowed, or disenfranchised from their families. These issues make crisis intervention often more complicated, but also allow for the crisis clinician to develop more comprehensive treatment planning. Due to the significant difficulties which elderly people experience during a major crisis, it is most beneficial to evaluate and treat them in their native environments, whenever possible. Clearly, an outreach approach will be most helpful.

CHILDREN

It is rather uncommon for distressed parents and extremely young children to present to an ER setting, or to call for mobile crisis assistance. However, such requests do occur and should be taken seriously.

> A distraught mother calls about her 5-year-old son. He is playing with matches and she cannot get him to stop. She has tried hiding them, but he explores until he finds them and then begins to burn things. During the past several weeks, he has burned her curtains, her clothes, and set her car on fire. She is desperate, and afraid of him. She is unable to set any limits on this behavior and wants him immediately hospitalized. "He's much stronger than I am," she says. "I'm afraid if he doesn't stop, I'm going to do something to him."

The mother's feeling is typical of how a parent might feel toward a child. Children can have temper outbursts, which many parents find extremely intimidating. Often parents doubt their own ability to parent and have difficulty defining and following through on behavioral consequences, which all children need. This distraught mother expected that a hospital could "cure" her child. A visit to the home helped the mother calm down, averted the need for hospitalization, and helped her set up a behavioral plan in the event the child again tried to obtain a pack of matches. Help with setting up an outpatient appointment was also given.

The typical reasons children present for a psychiatric emergency evaluation include:

- oppositional disorders
- ADHD
- depression
- psychotic symptoms (which are particularly common with depression in children)
- substance abuse

Going to the child's home will provide a great deal of data for a psychosocial assessment. If completely out of control, children must sometimes be brought into an ER for behavioral restraint. Much of the evaluation is similar to that used with adults and teenagers.

The Crisis Interview

Begin by introducing yourself and setting everyone at ease. Often, children are intimidated by adults. Do not hover above the child. Sit or squat to say hello to the child. With young children, it is best to begin the interview together with the parents or caregivers. Tell the child that after you hear the story from his parents, you might want to meet with him without his parents, but first you want him to get to know you so that he is more comfortable.

Ask the parents about the chief presenting problem. Be attentive to their needs and anxieties. Watch the child during the interaction. Is he sad, scared, unable to move away from the parents? Is he smiling, looking around, observing what's going on? Does the child have a "transitional object," for example, a teddy bear or other stuffed animal, and did the child or parent bring it along? Does the child have friends? Who? What does the child play with at home? Were there normal developmental milestones, such as crawling, walking, talking? Are there siblings? How do they get along with the patient? Does the child have problems with sleep, appetite, nightmares, sleep terrors, sadness, or thoughts of self-harm or wishing he wouldn't be around to "bother" his parents? Any bedwetting, cruelty to animals, or fire setting? Are there any family members with psychiatric problems? Were there any problems during the mother's pregnancy? Has the child ever experienced seizures? Head injury? How is kindergarten or school? Good grades? Do the teachers complain about bad behaviors in class or send home notes? Any medicines? Where does the child sleep? Does the child sleep alone? Any unusual sounds that the child makes, or motor tic movements? Any compulsions or school phobias? Any use of drugs or alcohol? Any anemia? Good or bad eating habits?

After an alliance is formed with the parents, and after the psychiatric questions are answered, ask permission to speak to the child alone. Ask the child for his ideas, if he has any. Is he worried? What does he think the problem is? Does he feel safe? Is anyone trying to hurt him or touch him in a bad way? Is he happy or sad? Keep in mind that depression is not uncommon in the child with a crisis.

> A mother and father rushed their 7-year-old daughter into an ER. They found her hanging by a rope tied to a bar above their bedroom doorway. The interview reveals that the girl knows that Daddy has been out of work for six months and now he and Mommy are arguing all the time about money worries. She thought if she killed herself, her parents would have less of a financial burden.

Fortunately, depression and other axis I disorders respond very well to biological treatments. Low doses of SSRI antidepressants are well-tolerated in children. If tricyclic antidepressants are considered, an EKG must be done in patients under the age of 18; the cardiac electrical conduction system is very sensitive in young children, and antidepressants may rarely cause instability in the heart rate of a young child.

Children and parents who need immediate help will often benefit greatly from the evaluation, support, and nurturance of a crisis clinician. Advice should always be given to families, with a focus on how to deal with the situation in a practical manner. If the child is suicidal, hospitalization is warranted, and, of course, firearms must be secured around young children. Crisis clinicians must also always rule out child physical or sexual abuse. Most children and families will require outpatient follow-up and further evaluation.

ADOLESCENTS

Remember not the sins of my youth, nor my transgressions . . .
— *Psalm 25*

Issues involved in treating adolescents in crisis certainly demand longer-term therapy than an emergency service can provide in a crisis situation. However, a mobile emergency psychiatric service can provide valuable ER and on-site community intervention as reinforcement for the longer-term therapeutic process. Crisis intervention techniques are similar to those used with adult patients, with some modifications.

Assessment

Rarely does the clinician assess and treat the adolescent in isolation. The adolescent often represents or acts out the much broader crisis within the family unit. Thus, in assessing the adolescent's current state of functioning, the clinician should screen and evaluate the parents and other family members as well. Since many adolescents do not live in a traditional nuclear family, it is important to understand the role of the main people involved in the adolescent's home life; these could include grandparents, foster parents, aunts, uncles, or older siblings. It is important to ask who is present with an adolescent in crisis, and also to understand who is missing. For instance, if the mother of a teenager brings her daughter to an ER because of a conflict over the daughter's boyfriend, one might ask why the father did not show up (assuming a nuclear family arrangement)? Was he too tired? Unavailable? At work? Or just fed up? Is there another woman in his life? Is he depressed? Or is the daughter reacting to his alcoholism? Such theoretical possibilities need to be explored.

GENERAL TYPES OF CRISIS PRESENTATION

In general, there are a few main reasons why an adolescent presents in crisis. The first concerns processes that occur directly *within the adolescent patient*. For example, an adolescent can develop signs of a genetic mental illness, such as schizophrenia or bipolar disorder. Or the teenager may develop a severe biological depression with weight loss, insomnia, and suicidal wishes. These disorders can occur within intact, psychologically healthy families, and in otherwise healthy teen-agers. Crisis intervention in such cases would involve a full medical and psychiatric evaluation, possible biological treatments, reassurance, and psychoeducation for the patient and the family.

The second type of crisis involves the relationships that an adolescent develops *outside the family system*, that is, relationships with girl-friends or boyfriends, relationships to peer groups, or relationships with teachers. Difficulties with these kinds of relationships may result in substance abuse, antisocial behaviors, or teenage pregnancy. Crisis resolution will involve working out some of the conflicts within such relationships as well as appropriate referral to treatment resources. The family or caregivers of the adolescent should be included in this process to the extent that the behaviors impact their system.

The third type of crisis involves interactions *inside the family system*. These issues often involve power struggles, conflicts around limit set-ting, lack of boundaries, and family members' feelings of powerless-ness. Parents and guardians may find themselves unable to create firm, necessary limits for adolescents because of a rekindling of their own adolescent conflicts. This can result in a lack of normal structure for a troubled teen. Thus, without structure and limits, the teenager's be-haviors may run wild. In this latter category of crisis, the family or caregivers often want to "dump" the adolescent patient on the crisis professional because of extreme frustration and exasperation.

A terrible verbal argument ensues between a husband and wife over their 15-year-old son, Michael. All three of them come into the ER. Three months ago, Mr. and Mrs. Simpson discovered that Michael was drinking alcohol on weekends with his friends. Mrs. Simpson is very concerned about him and demands that he be committed for alcohol abuse. Mr. Simpson is concerned, but underestimates the seriousness of Michael's experimentation with alcohol. Though well-meaning, he tells the crisis clinician, "You know how it is—all teenagers drink." Michael admits to the drinking, wants to stop, but feels his father "doesn't see it as a big deal" and doesn't understand why his mother is "putting up such a fuss."

The clinician speaks with the parents alone and asks, "Who is the disciplinarian in the family?" Mrs. Simpson says, "It's me—it's always been me." Mr. Simpson agrees and painfully admits that he's always had problems with setting limits with his son, explaining, "My old man was a violent alcoholic. He used to beat me when I was little, so I guess I run away from anything having to do with discipline." The clinician now has an empathic focus on why it's difficult for Mr. and Mrs. Simpson to enforce limits together. They negotiate how that can occur and then bring Michael in for further discussion. Everyone agrees to seek outpatient treatment and Michael hears that if he cannot abide by his parents' request to not drink, he will be "grounded next week."

Practical suggestions for limit setting and empathy for both the teenage client and the frustrated parents or guardians are necessary. It is important for the crisis professional to understand how parents or guardians can be in conflict with themselves over issues of discipline and child rearing. It's common for parents to fight with each other when they are really angry with their teenager. Such discord among those in the parenting role creates chaos and behavioral worsening. Unity is critical. Boundaries must be defined. Consequences for aberrant behavior must be clear and followed. Sorting through issues with parents and teenage patients can be extremely helpful. After striking an alliance with the adolescent and the guardians, the crisis expert can mediate for an effective outcome. For instance, if a parent insists that the teenager stop using drugs, but allows the teen to decorate his or her room with posters and paraphernalia that glorify drug use, the teenager will get a mixed message that results in much confusion. If the parents had abusive, abrasive, or cruel parents, they may become ineffective in providing discipline for their teenager in the fear that such strong actions mean they too are becoming abusive or coercive. Reassurance and clarification of roles and boundaries can bring great relief.

Another mistake that adults make is to think, "Well, when I was a kid, I felt this way" or "I know what kids need; I was a teenager once upon a time." This type of thinking is fallacious. First of all, every teenager is different. Also, times have changed. What worked in the fifties or sixties may not work in the nineties or beyond. Life is different. Divorce was rare in the forties and fifties, even in the sixties. Suicide among adolescents was rare in the fifties. Schools didn't need metal detectors. There were no 12-year-old alcoholics. Few teenagers had access to guns. If there was a disagreement among teenagers in the sixties, they'd fight it out. In the nineties, some kids take their own knives or guns and kill the person who "dissed" (disrespected) or angered them. Drugs were nonissues for kids in the fifties. Little children did not act as lookouts for crack dealers, that is, warn the dealers when the police patrols approach. Gangs were isolated. These are now major problems in some urban areas. Crisis clinicians have to help some parents see the dangers of living in the current fast-changing world.

Finally, the fourth type of crisis is the *developmental crisis*, for example, when the adolescent graduates from high school, goes to college, starts a first job, fails a course, or loses his or her virginity. Such developmental milestones can scare and overwhelm an adolescent. Support and reassurance is important, with referral to counseling if necessary.

As always, an important question to keep in mind during evaluation is, What is the least restrictive environment or the most practical treatment option or referral that will best meet the needs of the adolescent and the parents?

Often it is the crisis team and not the patient's primary therapist or caregiver who assesses the adolescent for hospitalization or alternative treatment settings. However, just like with every crisis patient, regardless of age, if the patient is in treatment, get in touch with that therapist or psychiatrist. Ask the patient and family how things are going in treatment. What are the treatment goals? Sometimes contacting a school counselor or teacher who has a working relationship with the teenager can help obtain a clearer picture of the adolescent's usual baseline. Corroborating information can aid in determining if the adolescent has difficulty in dealing with more than one environment. Does the adolescent display the same patterns at school as she does at home? It is important for the clinician to enlist the adolescent's permission to speak to other individuals. However, in an emergency situation, it is not necessary to have such permission, as long as the information gathering and discussion is pertinent to the emergency evaluation and treatment.

History Taking

It is essential in the history-taking process to obtain information pertinent to the *current* problem. Questions might include the following:

· What is the major difficulty going on *right now*?
· When did the symptom(s) or behavior begin?
· Is there a major psychiatric axis I disorder, such as ADHD (attention

deficit-hyperactivity disorder), substance abuse or dependence (e.g., gasoline sniffing ["huffing"] or crack cocaine use), or major depression?

- Has the patient had any unusual or severe illnesses or neurological problems, such as seizures, head injury, or meningitis?
- Does something or someone in particular seem to prompt or precipitate the behavior? If so, why might that be?
- What purpose, if any, does the behavior serve?
- What limits are placed on the adolescent when the behavior occurs? Are these limits consistent? Who sets these limits?
- Is the adolescent involved in criminal behaviors, and if so to what degree? Is there a childhood history of fire setting, enuresis (bed wetting), and cruelty to animals? A history of this triad of symptoms can be predictive of sociopathic behaviors.
- Could any current medications or illnesses contribute to the change?
- Are there any recent life changes or stressors, such as moving, divorce, abuse, or break up of a relationship?
- What about privacy? Does the adolescent have any "space," that is, his or her own room? Does he or she sleep alone in bed?
- Of course, the usual questions about psychotic symptoms, suicide, and homicide must be addressed, as well as questions about physical or sexual abuse.

By engaging the family in the history-taking process, the crisis clinician gives the indirect message that she is interested in all of them. She must quickly form an alliance with all parties, including the teenage patient and the parents or guardians. No one should be accused or seen as being at fault. Not only does the family history illustrate the context from which the family operates, but it also provides information on relevant family issues.

The Crisis Interview

Crisis situations involving adolescents are often volatile and anxiety-provoking. Technically, it is important for the crisis clinician to establish quick rapport and control of the situation. Security or police should be called in as needed to diffuse any potential for violence. Arguing family members should always be separated, whether in the ER or the home. The clinician should introduce himself to the patient and the family, making sure to identify the names and relationships of all present. The clinician can then explain to the parents or caregivers that he would like to speak first with the adolescent and then with the caregivers or guardians. This will establish rapid rapport with the teenage patient, restore boundaries, and also allow the family to see that the clinician is in control of the situation.

Ask the teenager what she would prefer to be called. Look at how she is dressed. Neat and clean? Ragged? Are there tatoos, body markings, pierced areas? Ask her to tell you about herself. What does she like to do? How's school? What bugs her about being in the crisis situation? What's her side of the story? Is she worried about herself, her parents, her family? Is she angry? At whom? How are her grades? What does she do after school? Is she alone in the afternoons or evenings? What kind of things does she like to do after school? Watch television? What's her favorite show? What kind of music does she like? Is she a musician? A good student? A gang member? If so, what's the gang's name, the colors, the initiation? Does she carry weapons? Why? What or who is she afraid of? Is she in a relationship? What's her girlfriend's or boyfriend's or best friend's name? What do they do together? Is she into drugs, booze? Does she have special talents, such as painting, writing poetry or prose? If so, can you see some if she has it with her?

The above questions help the crisis clinician achieve the most important part of the interaction with the patient — a therapeutic alliance or rapport. After this is accomplished, then the clinician can move to more specific assessment issues. Remember that even though some adolescents are quite large, they can still be child-like in thinking or impulsivity. Even the biggest teenagers can be fearful in times of crisis.

It is imperative that the clinician sees himself as allied with all family members, not just with the adolescent patient. It is of greatest importance that the clinician remain neutral; otherwise, successful crisis resolution may not be possible. Crisis clinicians must always monitor their own perceptions and countertransference reactions in these situations. After quickly assessing for the presence of major psychiatric syndromes, and after insuring that the patient is not dangerous, the clinician will need to focus a great deal of attention on allowing the parents or caregivers to project their frustration, hopelessness, helplessness, and anger. It is important for parents to understand that teenagers *must* seek more independence from their parents (they are biologically programmed to do so), that their impulsivity or careless-ness is often what allows them to think that they *can* grow up and leave the security of "the nest." However, teenagers need help staying within appropriate limits and controlling their often overwhelming impulses. Similarly, teenagers must understand that their parents are having a hard time figuring them out. They need to negotiate and explain their position to their parents or caregivers. A good philosophy for parents with teenagers is, "Give lots of love and lots of limits." One without the other often spells disaster.

Common Presenting Problems

In dealing with adolescents, the emergency worker is challenged by a multitude of presenting problems. Psychosis, poor impulse control, defiance, sexual acting out, running away, parent-child conflicts, sib-ling discord, aggression, substance abuse, depression, and suicidality are some of the most common presentations.

DEPRESSION

Major depression affects approximately 3% of school-age children and increases to approximately 6% in adolescents. Three-quarters of those with the diagnosis are comorbid for another diagnosis such as anxiety and behavioral disorders. Early onset of major depression is evidenced by poor academic performance. Grades will often deteriorate if a teen-ager is depressed.

A study of depressed adolescent females (Goodyer & Cooper, 1993) found that comorbidity for anxiety, behavioral, and obsessional disor-ders was as high as 40%, and that 80% of these adolescents reported increased irritability. Social withdrawal appeared to be the best pre-dictor of the likelihood of major depression. Depressed adolescents seem to exhibit high emotionality and become upset easily and in-tensely.

Depression in adolescence is often manifested through negativism and acting-out behaviors such as emotional outbursts and conduct disturbances. When dealing with a depressed adolescent, it is impor-tant to set limits to stop the acting-out behavior so feelings can be verbalized rather than displayed in a maladaptive manner. When a clinician conveys that he or she cares enough to set limits and wants to take the time to understand how the adolescent is feeling, it helps form a connection with the adolescent and aids in obtaining a clearer picture of his or her inner struggle. Although acting out is a common presentation for depressed adolescents, withdrawal and unwillingness or inability to discuss feelings or make eye contact is also common. Approaching this type of adolescent with pointed, direct questions concerning his or her feelings of depression can often result in further withdrawal and noncommunicative behavior. Beginning with general and neutral topics and questions and exploring the adolescent's interests can help him or her warm up to the examiner.

> A 16-year-old male is brought into an ER by his parents because they fear he is depressed. He will not speak to anyone in the ER. The three of them await the arrival of the crisis clinician, who is called in for the assessment. The clinician introduces herself to the three of them, asks the parents to please wait in the ER waiting area, and tells them she will speak with them after she interviews their son. She closes the door and sits on a chair across from the patient. He does not respond to her initial question of, "Can you tell me what happened to bring you here?" She notices he's wearing a Metallica T-shirt. She asks, "Are you a musician?" He looks up and smiles. The interview progresses.

It is important to determine if a specific situation or event has triggered the depression or whether any new life change or stressor occurred around the onset of the symptomatology. Fear of pregnancy, peer problems, problems in school, a new home or school environment, parents divorcing or forming new significant relationships, and sexual, emotional, or physical abuse can all trigger depressive responses. Adolescent depression often responds well to both antidepressant medications and psychotherapy.

SUICIDAL BEHAVIOR

Suicidality (particularly suicide "pacts" or recent suicides of close friends or peers) and homicidality should be explored. Guns, knives, other weapons, and pills, should be removed or secured in the homes of severely depressed adolescents—especially those who have made threats or past attempts.

Although children and adolescents have the lowest suicide rate of any age group in the United States, there has been a threefold increase over the last few decades—particularly in males. Strong indicators of suicidal risk in adolescents are prior suicide attempts, current suicidal ideation, major depression, substance abuse, recent attempt by a friend, prior inpatient hospitalization, and past or current psychiatric diagnosis (especially affective disorders, psychosis, and antisocial behavior). The highest risk group for successful suicide is older adolescent males who suffer from depression, who have made previous suicide attempts, and who abuse alcohol or other substances. The break-up of a romance or being "kicked out of the family" can also be a precipitant of suicide attempt.

Adolescent suicide attempts are often related to family dysfunction. The problems may be acute, due to a developmental milestone or a disagreement regarding friends or curfew, or the problems may be longstanding, such as a history of sexual or physical abuse. Adolescent suicide attempters are more likely to come from chaotic homes. Compared with nonsuicidal adolescents, suicidal adolescents tend to perceive their families as more dysfunctional, experience isolation within a perceived inflexible family system, feel that their families are disengaged and emotionally distant, and rate the family's ability to communicate lower.

Adolescents often are impulsive and have difficulty expressing powerful emotions in an appropriate or controlled manner. A suicide attempt can represent a maladaptive means of demonstrating and conveying to others one's internalized experience or pain. Studies indicate that the odds for a potentially suicidal adolescent killing himself increase 75-fold when a gun (handgun, rifle, or shotgun) is kept in the home. The presence of firearms may be associated with adolescent suicide even in the absence of psychiatric diagnosis, due to the extreme moodiness and impulsivity of the teenager under stress. It should be clear that in every serious crisis or psychiatric emergency, the presence of firearms must be assessed and guns *must* be secured.

In addition to assessing the usual information regarding suicide attempts, another important question is: How did the family respond to the attempt, and can they monitor the adolescent's safety and provide a supportive environment until follow-up is initiated? Sometimes parents, even well-meaning ones, feel so powerless and frustrated that they "just don't care what happens." Even if they don't mean that literally, the teenager can believe that it is so. If a family member is apathetic about an adolescent's suicide attempt, this should be seen as a potential danger sign; if the adolescent is not going to be hospitalized, extreme caution should be used and an alternative placement (e.g., another relative or temporary foster care) should be considered. Any suicidal adolescent who fires a gun, even in the air, should *always* be hospitalized because of the impulsivity of that action and the high lethality of such an act. Remember, when adults have an impulse, they still have some ability to think before carrying it out. Not so with the adolescent, whose brain and nervous system have not yet matured to that level of capability.

When outpatient treatment is indicated, crisis intervention specialists should be aggressive in ensuring continuity of care. Providing support until the adolescent is engaged in the follow-up process may include supportive and consistent phone calls, providing the family with emergency numbers if suicidality recurs, mobile visits to monitor the situation, initiating psychopharmacological treatment, and assisting in facilitating follow-up treatment. Such support will often help ensure follow-through with definitive treatment.

DEFIANCE AND AGGRESSION

Defiant and aggressive behavior in adolescents generally falls into three categories:

- typical "teenage rebellion"
- conduct disorders
- behavior related to a psychiatric illness

In the first category, defiant behavior usually takes the form of *teen rebelliousness* against parental structure. It is probably the most widely experienced and well-known adolescent behavior in society, as all teens exhibit it to some degree. In less severe cases, the adolescent tests limits around friends, curfews, house rules, assigned tasks, appearance, and attitude. While these conflicts can become a trial for beleaguered parents, such testing is a natural part of growth and allows the adolescent to find his or her own ground and identity, separate from the family. If parents are able to maintain fair and practical limits and structure, and can remember that despite the defiance the teen appreciates the safety of that structure, the adolescent years can be managed with the least difficulty.

In more severe cases, where the limit testing involves dangerous and/or illegal behaviors, parents may need to seek professional intervention to help reestablish structure and communication with the teen. Where parents begin to feel out of control and powerless to set limits, intervention should aim at clarifying parental roles and family system boundaries, as well as helping the parents understand what the adolescent's behaviors signify. At the same time, the teen can be assisted in understanding how his behavior is interpreted and how he can better get his needs met.

Conduct disorders, the next category, are chronic patterns of behavior where the rights of others and major rules of society are consistently flouted. Aggression is common, as is stealing, cheating in school, truancy, running away, and substance abuse. Recurring incidents with fire setting and cruelty to animals (especially from a young age) may indicate the onset of a severe and chronic problem. The adolescent in this category seldom expresses remorse or consideration for others and often blames others for his or her own actions. Home environments usually are chaotic with inconsistent discipline or none at all, and there are often absent or neglectful parents or a situation in which the adolescent moves from relative to relative. The teen in this case is susceptible to gang involvement as a replacement for the missing family and for a sense of security from harm. Clinicians may find that the teenager has previously been involved with counseling with little to no results, or a history of hospitalizations with minimal family involvement and little change in the teen's behavior.

In such cases, the most beneficial referral from the crisis clinician may be to the local Department of Juvenile Justice or its equivalent. The clinician may also need to involve the local Department of Social Services, Child Protective Division, and other agencies, which may include mental health or substance abuse treatment boards. The teen with this set of behaviors needs strongly imposed, concrete limits that clearly demonstrate the consequences of maladaptive behavior (i.e., the juvenile justice function). At the same time the adolescent needs an advocate to find a safe and structured home environment (the social services function). A social services case manager can also involve the teen in counseling where indicated if sexual and/or physical abuse has occurred. If available, home-based services for ongoing multisystemic family therapy can be very useful for young juvenile offenders.

The third category of defiance or aggression in the adolescent involves *behaviors that are the product of a psychiatric illness*. The teen who is depressed or manic may exhibit aggressive, defiant behavior resulting from irritability, frustration, powerlessness, hopelessness, and the feeling of not being understood. The teen with an impulse control disorder, learning disability, or attention-deficit/hyperactivity disorder may exhibit these behaviors but with a different flavor; that is, the behavior may appear more unfocused, energetic, and purposeless because, in fact, the teen *is* less able to focus behavior resulting from these disorders. However, such behaviors serve as outlets for the frustration of the teen experiencing a disorder over which he or she has no control. The key is in accurate diagnosis and treatment to help the adolescent and his or her family both understand and control the illness. Mood stabilizing pharmacologic agents (e.g., lithium, carbamazepine, or valproic acid) may be extremely helpful.

Adolescents suffering from psychotic disorders may also exhibit defiance or aggression, but for different reasons. If the teen becomes paranoid and delusional, he may feel the need to defend himself out of fear. The adolescent who experiences auditory hallucinations may be compelled to act on commands to protect herself or others she believes to be in danger. Any of the symptoms associated with a psychotic process can produce agitation and aggression in the adolescent. The key to treatment in this case is also accurate diagnosis and pharmacologic treatment, and hospitalization if necessary for safety and stabilization.

A crisis clinician will also encounter the adolescent who has suffered or is still suffering from sexual or physical abuse. Defiance and aggression in school and at home are common in the abused teen. These behaviors serve, however inappropriately or destructively, as a vent for the rage and betrayal the adolescent feels because of the abuse. The first step, always, when a clinician discovers physical or sexual abuse occurring, is to report it to the proper legal/social services agency to ensure both investigation of the situation and the adolescent's safety. The second step is to get the teen involved in treatment to help him or her deal with the many issues arising from such abuse. Treatment should aim at helping the adolescent talk about the abuse in a trusting and safe environment and begin to dispel the low self-esteem, mistrust, and anger such abuse engenders.

PSYCHOSIS

Extreme forms of aggression and mania with severe outbursts of anger may indicate the presence of a psychotic illness. It is important when dealing with psychotic adolescents to rule out medical etiologies for the psychosis—such as systemic infections with or without encephalitis, lead encephalopathy, epileptic seizures, AIDS, progressive diseases, brain injury, metabolic disturbance, and substance abuse.

Prepubertal schizophrenia is rare; the initial onset of the disorder more frequently occurs in late adolescence. Psychosis in adolescents is frequently a manifestation of psychiatric disorders such as major depression with psychotic features, bipolar affective disorder, mood disorders, mental retardation, and substance abuse. Psychopharmacological intervention in a controlled setting is usually best when treating early adolescent psychosis.

SUBSTANCE ABUSE

Adolescent substance abuse has its roots in a variety of sources—some environmental, some genetic, some psychiatric, some behavioral. While the family dynamics remain an issue in teenage substance abuse, as in other dysfunctional behaviors, the impact of peer behavior also plays an integral part in the development of adolescent substance abuse disorders.

When an adolescent grows up in a home where any substance is abused on a regular basis, he grows up with the message that such abuse is typical and therefore acceptable. Under these circumstances an adolescent may become a substance abuser at an early age. Not only is he mimicking what has been modeled as adult behavior in the home environment, but the teen may do so in an effort to act like an adult in the way that has been shown to him. That is, for the son of an alcoholic father or the daughter of a cocaine-abusing mother, wanting to make some connection with a parent can mean following in the path of that parent's addiction. Research has also discovered genetic predispositions to various types of addiction.

Of course, even if the home environment is one of moderate or no use of any substance, the adolescent may choose substance use as a means of rebelling against parental mores in the search for his or her own identity. The unfortunate consequence of this behavior may be addiction.

Peer pressure may also contribute to substance abuse. Again, in the search for identity and separation from the family, the adolescent may identify with and gravitate toward peers who abuse substances to rebel against authority. In a typical scenario, the harder parents try to stop this behavior, the more the teen runs to it, not understanding the medical dangerousness of possible addiction. This lack of comprehension or denial of possible difficulties also feeds into the general lack of comprehension about mortality in adolescent thinking.

Finally, the impact of an adjustment disorder or major depression may also contribute to substance abuse in the adolescent. As with every patient, it is critical to obtain history so that one can decide if a substance abuse problem is primary or secondary (to an anxiety, psychotic, or mood disorder); if it is secondary, that underlying problem must be treated.

Family upheaval, problems in school or with peers, or emotional or physical trauma can provoke an overwhelmed teen to escape through substance use or abuse. Given that adolescence is a confusing time under the best of circumstances, any type of trauma in addition to what is usual in the teenage years can lead to depression. The attempt to mask or avoid such feelings can lead to greater and greater substance abuse, which in turn can cause greater depression.

Treating the adolescent substance abuser again involves treating the entire family. If the parents are also substance abusers, they should be referred to treatment, as gently but firmly as the clinician can refer them. The adolescent should also be referred for treatment. The family as a whole should be referred for family treatment at a facility specializing in treating substance abuse.

If the adolescent is the primary substance abuser in the family, he or she should be referred for treatment to a substance abuse facility with specific programs for teenagers. These programs generally include family meetings to encourage dialogue among the family members about the problems at hand. Partial or day hospitalization is also an option when the teen's peer group consists of substance abusers, as a change in the teen's social setting is imperative in treating the addiction. The family should also be referred for treatment in dealing with the adolescent substance abuser, for example, educational classes at a substance abuse facility to help the parents understand the behavior and how to deal with it, or Al-Anon as a source of support and understanding.

Situations Warranting Hospitalization

Many factors should be considered before hospitalizing an adolescent. If substance abuse runs throughout the family system and the parents are unwilling or unable to look at their own substance abuse issues, hospitalization of the abusing teen may be the only way to motivate the family to unlock the silence around these issues. Hospitalization not only removes the teen from the environment but also creates a framework for the family to enter into treatment in a safe and structured setting.

In cases where physical confrontations occur between an addicted parent and an addicted adolescent, particularly if any weapon is involved, hospitalization can provide safety for the teen and offer a therapeutic environment to the whole family to begin the healing process. In cases where the adolescent exhibits depressive symptoms concurrent with substance abuse, the clinician should carefully screen for suicidality in the teen. As with adults, suicidal ideation in a teen who is actively abusing substances should be taken very seriously. The teen with substance abuse problems imposed on a depressive disorder should be considered at risk both for impulsive suicide attempts and attempts that are planned out. Again, special attention must be paid to any development of a plan for suicide, lethality of the method, and accessibility of weapons. If the adolescent actively uses substances, is depressed, has poor support at home or with peers, has a clear plan for suicide and the means to achieve it, hospitalization probably is the best course of action. A combination of any of the above problems can prove fatal. In summary, the overall three questions must still be asked, in order to reach a decision about whether a teenager needs to be hospitalized:

- Is he or she dangerous to self or others?
- Is he or she willing to follow treatment recommendations?
- Does he or she have a support system to go to, or can one be created?

As with every patient, the answers to these questions will allow the clinician to reach an intelligent decision.

ELDERLY PATIENTS

There is a common mistake that seems to occur with many elderly patients who present in crisis: Clinicians commonly believe that just because the patient is old, he or she must be suffering from a dementia. Not every elderly patient is suffering from dementia! Even if a patient has an established dementia, it can worsen suddenly for many reasons, such as stroke, pneumonia, or urinary tract infection with bacteremia (i.e., sudden spread through the body of the bacteria causing the infection). Therefore, a sudden worsening of an elderly patient's mental status should always warrant careful scrutiny. If the elderly patient has no history of psychiatric illness and suddenly develops a psychiatric disorder, *assume that this is caused by a medical emergency (i.e., this is a delirium) until proven otherwise!!!*

Assessment

Accept the occasional need for a lengthier evaluation, even in the rushed emergency setting. If the patient is not oriented, then a reliable history MUST be obtained from someone who knows the patient. A thorough assessment of the patient's psychosocial situation is necessary. Elderly abuse is clearly on the rise and must be explored if there is any evidence of neglect or trauma. Geriatric patients are often on numerous medications that can affect their thinking or mood. Depression is a risk for certain individuals who have retired, or for widowed people. Watch out for suicidal ideation!

Treatment

Metabolism changes dramatically with age, and thus geriatric patients experience increased sensitivity to side effects and a decreased capacity for drug clearance from the body. Therefore, watch out for *drug side effects.* Drugs with anticholinergic side effects (literally almost every drug prescribed in psychiatry) can cause marked confusion and memory impairment in older patients. It is not uncommon to find elderly people taking a half dozen or more medicines, which can lead to drug-drug interactions and toxicities.

On an epidemiologic risk basis, *suicide* is most common among the elderly, and the risk is increased by substance abuse, medical illness, or depression.

Treatment of geriatric crises usually requires both *acute intervention among complex multiple systems* and careful attention to follow-up services. Again, mobile outreach to homes or residential settings, coordination with family physicians, DSS, Adult Protective Services, and legal agencies will prevent the patient's crisis from worsening. Often, patients may need referral to nursing care facilities. Referral to DSS will be required.

In programs where crisis clinicians are only hospital-, ER-, or clinic-based, families and caregivers may often try to "dump" the elderly crisis patient into the ER or clinic setting. There is less likelihood of this occurring if the crisis care system is willing to mobilize to help treat the patient outside of a hospital setting. A *mobile response* can also support the family or system that is caring for the elderly individual. If, however, the history suggests acute illness or delirium, then ER evaluation is indicated. When in doubt, go out to see the patient, then decide.

Psychosocial referral is important to the elderly patient in crisis. Referrals to programs such as Meals on Wheels, Elder Support Groups, places of worship, ministers, priests or rabbis, and other community agencies can dramatically assist the older patient in need.

Dementia

Remember that dementia is a common reason for presentation in the elderly patient. Also recall that mood disorders, particularly severe states of depression, may result in so-called "pseudodementia." Patients with pseudodementia secondary to severe depression will often respond to antidepressants or electroconvulsive treatment (ECT).

If a patient is suffering from a dementia, find out why they are in crisis. For instance, is the patient delirious because of an infection, stroke, or change in their medication? How long have the symptoms been developing? (Remember, dementia is a chronic, longstanding decline in global cognitive function and skill. It is not an acute problem.) Ask about what has made the problem worse, if anything. Every patient who is diagnosed with a dementia should eventually be referred for a complete "dementia workup" (CT scan, spinal fluid analysis, blood and urine tests) since a significant percentage ____ of dementia-like illnesses are reversible (e.g., infection min B-12 deficiency, or normal pressure hydroceph done either on an outpatient or inpatient basis, needs of the patient.

If medication is used to calm the intermittent with dementia, high potency antipsychotics (e.g in very low doses (e.g., starting at 0.5 mg at night) can be helpful. Anticholinergic drugs should be avoided when possible, as these agents may worsen a patient's confusion or memory problems. There is some evidence that Tacrine may help the cognitive functions in select patients with dementia. (Note: Liver function tests must be followed when considering this agent.)

Finally, remember that agitated or violent elderly patients can be potentially very dangerous. Paranoid or delirious elderly patients, or those with profound mood or dementia disorders, may become dangerous. The crisis clinician should always be cautious. Do *not* assume that a 90-year-old frail woman with paranoia is harmless. She may be armed and agitated. A cane or other object may become a deadly weapon.

SUGGESTED READINGS

Children

Green, W. H. (1991). Child and adolescent clinical psychopharmacology. Baltimore: Williams & Wilkins.

Munger, R. L. (1993). *Changing children's behavior quickly*. Lanham, MD: Madison Books.

Adolescents

Adams, D., Overholser, J., & Lehnert, K. (1994). Perceived family functioning and adolescent suicidal behavior. *Journal of American Academy of Child and Adolescent Psychiatry, 33*(4), 498–507.

Bland, R., Neuman, S., & Orn, H. (1986). Recurrent and nonrecurrent depression: A family study. *Archives of General Psychiatry, 43*, 1085–1089.

Brent, D., Perper, J., Moritz, G., Baugher, M., Schweers, J., & Roth, C. (1993). Firearms and adolescent suicide. *American Journal of Diseases of Children, 147*, 1066–1071.

Brent, D., Perper, J., Moritz, G., Baugher, M., Roth, C., Bolach, L., & Schweers, J. (1993). Stressful events, psychopathology and adolescent suicide: A case control study. *Suicide and Life Threatening Behavior, 23*(3), 179–187.

Delga, I., Heinssen, R., Fritsch, R., Goodrich, W., & Yates, B. (1989). Psychosis, aggression, and self-destructive behavior in hospitalized adolescents. *American Journal of Psychiatry, 146*, (4), 521–525.

Goodyer, I., Ashby, L., Anthem, M., Vize, C., & Cooper, P. (1993). Temperament and major depression in 11–16-year-olds. *Journal of Child Psychology and Psychiatry, 34*, 1409–1423.

Goodyer, I., & Cooper, P. (1993). A community study of depression in adolescent girls. II: The clinical features of identified disorder. *British Journal of Psychiatry, 163*, 374–380.

Goodyer, I., Cooper, P., Vize, C., & Ashby, L. (1993). Depression in 11–16-year-old girls: The role of past parental psychopathology and exposure to recent life events. *Journal of Child Psychology and Psychiatry, 34*(7), 1103–1115.

Henggeler, S. W., Schoenwald, S. K., Pickrel, S. G., Rowland, M. D., & Santos, A. B. (in press). The contribution of treatment research to the reform of children's mental health services: Multisystemic family preservation as an example. *The Journal of Mental Health Administration.*

Henry, B., Feehan, M., Mcbee, R., Stanton, W., Moffitt, T., & Silva, P. (1993). The importance of conduct problems and depressive symptoms in predicting adolescent substance use. *Journal of Abnormal Child Psychology, 21,* 469–481.

Inamdar, S. C., Lewis, D. O., & Siomopoulos, G. (1982). Violent and suicidal behavior in psychotic adolescents. *American Journal of Psychiatry, 139,* 932–935.

King, C., Raskin, A., Gdowski, C., Butkis, M., & Opipari, L. (1990). Psychosocial factors associated with urban adolescent female suicide attempts. *American Academy of Child and Adolescent Psychiatry, 29,* 289–294.

Low, B., & Andrews, S. (1990). Adolescent suicide. *Medical Clinics of North America, 74*(5), 1251–1261.

Lewinsohn, P., Rohde, P., & Seeley, J. (1994). Psychosocial risk factors for future adolescent suicide attempts. *Journal of Consulting and Clinical Psychology, 62*(2), 297–305.

Miller, K., King, C., Shain, B., & Naylor, M. (1992). Suicidal adolescents' perceptions of their family environment. *Suicide and Life Threatening Behavior, 22*(2), 227–239.

Paluszny, M., Davenport, C., & Kim, W. (1992). Suicide attempts and ideation. *Adolescence, 26,* 209–215.

Puig-Antich, J. (1982). Depression and conduct disorder in prepuberty. *Journal of the American Academy of Child Psychiatry, 21,* 118–128.

Rich, C., Sherman, M., & Fowler, R. (1990). San Diego suicide study: The adolescents. *Adolescence, 25*(100), 854–865.

Rosenberg, M., Mercy, J., & Houk, V. (1991). Guns and adolescent suicides. *Journal of the American Medical Association, 266*(21), 3030.

Shaffer, D. (1988). The epidemiology of teen suicide: An examination of risk factors. *Journal of Clinical Psychiatry, 49,* 36–41.

Shaffer, D., Garland, A., Gould, M., Fisher, P., & Trautman, P. (1988). Preventing teenage suicide: A critical review. *Journal of the American Academy of Child and Adolescent Psychiatry, 27,* 675–687.

The Elderly

Ellison, J. M., Hughes, D. H., & White, K. A. (1989). An emergency psychiatry update. *Hospital and Community Psychiatry, 40,* 250–260.

Rowland, M., & Burns, B. J. (in press). Outreach services for elderly populations. In S. H. Henggeler, & A. B. Santos (Eds.), *Innovative services for difficult populations.* Washington, DC: American Psychiatric Press.

Chapter 16

MANAGING OTHER SPECIAL POPULATIONS: THE HOMELESS, PRISONERS, THE MENTALLY RETARDED, AGORAPHOBICS, AND V.I.P. PATIENTS

> I am become a stranger unto my brethen.
> — *Psalm 69*

> Everyone likes flattery; and when you come to Royalty
> you should lay it on with a trowel.
> — *Benjamin Disraeli*

THE HOMELESS MENTALLY ILL

THE HOMELESSNESS of many persons with chronic mental illness means more than lack of a home; it also represents a profound disconnection from other people and from social institutions. The homeless mentally ill have lost their "social margin"—that is, the set of relationships and resources that individuals draw on to advance or survive in society.

Statistics are contradictory, but indicate that among the total population of homeless persons, up to 40% may have a psychiatric diagnosis. The most common psychiatric problem among homeless people is probably alcohol dependence and drug abuse. They have numerous biopsychosocial needs, and often are medically ill as well (e.g., resistant strains of tuberculosis have been reported in shelters).

The psychiatrically impaired homeless often avoid contact with the health care system, even though they suffer from a multitude of medical and behavioral disorders; their basic survival needs are more urgent than treatment for their mental illnesses. For this reason, mobile outreach services are ideal resources for treating this population. Many homeless people with mental illness live in shelters, streets, parks, or even in unusual places, such as garbage dumpsters, and often travel around the country, migrating south or west in wintertime, and north or east in the summer.

However, these patients may show up in busy ER settings to vigorously demand services. Homeless people with paranoid schizophrenia may be too frightened to go to traditional settings for services due to their delusional fears and beliefs. Sometimes, climate changes (e.g., freezing temperatures) will precipitate a crisis need for shelter or demands for immediate hospitalization. Drug-using homeless persons may demand admission if someone on the street may be out to harm them. Crisis clinicians need to be flexible in dealing with the numerous needs of these disenfranchised people. The astute crisis clinician should try to understand and deal with the precipitants of the crisis — why the patient is presenting for services *now*.

Outreach is critical. Many homeless patients may be paranoid or too anxious to come into traditional treatment settings. Crisis clinicians should keep in mind that many homeless people *routinely* carry weapons, (e.g., knives or box cutters) for self-defense when living on the street ("camping out"). Although most will present little potential for harm, if the patient is acutely agitated, confused, psychotic, or paranoid, *be alert*. Some homeless people have severe personality disorders that contribute to their lifestyle. Others are substance dependent or have major psychiatric mood or psychotic disorders, and many are "dually diagnosed." It is always wise to be cautious and to use police assistance when warranted.

Homeless shelters are safe, controlled environments in which residents must exhibit a certain degree of calm in order to stay there. Thus, patients can be evaluated more easily in a shelter, where they are frequently less agitated (unless their mental illness is escalating) than if they are "camping out." Directors of crisis programs should advocate for the presence of clinical counselors and psychiatric coverage in a given community's main shelter for the homeless. This is an excellent way to complement the availability of an outreach-oriented crisis service, and to provide entry into the mental health care system by the homeless in a more natural way.

Common Causes of Agitation

Homeless people may become agitated due to mood, psychotic, and/ or substance abuse syndromes. Drug and alcohol withdrawal, delirium states, and severe medical problems (e.g., pneumonia or foot infections) may also cause agitation or escalating behaviors. Sometimes a homeless person may suffer with a schizoid, schizotypal, passive-aggressive, or borderline personality disorder, with a concomitant sense of entitlement; for example, an axis II problem may encourage him or her to remain in a public place in spite of police orders to leave. (Such a person may have to be removed by legal means, if they are not acutely mentally ill.) On the other hand, the person may truly be in severe crisis and may require involuntary hospitalization. Medical problems can also cause agitation; keep in mind that homeless people are exposed to the elements, have poor nutrition, and are susceptible to numerous medical illnesses and infectious diseases. In addition, they are often the victims of crime and will often be physically abused or beaten on the streets.

> The crisis team goes to see a homeless man who is psychotic and living on the street. He is originally from Chicago, but is now in the south for the winter. He has been "camping out" for over five years. Plagued by the voice of Satan, he is distracted by voices he is hearing. He is disheveled, emaciated, and fearful of the psychiatrist who has come with the clinician. After much coaxing, the patient is willing to take 5 mg of Navane, an antipsychotic, in order to relieve some of the voices he's hearing inside his head. At first, he was mistrustful of "mental health," since he had never known clinicians to meet with him "out on the streets." He agrees to stay in the shelter that night. The shelter staff will remind him to take more medicine. The clinical team will meet him the next day.
>
> On the following morning, his symptoms are worse, and he agrees to a short hospitalization. "I trust you guys," he says. "You came to me."
>
> The emergency psychiatrist has no further contact with this man until one year later. At that time he is married, has gained 30 pounds, regularly attends his appointments at the mental health center, and has a job delivering auto parts.

The above story seems far-fetched, but it is true. The key to working with homeless people in crisis is to keep hope alive! You can do much to help them.

PRISONERS

It is not uncommon for people who have just been incarcerated to feel out of control, humiliated, disinhibited by alcohol or drugs, depressed, and hopeless. Studies have estimated that 5–10% of the jail population suffers from chronic mental illness. If substance abuse and dependence and personality disorders are included, this percentage skyrockets. Some county prisons hold more mentally ill persons than do psychiatric hospitals.

Furthermore, one study suggests the suicide rate among jail inmates is as high as 8 times that of the U.S. population (DuRand et al., 1995). In 1986, national criminal justice statistics reported 399 suicides among jail inmates (i.e., individuals serving terms of two years or less) and 85 among sentenced prisoners in state and federal prisons (i.e., those serving longer terms). Hanging is the most common method of suicide in jail. The first 24 hours after arrest is felt to be the time of highest risk. Adolescents may be particularly vulnerable due to feelings of fear, isolation from their peer group, and humiliation. People charged with murder may be at highest risk due to their generalized impulsivity.

In most states, law enforcement officials are not allowed to "book" prisoners into jail if they are deemed truly suicidal. Therefore, emergency mental health services will often be called in to evaluate "jail clearance."

Evaluation

There are certainly people with severe mental illnesses who commit crimes; there are others who feel suicidal after arrest; and still others who feign suicidal ideation as a way to avoid incarceration. A good philosophy for the crisis clinician is this: If the patient is acutely and severely ill, and mental health services cannot be provided in the jail, then hospitalize the patient for treatment. If the patient does not appear to be acutely mentally ill, then send him or her to jail, on suicide precautions if necessary.

Remember, police and jails are adept at issues of security, but have little expertise in maintaining jail environments for suicidal inmates or for prisoners with severe mental illness. Also, it is important to know the limit-setting capabilities of the jail system. For example, if a sociopathic inmate is trying to cut himself or smash his head on the bars in order to get out of serving jail time, does the jail have the ability to hold and restrain this person through the use of special cells or chairs? Can this be a limit-setting measure with inmates who are malingering and manipulating (e.g., the sociopathic patient in the emergency room who tells a crisis clinician, "I'll kill myself if I go to jail")?

"Jail clearance" patients may be the most difficult to assess. Sociopathic patients have secondary gain for "possessing" psychiatric symptoms and often know the catch words to use (e.g., "I see a little green man" or "I want to kill myself" or "I hear voices telling me to kill myself and others"). Patients who come in for suicide evaluation after being arrested need to be asked when their suicidal ideation began (if only after arrest, they could be manipulating). Patients who are intoxicated and markedly agitated and disinhibited from drug or alcohol use should have their clinical states stabilized with time and necessary pharmacologic treatments prior to being sent back to jail. Most patients will no longer have suicidal intent after returning to sobriety. This often requires a significant period of time for an emergency department, so close coordination with the ER director is required.

PREDICTABLE CRISES

There are some crises that occur predictably over time following arrest. *Immediately following arrest* one will see:

- psychological decompensation due to shame, humiliation, anger, and fear of confinement.
- disinhibition from intoxicants or withdrawal phenomena. These should be treated medically.
- trauma. For example, patients may have fallen and injured their head, or injured themselves by scuffling with police, or may be hypothermic from the cold. ER treatment may be required—sutures, butterfly bandages, etc.
- malingering. Again, if given the choice of a hospital or jail, what would any reasonable person choose? After psychologic support and limits are provided and reality sets in, these patients should go to jail and then be encouraged to obtain mental health services either in jail or when they are released.

- acute medical illnesses (e.g., hepatitis, AIDS-related diseases), which require medical treatment.
- acute mental illnesses, which often require emergency stabilization, pharmacologic treatment, and, sometimes, hospitalization. Follow-up in the jail is essential, if available; if it is not available, arrangements should be made and coordinated to bring the patient to a clinic for further treatment.

During the first week following arrest, one will see:

- delirium secondary to abrupt cessation of drugs/alcohol.
- depression secondary to incarceration. Initiation of SSRIs may be useful. Tricyclics should not ordinarily be prescribed, since inmates often hide their medicines in their cell to be used for an overdose.
- adjustment disorders, which are frequent but respond to psychologic support, brief medication treatment, and resources such as, AA, NA, or mental health follow-up after release.
- psychosis, if the patient has a severe mental illness and has not been given medication in the jail.
- seizures, secondary to alcohol or sedative drug withdrawal, or of not getting anticonvulsants if the patient has a seizure disorder.
- the inmate's family going to court in an effort to have the person transferred from jail to a psychiatric treatment facility. This may be inappropriate, unless the patient is acutely mentally ill. Every effort must be taken to provide consequences to sociopathic behaviors, otherwise, the mental health care system may reinforce deviant behaviors.
- rape. It has been estimated that over 1 million men in the penal system are raped each year. The patient should be examined and counseled like any other rape victim. A secure, isolated holding environment should be arranged if he is to be returned to jail, and follow-up with crime victim services or other programs should be arranged.
- malingering, which can be seen at any time.

During long-term incarceration, one will see:

- mood disorders, due to the extreme stress of chronic incarceration.
- AIDS/opportunistic infection. Given the high risk behaviors for HIV illness, AIDS-related illnesses may manifest while a person is incarcerated.

- acute and chronic psychiatric or physical illnesses.
- malingering.

In summary, prisoners may have the following mental disorders:

- acute, intoxication and agitation or extreme dysphoria
- psychoses
- severe axis I and comorbid axis II disorders
- mood disorders
- organic mental disorders, such as withdrawal delirium

Prisoners may also

- have been raped.
- have a history of significant suicide attempts.
- become suddenly and inappropriately happy (are they happy about a final decision to commit suicide?).
- have a history of violence and impulsivity.
- have a family history of completed suicide.
- have lost a significant romantic relationship.

Treatment

For people brought into crisis settings for "jail clearance," reserve hospitalization only for those who have a severe acute syndromal psychiatric disorder, that is, those who are *severely ill* from a psychiatric standpoint.

Empathize with the patient who is not truly suicidal or psychiatrically ill. Say, "I can understand your desire to go into the hospital. If I had the choice of going to jail or to a hospital, I'd pick the hospital too. But unfortunately, the hospital can only be used for patients who are very sick. Fortunately, you are not psychiatrically ill. But we will set you up with some resources to help you out." Resources could include follow-up visits by a counselor (if one works in the jail system), AA, or counseling upon release, or the jail may transport the patient to a mental health clinic for further evaluation and treatment.

A manipulative "suicidal" patient may be returned to jail under direct observation and suicidal precautions. Document that:

- He should remain in the observation area on constant watch.
- Follow-up is necessary with local mental health resources for re-evaluation and treatment.

If a patient manipulates by threatening to harm himself if he is placed in jail, ask jail personnel to carefully and directly observe that inmate and to set appropriate limits. Explain to this type of patient that it is understandable that he would wish to go to a hospital, but the hospital must be reserved for sick individuals. Also, explain that if he does something to harm himself, for instance, stab himself with a broken toothbrush, he will be treated for this in the jail infirmary or ER and then immediately returned to jail under tighter security. An inmate should also be told that hospitalization will not decrease his sentence, or the time he must serve. Offer medication to reduce agitation, and advice on how to obtain counseling and mental health care while in jail (e.g., arranging visit to a mental health clinic or ER, AA or NA meetings in jail, availability of jail outreach, treatments after release, etc.). If a patient manipulates his or her way out of jail, then a crisis service may actually see an increased number of patients from the jail setting, as word spreads. Finally, clinicians must remember that severe mood or psychotic illnesses can develop in manipulative, sociopathic individuals, as well as in any other person, so a high degree of suspicion for the development or worsening of psychiatric illness should be kept in mind.

One final caveat. *Be careful.* Always be vigilant around prisoners. You can be their "ticket out." So, if you travel to jail settings, be certain that you are in a secure area. Do not evaluate a patient in an "open unit," where prisoners are roaming free. Similarly in an ER, make sure that violent prisoners are handcuffed *behind their backs* so that they cannot injure you or hold you hostage.

THE MENTALLY RETARDED

According to DSM-IV (which codes mental retardation [MR] on axis II), a person is considered mentally retarded if before the age of 18 he or she is found to have an IQ of 70 or below and demonstrates impairments in adaptive functioning (e.g., inability to meet cultural standards in such areas as social skills, daily living skills, independence, responsibility, and self-sufficiency). Common causes of MR include Down's syndrome, or Fragile X syndrome. Both of these are caused by chromosomal abnormalities. Mentally retarded persons represent about 1% of the population.

Patients with MR often present to emergency psychiatry services when staff or family notice a change in functioning or observe an unacceptable behavior. Sudden changes in the structure of life (e.g., death in the family, move to a different setting, etc.) may cause *dramatic* changes in a person with MR. Crisis clinicians should not explain away new onset of out-of-control behaviors with, "Well, what do you expect? He's mentally retarded." Mentally retarded individuals can and do develop psychiatric disorders, just like other individuals without mental retardation; in fact, other mental disorders are 3 to 4 times more prevalent than among the general population.

A 50-year-old woman with mild mental retardation (MR) had been calling EMS services several times a week for two years. She would dial 911 and demand to be taken to the ER. Once there, she would demand to be admitted to the psychiatric unit because she was "suicidal"; she would moan and repeat, "I feel bad. I'm suicidal." However, she never made any suicide attempts, even if not hospitalized, and had no history of mood disorder. Everyone thought she did this "because of her mental retardation." Thousands of dollars in health care treatment costs were spent, but no one could stop this pattern of calling 911. Finally, a crisis clinician happened to question the patient about symptoms of panic disorder and discovered that she met criteria for having panic attacks.

In retrospect, people realized that this patient with MR was having numerous panic attacks, but because of her MR disorder, she was not able to explain and characterize the symptoms to anyone. She could only call 911 and ask for transport to the ER. Because of the fear these attacks engendered and her agoraphobic feelings, she would try to get into the hospital by saying she was suicidal. This also explained her reluctance to leave her home on occasion. Once the panic was treated pharmacologically, the 911 calls ceased and the patient has since functioned at a very high level.

Emergency Evaluation

Essentially, evaluation of the mentally retarded person involves the same careful process required of all psychiatric evaluations—with some adaptations. Most requests for services are not initiated by the mentally retarded person, but by staff or family. Effective interventions in the emergency setting will meet the needs of both the patient and those who care for him or her.

- Have the patient stay with a familiar person (family or staff) while waiting for the crisis clinician to begin the evaluation. This minimizes the patient's anxiety and thereby diminishes the likelihood of escalating agitation.
- Have frequent interactions with the patient. Infrequent contacts will increase the patient's anxiety. Use food, snacks, or drinks to make the patient more comfortable. An MR patient who refuses to do something will often respond to kindness and the offer of a candy bar or snack.
- Mentally retarded patients who are agitated will often respond well to pharmacologic treatment. Lorazepam or droperidol may end a crisis immediately. Physically restrain the patient if no other means of containment work.
- Allow time for the person to express his or her experience. Family members or staff can often "translate" the issues, and can explain what the patient's usual baseline is.
- Avoid jargon; adapt vocabulary and concepts to the developmental level of the patient. Some patients with MR are very functional, for example, able to manage independent living or group living, or to balance a checkbook. Others may be severely impaired. A major decline in mental status in a patient with MR (e.g., from mild to profound changes in intellectual function) could result from a severe depression or other illness.
- Inappropriate affect may have a different meaning in the MR population. For example, failure to comprehend a situation may lead to inappropriate smiling or loud, sometimes frightening vocalizations.
- Mentally retarded persons are capable of true suicidal behavior, but this must be distinguished from self-injurious behavior that may result from self-stimulation or an attempt to attract attention. One syndrome that is accompanied by profound mental retardation, the Lesch-Nyhan syndrome (a problem in metabolism), is also accompanied by severe self injurious behavior (note that this is a rare syndrome).

- The more severe the mental retardation, the greater the likelihood that the patient will have a seizure disorder and will be on some type of anticonvulsant medication. Addition of a psychotropic medication may cause a fall in the blood level of anticonvulsant; conversely, discontinuing a psychotropic medication may lead to a rise in anticonvulsant blood level. Adding Tegretol to a patient's regimen of Haldol will cause a decrease in Haldol levels. Drug-drug interactions should be monitored. A low anticonvulsant level can cause agitated behaviors because the patient is having partial-complex seizure activity or brain irritability.
- Aggressive behavior is a frequent presenting symptom for mentally retarded patients. Lay people may erroneously demand that the patient be placed on antipsychotics. This is not necessarily the best form of treatment. Target behaviors must be used; patients can be agitated secondary to depression, psychosis, bipolar swings, surreptitious substance abuse, etc.
  1. Sudden changes in the patient's life situation or environment can cause profound agitation.
  2. Recurrent violent outbursts suggest either a psychiatric or neurological disorder.
  3. Low frustration tolerance and secondary agitation may be associated with mental retardation syndromes, and may derive from comorbid psychiatric or medical conditions. Mood stabilizers, anticonvulsants, or high dose beta-blockers (which must be started at a low dose and slowly increased) may be helpful in patients who exhibit longstanding, intermittent, and unpredictable violent spells. Combinations of these drugs, or possibly buspirone, can ameliorate this type of aggression.
  4. Any serious medical illness may cause agitation in a mentally retarded person.

In mentally retarded patients, target symptoms must be defined and chosen if one is to recommend any possible pharmacologic treatments. Longstanding hyperactivity or attention deficits may respond to stimulants or clonidine. Depression and decline of intellectual skills may require a trial of antidepressant treatment. Mood lability will require mood stabilizers (e.g., lithium, valproate, carbamazepine). Some general information on these medicines can be found in chapter 22.

HOUSEBOUND AGORAPHOBIC PATIENTS

A few patients with the most severe forms of panic disorder will develop complete agoraphobia and states of being housebound, or even roombound, due to the overwhelming fear they experience from panic attacks. Panic disorder may affect almost 2% of the population, and may be more prevalent in emergency psychiatric populations. Panic has been linked to being a potential variable in completed suicide, and causes severe psychiatric morbidity in afflicted individuals. Depression and substance abuse are risks to the patient with panic disorder.

Panic attacks cause severe fears of death or losing control or "going crazy." In addition, the extreme autonomic symptoms (e.g., chest pain, numbness, dizziness, and depersonalization or derealization) may indeed make people believe that sudden death is imminent. These attacks are associated with such intense fear and anticipatory anxiety that the patient with panic begins to avoid places where panic attacks occur. In the most severe cases, people become completely housebound. Then they are at risk for depression, suicidality, and substance abuse.

Agoraphobic, housebound patients find it impossible to come into clinics for an appointment. Sometimes, they call crisis programs for assistance. Often, once therapy is initiated it may take several months to achieve a return to normal or even seminormal functioning. With the proper assistance, however, the prognosis of these patients is excellent.

Mobile outreach is mandatory in the beginning phase. A trusting alliance must be developed. A brief physical examination is helpful to rule out "organic" causes of panic, such as hyperthyroidism or other endocrine illnesses.

Crisis clinicians should explain that the patient's panic disorder is coming from an autonomic part of his or her nervous system, and it is as though "a switch is thrown in the nervous system," which sets off a chemical explosion, which in turn goes through the entire brain and body, causing the symptoms of panic.

Medication should be started to diminish the patient's anxiety and panic. Clonazepam is an excellent starting medicine, and once the patient's anxiety is diminished, antidepressants can be used to control and treat the patient's panic.

Once the patient's panic attacks are controlled, the clinician must make a "behavioral hierarchy scale" to desensitize the patient's fear. For instance, a patient should be asked to rate on a scale from 1 to 10 (1 being least fear, 10 being the most fear) how much fear they have doing certain things. For example, the patient may rate going to the corner of their yard a 3, going to their front mailbox a 2, and going to the front step and standing there a 1. The patient can then be instructed to go to the step and stand every day, until all anxiety has disappeared. When that occurs, the patient should then go to the mailbox every day and stand there until all anxiety disappears. If that's too hard, then she can go half-way, or one-fourth of the way, etc. As the patient masters each step, she is reprogramming her nervous system to not have as much fear. Since the medication is blocking her attacks of panic, she learns that the world is a safer place.

Finally, after weeks to months, the patient will be able to go to a clinic setting to see the therapist (often, the patient will need to go with someone). The appointment should be on the first floor, for these patients will be terrified to ride in an elevator for a long time to come; they will fear having a panic attack while stuck in a crowded elevator).

Progressive relaxation techniques and tapes are also useful for helping patients to master their anxiety during the desensitization phase of their treatment. The entire sequence of treatments is effective and the patient's progress and recovery are very rewarding for patient and crisis clinician alike.

THE V.I.P. (VERY IMPORTANT PERSON) WHO IS A PATIENT

Occasionally, crisis programs are called on to respond to important people in the community, such as politicians, police, celebrities, bank presidents, university officials, wealthy citizens, business leaders, doctors, lawyers, and other professionals.

It is *critical* in these cases, especially if a crisis clinician feels awkward or uncomfortable, for the clinical staff to deal only with the clinical issues and for the administrative staff to deal with any appropriate VIP-related administrative or political issues. Otherwise, the patient will not be treated with the dignity and objectivity that is needed, and the clinicians will be too anxious to think of appropriate evaluations and treatments.

The crisis clinicians and administrators must ask, "Are we treating this patient with the same standard of care that we would give to any other patient with a similar clinical presentation?" If the answer is "yes," then the case is being handled well. If the answer is "no," then more consultation or supervision is required.

These types of cases should always be handled according to policy. Ideally, everyone must be treated equally and with the same level of high quality care. To treat a patient any other way is simply inappropriate and could even be dangerous.

Remember, tragedy may occur if patients are given substandard treatment recommendations, or if dangerous situations are not handled by routine procedure, *even* with someone famous or influential. For instance, police must always be involved when clinicians decide to go to the home of an agitated or suicidal patient with a gun. Anything less is inappropriate. Never let a VIP convince you that you should not follow your standard operating procedures. Remember, the VIP is a human being, like anyone else.

> A well-known political representative asks the police to accompany him to the home of his son. His son is bipolar-manic, psychotic, and dangerous. His son had told the father that he'd kill anyone who returned to bother him, especially the police. The father insisted that only one officer accompany him. Feeling under pressure, the police officer agreed, and apparently neglected to wear his bulletproof vest. They entered the home. The son shot and killed his father, then the officer, and then himself.
>
> Sometimes a VIP person or system will make unusual demands. In these cases, the crisis program's supervisor must be involved, and must shield the crisis clinical team from external VIP pressure that can, ultimately, have a negative impact on effective crisis management.

> A man with a bipolar disorder calls the White House. He says he can be a very dangerous man if something isn't done to help him. The White House liaison calls the governor's office. The governor calls the department of mental health. The mental health officials call the director of the mental health center and demand something be done. The director calls in the crisis team. The administrators of the team talk with the director, the regional mental health director, the state officials and the White House liaison. While all of that is going on, the clinicians call the patient, establish an alliance over the phone, and he allows them to visit him at his house. He is found not to be suicidal or homicidal, and is agreeable to starting medical treatment for his mood disorder and ongoing psychotherapy. Political anxieties and pressures are kept at the ad-

ministrative level, filtered away from the patient and the clinical team so that they may have the judgment needed to do their necessary clinical care.

SUGGESTED READINGS

Homeless Mentally Ill

Lamb, H. R. (Ed.). (1994). *The homeless mentally ill: A task force report of the American Psychiatric Association.* Washington, DC: American Psychiatric Association.

Prisoners

Marcus, P., & Alcabes, P. (1993). Characteristics of suicides by inmates in an urban jail. *Hospital and Community Psychiatry, 44*(3), 256–261.
DuRand, C. J., Burtka, G. J., Federman, E. J., et al. (1995). A quarter century of suicide in a major urban jail: Implications for community psychotherapy. *American Journal of Psychiatry, 152,* 1077–1080.

The Mentally Retarded

Stavrakaki, C. (Ed.). (1986). *The psychiatric clinics of North America* (Vol. 9, No. 4). Philadelphia: Saunders.

Agoraphobics

Ballenger, J. C. (Ed.). (1996). *Biology of agoraphobia.* Washington, DC: American Psychiatric Press.
Ellison, J. M. (Ed.). (1966). *Integrated treatment of anxiety disorders.* Washington, DC: American Psychiatric Press.
Sheehan, D. V. (1983). *The anxiety disease.* New York: Scribner's.

V.I.P.s

Smith, M. S., & Shesser, R. F. (1988). The emergency care of the VIP patient. *New England Journal of Medicine, 319,* 1421–1423.

Chapter 17

RESPONDING TO CRITICAL SITUATIONS WITH LAW ENFORCEMENT

Thou shalt not be afraid for the terror by night;
nor for the arrow that flieth by day.
— Psalm 91

ONE OF THE MOST difficult situations encountered by mental health professionals, police officers, and crisis intervention teams is the "critical situation." These situations often involve a "barricade situation," where an individual may be locked in a room threatening suicide or homicide, standing with a knife or gun held to his chest or head, or threatening to jump from a bridge or rooftop. Such critical incidents involve physical or emotional barricades that present enormous challenges to crisis workers. As demonstrated by the playout of events in Waco, Texas, each time a barricade situation occurs, the potential exists for tragic consequences.

As economic realities force change in mental health care systems, inpatient psychiatric care will decline and a focus on rapid crisis intervention will emerge. Given the increase in violence in our society, more mental health professionals may be called upon to intervene in critical situations. The purpose of this chapter is to examine practical

We thank Maria Durban, M.Ed., Deborah McAlhany, M.A., Susan J. Hardesty, M.D., and Shannon Tyson, M.D., for their contributions to this chapter.

issues in responding to such calls and to share experiences and success-ful operating strategies in dealing with life-and-death situations.

Much of the current literature on critical situations is based on the experience of negotiating teams whose training has focused primarily on dealing with terrorists or criminals in hostage situations. This train-ing often assumes that there will be specific demands around which negotiations can be focused. There is much debate about the role of mental health professionals during a critical situation. Opinions vary, from the rigid view that there is no role, to the experience of using trained civilian volunteers for some crisis response teams.

We believe that close collaboration between law enforcement and mental health can allow both sides to complement each other in resolv-ing acute emergencies. Much of the success of this approach lies in ongoing, open communication and advance planning between law en-forcement agencies and the psychiatric emergency team. At times crisis clinicians may serve as primary negotiators while at other times they may serve as background consultants.

There are several basic principles that can be applied to critical situations to maximize the chances for a successful, nonviolent resolu-tion. In most critical situations, we are dealing with a frightened indi-vidual who may be acutely mentally ill. For this reason we will restrict our observations to those situations in which the negotiating team is dealing with an individual and in which no hostages are involved. Mental health professionals have little to offer if the situation involves a sociopath who has taken hostages for purely personal gain (e.g., to get out of jail or in a foiled robbery attempt). Such negotiations involve "business transactions" between criminals and police. However, if the person involved is acutely mentally ill, then a collaborative approach will more likely result in a positive outcome.

Although each critical incident is unique and requires flexibility of approach, several basic principles apply, including the importance of:

· constant documentation and good record keeping.
· exhausting every resource when attempting to communicate with the barricaded individual.
· working in partnership with the police and understanding each oth-er's roles at the scene.
· debriefing for all involved in the work.

These principles will become more clear as we move through the stages of responding to a critical situation.

STAGE 1: RECEIVING THE CALL

- Rapidly assess the situation. Assessing the type of emotional stress or mental illness of the subject is critical because it affects all other phases of the process.
- Make decisions on staffing. Who should go? Are supporting staff needed? If so, what are their roles?
- Contact police to meet crisis workers at the scene if police are not already at the scene. Find out the name of the officer in charge.
- Begin thorough documentation and history taking. Get the basics:
  1. name of subject
  2. exact description of the situation, including location of the barricade and patient
  3. types of weapons available to the subject
  4. safe access routes to the vicinity
  5. whether hostages have been taken
  6. pertinent medical, psychiatric, and/or substance abuse history
  7. names of family members and treating professionals to facilitate data gathering
  8. name of the primary contact at the scene (i.e., officer in charge). Names and phone numbers of *all* contacts should be noted in the record.
  9. Keep all notes.
- Before going to the scene, take necessary personal items and stop for a "bathroom break"; the case may last many hours. Make sure all clinicians have ID badges to get through police perimeters (in dangerous standoffs there are usually an external and an internal perimeter).

STAGE 2: EN ROUTE

- Continue gathering data using cellular telephones or even portable fax machines, but remember that these cellular telecommunications may be monitored by the media or others. Be sure to document

significant times in the record (important from the legal perspective).

· Attempt to contact the officer in charge if the police are already
present, or some other reliable informant at the location.

· Find out whether anyone has been in direct contact with the subject
and what the quality and means of that communication has been. If
negotiations are under way and going well, do not interfere. If no
communication has occurred, or if communications are not going
well, ask permission to establish contact with the person by phone.

STAGE 3: AT THE SCENE

The primary concern at the scene is the safety of all involved.

· Define clearly each team member's role when they reach the scene.
· Law enforcement officers will establish a safe working perimeter
and deal with crowd control. Media and family or friends must be
kept at a safe distance.
· Crisis workers should report to the commanding officer at the scene
and be sure that they understand the chain of communication.
· The presence of an emergency mental health team can decrease the
sense of urgency and the need to act, allowing more time to think
and develop a plan and diminishing the likelihood of premature
action. An important role of the presence of the crisis professional
is to dampen the anxiety of the officer in charge.

STAGE 4: DEALING WITH THE PATIENT—EARLY PHASE

The initial challenge is to establish contact with the patient. This is
the *most important step* for a successful outcome.

· If someone is talking to the patient, and all is going smoothly, allow
that interaction to continue.
· If you become the primary communicator with the patient, *assume
that you will have a positive outcome!*
· DO NOT allow anyone who precipitated the crisis to speak to the
patient. Sometimes, patients will insist on this. Early in a situation
involving a suicidal patient, the patient may wish to have the person

who hurt his emotions witness his self-destruction. Or, sometimes the patient may wish to say goodbye to a loved one and then kill himself. Use every wish as a potential negotiation tool, but do not agree to demands prematurely.

- Sometimes patients who are barricaded will not respond to initial attempts at communication. Multiple attempts may be required; continue relentlessly. If phone calls don't work, be creative — try large painted signs, if necessary, or a "beep" if the patient has a pager.
- Offer communication with a doctor, counselor, police officer, minister, or family member, *provided* that you know they were not involved in precipitating the crisis.
- Avoid bullhorns except as a last resort; they may sound frightening and/or be indistinct.
- Initially the patient may communicate angrily. Don't take the hostility personally.
- Expect and even welcome the fact that the patient will initially make you feel helpless. Allowing the patient to externalize and project his helplessness or rage gives him the feeling of more control. Patients barricade themselves, or threaten to jump or shoot themselves because they feel helpless to do anything else. They need to project that feeling somewhere else in order to diminish their lethality, which is why a crisis clinician must absorb the patient's projections and frustrations. This is often psychologically frightening to a clinician, but it is the conduit through which a rapport will develop.
- Allow the patient to believe he is in control.
- Repeatedly clarify to the patient that you are there *for him*, not for the benefit of the police (remember, however, that you are a consultant to the police).
- If the patient is armed, and you are speaking from a telephone or car cellular phone, do not give the patient your location. You do not want the patient shooting in your direction. Keep in mind that these situations are most dangerous and volatile at the beginning and ending phases (just like airplane crashes are most likely on take-off or landing). In the beginning phase, while the suicidal patient is still hopeless, he may not want you, "that nice counsellor," to suffer any longer on this "terrible earth" either, so may want to "take you with him." Remain safe at all times, out of range.

- Find out the story. What caused the situation or hurt?
  1. Don't underestimate the value of empathically hearing the patient's description of the problems and feelings he or she is experiencing.
  2. Also obtain as much objective information as possible from family, friends, observers, treating professionals, hospitals, etc. It takes a minimum of two people to do this job: one to negotiate or to psychologically support the negotiator and the officer in charge, and the other to obtain as much history as possible in order to develop a theoretical psychiatric and psychologic formulation of the patient.
  3. Find out if the patient used any substances immediately prior to the barricade situation and if the patient is intoxicated. If so, the passage of time will help him sober up and feel more in control. If the patient is still using alcohol or drugs, ask him to please stop.
- Get history from the patient or others regarding what possible psychiatric syndrome (if any) you are dealing with. Control returns with sobriety; paranoia requires careful reassurance and that you ask permission of the patient before taking any action or before even asking a question; mania requires support of the person's narcissism, but not inappropriately; and mood lability requires waiting for short moments when the erratic mood stabilizes. This is where the clinician's training with severely ill patients in ER and other settings really comes in handy.
- Be empathic but not patronizing. Avoid statements like "I'm here to offer you help." The person may not be interested in help. However, the question "How can I be of help to you?" may be better received. Be gentle yet firm. Be reality-based. For instance, patients may say, "Come on in here and talk to me"; if they are armed, you might reply, "I'd love to. Once you can put down the weapon, and we know you're safe, then we'll figure out how you and I can meet face to face. Right now, you know I can't do what you want me to. So let's talk about how we can meet."
- *Never* lie, but do not tell the whole truth if it is not necessary. You must make good on any promises.
  1. If you don't know the answer, say so.
  2. Do not let others at the scene make you aware of information that may jeopardize your ability to be truthful. For instance, if a

patient has shot a loved one, do not try to find out the extent of the loved one's condition until the patient is secure. The hope that the loved one is alive might be keeping the patient alive.

- Patients may insist on being allowed to talk with someone who may have precipitated the crisis (e.g., girlfriend, father, grandmom, doctor, boss). Respond to this as a possibility, as soon as everything is safe and secure. Never allow the person to get you to concede to such requests prematurely. An appropriate answer might be, "You know I cannot do that until I know that you and they will be safe. So let's talk about how we can make that happen."
- As the alliance builds, move the patient toward face-to-face contact.
  1. Offer drinks, food, cigarettes, etc., as a symbolic gesture of nurturance and empathy. Do not do this prematurely or the patient will think you are trying to "trick them" with psychological techniques.
  2. Talk about your safety and that of the patient. Let him or her know "you're in this together."
  3. Ask for the patient's trust.
- Again, work in pairs during these negotiations.
  1. Never hesitate to step back and discuss the next step with your partner or with the officer in charge. If you need someone else to negotiate (e.g., due to fear, anxiety, rage, helplessness, needing a break or snack or trip to a bathroom), inform the patient about such changes.
  2. Never hesitate to consult with another colleague or supervisor, even if they are not at the scene.
  3. Ideally, both partners can become involved in the alliance with the patient so they can take turns and relieve each other.
- Police departments and SWAT teams will often be video recording these events for legal protection. Make sure that the police video camera is not visible to the patient throughout the entire process. This is particularly true when the situation involves a person who is paranoid.

STAGE 5: DEALING WITH THE PATIENT—MIDDLE PHASE

- Police or others may ask, "How long will this take?" The answer is, "Once communication is established, it will take as long as it takes."

When communication is established and going well, time is on everyone's side.

- Media people may put tremendous pressure on a chief of police to make a public statement. Help them to do so, if asked. Off camera, explain to the media that you need their help, that responsible reporting is A MUST, that the person who is barricaded in might have a TV or radio, and anything that shames or humiliates that person may cause a negative outcome. No mention of names should be used until the person is secured (often, at the conclusion of such an event, everything will be known to the public). The media will almost always publicize a person's name (they want to get the "big story"), but even the most "rabid" reporter will honor the sincere wishes of a police chief or sheriff, especially if advised by a crisis professional. Never share any specifics about the patient.
- Once the patient trusts you, it's all right to give some more options, such as putting down the phone to take deep breaths, sitting down, taking psychiatric medicine if they were on any. The patient will now slowly begin to become exhausted as his adrenaline wanes.
- If the patient is having difficulty trusting you, point out that you have done nothing to harm that trust.
- Tell him that you need to meet face-to-face, or that he must put down the gun or knife, or move away from a danger point (roof edge, bridge span, etc).
- If weapons are involved, begin asking the patient to relinquish them by placing them at a neutral point.
- After a patient puts down a weapon, it may be too threatening for him to come out of a barricaded home or room. If so, ask the patient if someone may come in. Explain that you want to see him in person, but need to do so in a safe manner; that is, they must come out or guarantee that there are no weapons. If there is a weapon, or even if he or she guarantees that no weapons exist, you MUST insist on allowing the police to secure the environment. Police negotiators can advise on how to proceed.
- Do not rush the process once initial concessions are made by the patient.
- The patient must feel as empowered as possible within the limits of reality. Give where you can give. At all times move away from a contest of wills.

STAGE 6: DEALING WITH THE PATIENT—
DE-ESCALATION AND RESOLUTION PHASE

- If things are going well, don't involve anyone else in the process.
- As the patient's dysphoria and adrenalin wane, you can be more specific and directive.
  1. Tell him you are concerned for him and worried about his medical condition, since he may be dehydrated and exhausted.
  2. Don't hesitate to back away if the patient's response is aggressive.
- Make a clear plan with the patient about how each of you will handle closing the standoff. It is important that you and the police officers at the scene also agree on these steps to ensure the safety of all concerned. The crisis clinician should coordinate with an officer on how to direct the person from a barricade.
  1. Such directions must be specific. For example, "You will open the front door, take two steps out and lay the knife down" or "You'll come out with your hands on top of your head, and you'll sit down" or "A police officer will search you, then you and I will sit on the steps and talk."
  2. If you have not been in visual contact with the patient, describe yourself so he can recognize you, and ask the patient to do the same.
  3. Do not agree to see the patient alone.
- When the patient does make it possible for the standoff to end, thank him for his trust and as much as possible help him prepare for what will happen next.
- Sometimes patients are too afraid to come out of their safe environment. You must imagine a barricaded person as a turtle; you are asking a person to relinquish all security. It would be like asking a turtle to live without its shell, which is virtually impossible. You must make the external environment safe enough so the person may leave one secure place for another. Sometimes, introducing close friends or loved ones at this point can help facilitate this process. Again, do NOT involve friends or family who precipitated the crisis.
- In a tense standoff, alert the police to the possibility that the patient may still come out with a gun or knife. If so, face-to-face negotiations will be in order directly with police; face-to-face negotiation with an armed individual would be too dangerous for a clinician.

STAGE 7: AFTER THE PATIENT IS SECURE –
LAST MINUTE DETAILS

- Patients involved in barricade-type situations who do not have legal charges against them (so that they need immediate placement in a jail setting) should ALWAYS go into a hospital for further evaluation. When sending a patient to an ER, the crisis clinician should always relay the information to the ER attending physician in charge or the charge nurse. Advise him or her to watch the patient carefully, to address any specific medical concerns that you have discovered, and that the patient should not be discharged!

- When a patient comes out from a critical standoff, it is amazing how quickly he is left in the presence of mental health professionals on the scene, and how rapidly law enforcement officials "disappear." *Do not let this happen.* Until the patient has been adequately searched and secured, and until the patient's extreme fear and anxiety has dissipated, the patient will have potential for running, becoming aggressive, or feeling paranoid. Before the patient comes forward, request that police stay with you and the patient until you are comfortable that the patient is calm and no longer fearful. Often, the patient will need direct transport to a hospital, or, if medical evaluation is required for injury, illness, rapid tranquilization, or treatment of dehydration, the patient will need to be taken to an ER. Have police or EMS on standby.

- Thank everyone involved. At this point (and during critical junctures of a highly visible situation where the media is involved), the commanding officer may request that you accompany him or her while a media statement is released. If possible, honor this request. Never give any specific information to the media. Give credit to others; never allow all credit to be given to the crisis clinicians. Praise the police for an excellent job.

- If the case is a highly publicized situation, and the patient is ultimately placed in a psychiatric facility, it is advisable to speak to the clinical or administrative leadership of that institution and caution them against allowing any information to be reported to the media. It is easy for clinicians and others to be seduced by "media hype" and notoriety. Be polite to media, but do not divulge any specific information that would jeopardize the patient's confidentiality. Reporters are aggressive. They will try to sneak into ERs, monitor police broadcasts, or go onto psychiatric units in an effort to speak with such a patient. Anticipate this and alert your colleagues. In addition, be humble. Don't get caught in the publicity!

· Debrief and review with colleagues. Did all go well? Was policy adhered to? How could things be improved upon next time? Police and other officials may need debriefing prior to leaving a scene. Take a few minutes to speak to them. Congratulate the officer in charge. Then, find a few colleagues and get debriefed too. Clinicians need to express their joy, anxiety, and fear in order to restore their sense of psychological equilibrium. This "debriefing" should be done with a colleague. Mental health professionals are good at debriefing others, but sometimes not the best at debriefing and supporting themselves. Abide by the well-known advice to the physician, "Heal thyself."

IF AND WHEN NEGOTIATIONS FAIL

Even the best negotiators and crisis teams cannot always establish an alliance with the patient. At times, crisis teams may not even be able to establish contact with the barricaded person. If no communication can be established, a crisis expert can do little to assist a barricaded individual. At such times the role of the crisis team changes from direct interaction with the patient to support for police and emergency services personnel.

· Offer suggestions, depending on the tactical situation, but remember that the police are responsible for the scene.
· If a SWAT team must "storm a house" or other facility, crisis clinicians should leave the premises and not watch the operation.
  1. If the patient is injured, such a scene can cause posttraumatic stress disorder (PTSD) in a mental health professional.
  2. Such situations are also potentially dangerous. Bullets can fly.
· In such situations, one last valuable role for the crisis team may be debriefing of officers, family, and bystanders at a barricade scene, particularly when the incident involves injury or death.

Following are a number of case examples that illustrate possible solutions to specific problems that can arise in a critical situation.

When the mobile crisis team arrives at the scene, a young woman is standing on a fourth-floor ledge of a hotel. She is threatening to jump if she is not reunited with her estranged husband. From within the woman's hotel room, the clinician introduces himself to the patient as a consultant to the police department. The patient, Ms. Volling, is disheveled, appears intoxicated, and has pressured speech. Conversation is difficult because the hotel window can open only six inches and then locks into place. The young woman believes she can float to the street below or that a giant bird will pluck her from the ledge. The patient is in danger of falling or jumping at any moment. At one point, she is holding on by two fingers and swinging half her body away from the ledge.

As the clinician talks to Ms. Volling and their rapport increases, he is able to direct her to stop such behavior. His immediate goal is to develop a rapid therapeutic alliance with her and to provide for her safety by "holding" her on the ledge through conversation until a rescue net can be placed below her. Once the key to the window is found, the team stationed downstairs move into position with the net. When the patient is distracted by this development, the window is unlocked, and she is pulled to safety.

Later, in the emergency room, Ms. Volling's history of bipolar disorder and polysubstance abuse is confirmed. She had exhibited increasingly bizarre, manic behavior over the preceding three weeks, quit her job, and increased her consumption of alcohol. The clinician commits the patient to the hospital's inpatient psychiatric unit.

Mr. Xiang, a young, depressed man, is drinking vodka and begins an argument with his wife. As she runs out of the house, he shoots her in the back and then barricades himself in the house. An ambulance takes his wife to the hospital, and Mr. Xiang begins an angry encounter with police who arrive on the scene. Several shots are exchanged, and the SWAT team is called in. All utilities, including the telephone, are cut off by police, and the area is evacuated.

Two team clinicians are called to the standoff several hours later to talk Mr. Xiang out of the house. One clinician takes a psychiatric and substance abuse history from the patient's family and friends, and a special phone line is connected so that only the other clinician can talk to the patient. After many rings, Mr. Xiang answers the phone. He is extremely dysphoric, irritable, and labile. He tells the clinician that he has killed his wife and there is no reason to live, so he "may as well kill some police" and then himself. He is told that at last report his wife was still alive and there was still hope. The clinicians insist that no one share with them further information about her condition so they would not exacerbate the situation or need to be untruthful in the intervention.

The clinicians want Mr. Xiang to know that they understand how desperate he feels, and that they care for him. They also want to keep him talking, since over time his blood alcohol level will diminish, allowing him more control. After an hour of rapport building and reassurance, the patient is asked to put down his rifle and walk out. He does so, gives himself up peacefully, and is escorted to jail.

As the clinician enters a trailer with police protection in response to a critical situation, she sees a young man holding a knife to his neck. He is against the wall and looks at her as she slowly enters his living room. The clinician sees the bounding pulse of his carotid artery moving the knife's blade in and out. He holds it against his skin, but has not cut himself. The young man begins to cry and asks, "Have you ever seen someone cut their throat and bleed to death in front of your eyes?" If the clinician says yes, he might say, "Well okay, see it again," but if she says no, he may say, "Well, you're gonna see it now."

One cannot respond simply to such a question. The clinician might avoid a direct response; a possible answer could be, "Your question scares me to death and I don't even know how to respond. But I can help you if you let me." The clinician's job here is to create an environment in which the patient can tell his story.

A man has been jilted by his lover. He climbs 250 feet onto a radio tower and threatens to jump down. All crisis clinicians called to the scene are afraid of heights. A fire fighter agrees to climb onto the tower from the extended ladder of the hook and ladder truck, and to communicate with the patient through a bullhorn. However, he doesn't know what to say. He takes a walkie-talkie, so he can communicate with the crisis experts below. The air temperature is 100 degrees, and it is mid-afternoon.

The key in this situation is to help the fire fighter build an alliance and gain the patient's trust. In this case, after a few hours, the fire fighter says to the patient that he is extremely hot and is sending down for a drink. The patient agrees to come down for a cool drink, and also expresses regret that the fireman is so uncomfortable. After further alliance building, they both climb down together.

A young man is told by his lover to get out of her home. He then grabs a knife, holds it to his chest and threatens to kill himself. She runs out, and calls the police. Law enforcement personnel and crisis counselors are called in but are held at bay for several hours. Finally, the young man agrees to come out if his lover comes to meet him across the street. Hostage negotiators agree to this.

When the girlfriend appears, he jumps through the front window, knife in hand. Luckily, he had neglected to notice a small steel bar near the top of the window, and he knocks himself out. If he had succeeded in jumping through, he would either have killed her, or more than likely he would have been killed by the police surrounding her house.

The scenario emphasizes the importance of *not* allowing family members or others who may be involved in causing the patient's distress to be present at, or return to, the scene, until the patient is secured. A better tactic might have been to help the patient de-escalate and work with him to establish a future time during which he could talk to his girlfriend.

A court order for a psychiatric evaluation is issued by the Probate Judge. When officers go to pick up the man involved, he meets them at the door with a gun, fires one shot and retreats into the house. From that point on all attempts to communicate with him fail. The available history leads the team to realize that the man has a history of military service and has also been paranoid for several years. After seven hours of failed attempts to contact the man, the SWAT team feels that the need to protect the neighborhood dictates that he be taken into custody by force.

The mobile team recommends against it, as the man is paranoid, and the loss of power and control would only raise his anxiety, increasing the likelihood of a negative outcome. The police considered their recommendation and decided not to take control. The man peacefully surrendered an hour later.

Here, an understanding of the underlying psychopathology is critical in preventing an incident from escalating to tragic proportions.

Hopefully, these case examples have introduced the crisis professional to some of the issues at hand in dealing with life-and-death situations. Crisis clinicians should consult with local law enforcement agencies, and get to know the hostage negotiations teams. Ask for further specialized training from those individuals and offer your skills and expertise in return. For professionals interested in this type of intervention, the rewards are many. However, it is not for everyone, as the work is also potentially dangerous and tragic, even in the best of circumstances.

SUGGESTED READINGS

Bard, M., & Berkowitz, B. (1967). Training police as specialists in family crisis intervention: A community psychology action program. *Community Mental Health Journal, 3*, 315–317.

Barker, G. A., & Hillard, J. R. (1987). The patient on the ledge: Evaluation and intervention. *Hospital and Community Psychiatry, 38*, 992–994.

Baumann, D. J., Schultz, D. F., Brown, C., Paredes, R., & Hepworth, J. (1987). Citizen participation in police crisis intervention activities. *American Journal of Community Psychology, 15*(4), 459–471.

Bengelsdorf, H., & Alden, D. C. (1987). A mobile crisis unit in the psychiatric emergency room. *Hospital and Community Psychiatry, 38*, 662–665.

Bonovitz, J. C., & Bonovitz, J. S. (1981). Diversion of the mentally ill into the clinical justice system: The police intervention perspective. *American Journal of Psychiatry, 138*, 973–976.

New York City Health and Hospitals Corporation, Offices of Mental Hygiene Services and Strategic Planning. (1989, January). *Crisis in mental health: Issues affecting HHC's psychiatric inpatient and emergency services: Summary data.* New York: Author.

Ebert, B. W. (1986). The mental health response team: An expanding role for psychologists. *Professional Psychology: Research and Practice, 17*(6), 580–585.

Fuselier, G. D. (1981, June). A practical overview of hostage negotiations: Part I. *FBI Law Enforcement Bulletin,* 2–6.

Fuselier, G. D. (1981, July). A practical overview of hostage negotiations: Conclusions. *FBI Law Enforcement Bulletin,* 10–15.

Fuselier, G. D. (1988). Hostage negotiation consultant: Emerging role for the clinical psychologist. *Professional Psychology: Research and Practice, 19*(2), 175–179.

Gillig, P. M., Dumaine, M., & Stammer, J. W. (1990). What do police officers really want from the mental health system? *Hospital and Community Psychiatry, 41*, 663–665.

Gilliland, B. E., & James, R. K. (1993).*Crisis intervention strategies* (2nd ed., pp. 503–536). Pacific Grove, CA: Brooks/Cole.

Gist, R. M., & Perry, J. D. (1985). Perspectives on negotiation in local jurisdictions. Part I: A different typology of situations. *FBI Law Enforcement Bulletin,* 21–24.

Gist, R. M., & Perry, J. D. (1985). Perspectives on negotiation in local jurisdictions. Part II: Negotiation strategies for escalated situations. *FBI Law Enforcement Bulletin,* 5–12.

Lanceley, F. J. (1981). The antisocial personality as a hostage-taker. *Journal of Police Science and Administration, 9*(1), 28–34.

Manglass, L. (1986). Psychiatric interventions you can use in an emergency. *RN, 49*(11), 38–39.

Mann, P. A. (1973). *Psychological consultation with a police department: A demonstration of cooperative training in mental health.* Springfield, IL: Charles C. Thomas.

Matthews, A. R. (1970). Observations on police policy and procedures for emergency detention of the mentally ill. *Journal of Criminal Law, Criminology, and Police Science, 61*, 283–295.

Perrin, A. (1989). When crisis intervention gets physical. *RN, 52*(3), 36–40.

Powitzky, R. J. (1979). The use and misuse of psychologists in a hostage situation. *The Police Chief,* 30–33.

Reiser, M. (1973). *Practical psychology for police officers*. Springfield, IL: Charles C. Thomas.

Reuth, T. W. (1993). Onsite psychological evaluation of a hostage taker. *Psychological Reports, 73,* 659–664.

Sowder, B. J., & Lystad, M. (1986). *Disasters and mental health: Contemporary perspectives and innovations in services to disaster victims.* Washington, DC: American Psychiatric Press.

Strentz, T. (1983). The inadequate personality as a hostage taker. *Journal of Police Science and Administration, 11*(3), 363–368.

Strentz, T. (1986). Negotiating with the hostage-taker exhibiting paranoid schizophrenic symptoms. *Journal of Police Science and Administration, 14*(1), 12–16.

Strentz, T. (1991). Crisis intervention with victims of hostage situations. In A. R. Roberts (Ed.), *Contemporary perspectives on crisis intervention and prevention* (pp. 104–120). Englewood Cliffs, NJ: Prentice Hall.

Tufnell, G., Bouras, N., Watson, P., & Brough, D. I. (1985). Home assessment and treatment in a community psychiatric service. *Acta Psychiatrica Scandinavica, 72,* 20–28.

Turner, J. T. (1988). Hostage-takers in health care settings. *Psychiatric Clinics of North America, 11*(4), 649–664.

Wilson, J. P., Harel, Z., & Kahana, B. (1988). Human adaptation to extreme stress: From the Holocaust to Vietnam. New York: Plenum.

Zealberg, J. J. (1992). A mobile crisis program: Collaboration between emergency psychiatric services and police. *Hospital and Community Psychiatry, 43*(6), 612–615.

Chapter 18

RESPONDING TO DISASTER: THE CHARLESTON HURRICANE EXPERIENCE

I have seen tempests when the scolding winds have rived the
knotty oaks, and I have seen th' ambitious ocean swell and rage
and foam to be exalted with the threat'ning clouds.
— *William Shakespeare*

DISASTERS ARE A PART of life. Most people will witness or live through
a natural or human-caused disaster sometime during their life. Such
events — hurricanes, earthquakes, tornadoes, fires, accidents, explo-
sions, and floods — are universal and create predictable psychological
responses. If such responses are left untreated, they may evolve into
longstanding, chronic syndromes such as posttraumatic stress disorder
(PTSD). They may also exacerbate existing psychiatric or emotional
conditions. Therefore, timely delivery of crisis intervention services
and mental health emergency care is an important component of a
community's response to disaster planning and intervention.

Traditional mental health programs cannot respond adequately following disaster; they are not usually community- or outreach-based,
but are more often situated within institutions, hospitals, clinics, or
emergency departments. In the immediate aftermath of a disaster, few

---

We thank Nancy Carter, M.S.W., and Susan J. Hardesty, M.D., for their contributions to this
chapter.

psychiatric emergencies are brought to ERs, and the false impression may develop that crisis services are unnecessary. Disaster victims are often overwhelmed, afraid, or traumatized, and may have difficulty accessing traditional ER clinical services. Lack of transportation, need for attention to basic needs, family security concerns, or disaster-related injuries may prevent victims from going to ERs. After a disaster, few people wish to leave property unguarded and open to looting or robbery.

If disaster victims who require psychiatric assistance do manage to get to the ER, they may not receive optimal treatment. In postimpact phases, ERs are often crowded with trauma victims (as a result of falls, auto accidents caused by lack of traffic signals, stepping on roofing nails, chain saw accidents, etc.) and those suffering with acute, serious medical conditions. Physicians' offices, hospitals, and neighborhood pharmacies may no longer exist, or may be completely inaccessible. Patients may have lost their anticonvulsants, insulin, or antihypertensive medications. ERs quickly become crowded, overburdening a stressed emergency medicine staff.

For these reasons, mobile crisis teams are a preferred method of response for providing emergency psychiatric care to a community of disaster victims. Mobile crisis responses can allow overtaxed law enforcement and EMS systems to focus more on their areas of expertise: police on traffic and looting control, dealing with domestic disputes, patrolling neighborhoods, and relieving severely affected colleagues; EMS on delivering physical aid and transport services to severely ill or injured patients. Mobile teams can travel into disaster impact areas, and are therefore capable of directly assessing the emergency mental health needs of a community. On-site evaluation and treatment may circumvent the need for transport and admission to busy ERs and psychiatric hospitalization. This not only saves dollars and cents, but also energy in an emotionally distressed system.

This chapter concentrates on one specific type of disaster—hurricanes. It presents an overview of the severe trauma that exists after a major natural disaster and some practical approaches for mobile emergency interventions. The suggestions we offer are derived from the experiences of our Emergency Psychiatry Service/Mobile Crisis Program (EPS/MCP) during hurricanes Hugo and Andrew. Our program is a public-academic collaboration between the Charleston/Dorchester Community Mental Health Center (CDCMHC) and the Medical University of South Carolina (MUSC). It is state-funded and administered through the CDCMHC. EPS/MCP was given responsibility for coordination and delivery of mental health services to the Charleston, South Carolina, area after Hurricane Hugo. Three years later, in the fall of 1992, staff members of EPS/MCP traveled to Dade County, Florida, following Hurricane Andrew as a spearhead team to identify how best to utilize groups of volunteers from the South Carolina Department of Mental Health (SCDMH). Based on these experiences, we discuss pragmatic solutions to the issues and problems that confront emergency mental health professionals (MHPs) in response to a severe hurricane.

It is crucial to understand that responses to a disaster in one's own community—when mental health professionals may themselves be disaster victims—will necessarily differ from responses as outsiders traveling to another community that has been devastated. We will first discuss the issues involved when a mobile crisis team responds to a disaster within its own community, and will then outline some issues that exist when an experienced group travels to a distant community where a hurricane has struck.

WHEN A HURRICANE AFFECTS ONE'S OWN COMMUNITY

Long-Term Preparation: Months or Years Before Disaster Strikes

Each community should have a civil defense/emergency preparedness plan in place. Every emergency psychiatric service (EPS) should know the plan and understand how EPS integrates into the community disaster plan, what reporting relationships and communication networks exist, and the appropriate back-up plans. Staff members should know well in advance what their administrative and clinical duties will be in the event of a disaster.

It is important to have established disaster protocols through meetings with the key contacts in a state's department of mental health (DMH), since the state agency is often responsible for coordination with the Federal Emergency Management Agency (FEMA) and other federal disaster assistance programs.

EPSs should be concerned with two main populations: patients who are actively in treatment within the mental health system; and people who have no previous history of mental health care but who have become victims of the storm.

PEOPLE ALREADY IN MENTAL HEALTH TREATMENT

Staff should understand that patients in treatment at their local community mental health center (CMHC) will attempt to return to the CMHC site after the storm in search of follow-up care. This may happen even if the CMHC main buildings are destroyed. Therefore, this eventuality should be considered during the planning phase. Patients should be instructed that in case of loss of the main CMHC, the local emergency operations center (EOC) will have a mental health representative to instruct them, and that all police, EMS, and National Guard will be aware of the headquarters location. In addition, this information should be reported to the community by newspaper, radio, and television. Designated places to reestablish "command central" after the storm should be defined, and back-up plans should be created (during Hurricane Hugo, seven out of nine mental health center offices in Charleston were destroyed). Care plans for patients may be destroyed by the disaster, and it is important to make plans in advance for recreating them. Simple things like going to the drug store to have a prescription filled may become impossible. Getting to a lab to have a blood level drawn may be unworkable. For some time following the disaster, regular appointments may be hard to obtain. Special care for these eventualities must be planned prior to the event.

PLANNING FOR SHELTER: DISASTER VICTIMS WITH
NEW ONSET MENTAL HEALTH CARE NEEDS

Shelter during and after the hurricane may spell the difference between life and death. Locations that will serve as shelters for those who do not evacuate the area must be designated as part of the long-term disaster preparedness plan. Contingency plans should be made for dealing with crises at shelters. Typical crises may include medical problems, emotional problems (e.g., panic attacks, fighting, intoxication, etc.), and physical damage to the shelter from fire, wind, or rising water. During Hugo, at least one shelter was flooded by more than eight feet of water, necessitating evacuation through the ceiling into the attic. A baby was delivered at another shelter. It is advisable in shelter planning to identify medically trained personnel (MDs, nurses,

EMTs) willing to assist in emergencies. At this time, too, it is helpful for shelter officials to update contingency plans for coping with absence of electricity, water supplies, and sanitation facilities after the storm. A back-up plan for shelter evacuation should also be thought out in advance because shelters may become flooded or destroyed. Shelter exit doors must be unlocked prior to a storm's arrival, as evacuation may need to take place in total darkness.

Short-Term Preparation: Days to Hours Before

When an EPS receives warning that a hurricane is approaching, clinical and administrative records should be secured and moved to high ground. Phone and beeper numbers of all clinical and administrative leadership staff should be made available. Plans to evacuate, including choosing a destination, should be a priority. Those who choose to stay behind "in harm's way" should be equipped for their own survival and should be prepared to contact the emergency preparedness coordinator of the CMHC as soon as possible after the storm.

Residents of coastal areas are often ordered to evacuate by government officials. Paging systems may be "down," so cellular phones should be obtained if possible, and cellular phone numbers should be shared among staff before evacuation. If all phones are down, a written message "train" can be established from the center director to all members of the crisis staff. This is more effective and cuts down on the confusion of word-of-mouth. Mobile crisis vehicles should be parked on high ground and supplies removed to prevent looting immediately after the storm.

A number of important supplies should be collected for use by the team (table 18.1). Psychopharmacologic emergency medicines should be secured. It may be helpful to distribute basic medicine supplies among the medical staff to ensure "survival" of most supplies. A running inventory should be kept whenever possible. Benzodiazepines should be available to assist people who may become anxious or agitated from the storm's effects and subsequent losses.

PROFESSIONALS WHO CHOOSE TO HELP DURING
THE IMPACT PHASE

If emergency psychiatry personnel remain in the community, they should now move to their designated stations and deliver mental

Table 18.1
Disaster (Hurricane) Supplies Checklist

Waterproof flashlights and lanterns

Flashlight batteries

Backpack

Medications

Hip boots or waders

Phone numbers of agencies and community resources

Battery-operated radio

Bottled water

Nonperishable snacks

Tire inflater pump (and check air in spare tire)

Insect repellent

Area Maps

Beepers

Laptop computer (if possible) with cord to plug into
    car cigarette lighter

Cellular telephone (if possible) with cord to plug into
    car cigarette lighter

---

health services throughout all phases of the storm; this should be coordinated with civil defense authorities at the local EOC. Crisis team members who choose to assist shelter officials in community shelters should be equipped with basic supplies, medications, cellular phones, flashlights, etc., to facilitate their efforts and to help resume rapid contact with others who remain in the community during the storm. Initially, there often are no "official" coordinators in hurricane shelters; school principals, teachers, EMS workers, police, Red Cross, or other volunteers may be in charge. Often anxiety runs extremely high. If EPS clinician staff remain in shelters, they can be extremely useful in helping evacuees prepare for the stress of a hurricane.

Community Evacuation to Shelters

Once evacuees arrive at a shelter, giving them an idea of what is to come helps diminish anxiety. At this time, shelter coordinators are generally concerned with provisioning and insuring physical security of the shelter. School buildings are often used as shelters, so the school principal or a member of the police force often serve as shelter director. EPS personnel coordinate with designated shelter directors. EPS staff can instruct evacuees in basic safety rules for the shelter as determined by individual shelter authorities. Volunteers from within the shelter may also be instructed on how to circulate throughout the shelter complex to reassure people and help them remain calm.

EPS staff may warn people to expect power outages and to anticipate that all television and radio communications will be silenced by hurricane force winds; this unexpected experience can be very frightening, since we are "information-dependent." People should be instructed to locate flashlights ahead of time and to expect deafening noise, wind, rushing and roaring sounds, and sounds similar to freight trains all around the shelter. Everyone should be encouraged to attend to restroom and sanitation needs before the storm hits, as plumbing pipes are often destroyed and water pressure or availability ceases.

Prior to the storm there is often a strange, eerie silence and calm, followed by rising wind and intermittent rain. As the storm intensifies, one can hear exploding transformers, followed by hours of intense wind that sounds like battering rams against the doors and windows. Throughout the storm one hears the high-pitched snapping and heavy thuds of large trees sheared by the wind. There may be intense lightning, hail, tornados, and rain. Tidal surges of up to 20 feet may cause severe flooding; in coastal or shallow flood areas, flying and floating debris is everywhere. Emergency back-up generators fail, and windows and roofs blow off, even in shelters. This is the time to expect some uniform sense of panic.

Impact: The Hurricane Strikes

In the shelters, crisis efforts should be directed at maintaining calm and coping with any problems in a confident, reassuring way. Structural damage or flooding may require evacuation from one part of a shelter to another during the height of the storm. Volunteers should try to calm adults and children who may be suffering from acute, severe panic and terror. People often use the metaphor that "the devil" is outside the shelter, looking for victims. As the intensity of the storm continues, comfort—spiritual, emotional, and physical—is appropriate and necessary.

Suddenly, there is an abrupt surreal silence as the eye passes over, bringing some minutes of reprieve. People should be instructed to remain in the shelter, and crisis efforts should be directed at stabilizing any problems that have arisen during the first half of the storm. The return of the storm is abrupt, with little warning, and may trigger further panic and hysteria in those who were falsely reassured by the lull. At this point, however, people are often emotionally exhausted and should be encouraged to sleep and relax in preparation for what lies ahead—the winds of the tempest suddenly returning from the opposite direction.

Postimpact

When daylight comes, the entire community is changed. Often, over hundreds of square miles, thousands of people will be without shelter, basic utilities, or even food and water—a situation that may last for weeks in many locations. Areas flooded under huge tidal surges are now rubble, and others look as if they had been bombed. Trees block sections of roads and cut through houses. Boats lie on highways. Virtually every powerline and pole, the entire power distribution system, may be down, leaving hundreds of thousands of people without electricity. Where forests and woods once stood, broken stumps remain. Houses have collapsed or are severely damaged, leaving thousands homeless. Sanitation systems are largely inoperable. Imminent dangers arise from debris, snakes, lost and frightened animals, open gaslines, and a few predatory looters who hope to profit from the tragedy. There are no open grocery stores or places to buy ice or gasoline. Some who failed to heed the evacuation warning are dead. In one night's passing, the entire face of the community has been altered. The devastation is overwhelming, nightmarish, and unrelenting. No matter where one turns there seems to be no escape.

As the storm abates, contact should be initiated as soon as possible with the local and/or state central EOC. Portable cellular telephones and gasoline-powered generators allow staff to organize central communication and treatment centers for mental health patients and walk-in emergencies. However, at times phones may be unusable and the only way of linking up and communicating with an EOC is to make several car trips per day. It is important to centralize communication facilities so that major needs are addressed and resources distributed in a coordinated and efficient way. In the face of a disaster, one's usual job description is completely meaningless; in the first few days there is little coordination or availability of services, and psychiatric emergency workers may have to deal with many medical problems that patients are experiencing. As newspapers and radio and television transmission become available, the command post for the community mental health center will be able to publicize widely that emergency mental health services are available at local hospital emergency departments, at the CMHC, and directly in the community via mobile crisis intervention.

In a disaster, everything changes. The real suddenly becomes unreal; the familiar, unfamiliar. The result is extremely disorienting and anxiety provoking. Familiar places become almost unrecognizable due to lack of lighting, signs, or other means of obtaining orientation and direction. Food, ice, batteries, and generators are scarce, and water is undrinkable in many areas. People are irritable, and looters and profiteers quickly appear. These changes make security concerns of paramount importance as volunteers enter devastated areas.

After Hurricane Hugo, the Charleston newspaper, which had moved out of town to publish, was the most dependable information source in the first few days when most people did not have access to electric power or adequate battery supplies to maintain a television or radio. It is also notable that many areas were so damaged by the storm that no communication existed and transportation was limited. Mental health providers must be alert to the need to seek out these areas and help provide resources.

Few psychiatric emergencies present in the first days after a hurricane. Most people are in a state of denial and shock, glad just to be alive. In the face of such massive destruction, people feel that their most important possessions (material items, belongings, and personal property) suddenly become less important than basic needs: Am I alive? Do I have food? Do I have water? Attending to basic needs blunts the pain of the immediate trauma. For example, people say, "I have lost my house but the guy up the street lost his house, his boat, and his car. I guess I'm really lucky." This change in perspective helps people through trauma that otherwise could damage their psychological well-being. Many describe a form of survivor's guilt, especially those who are less affected by the storm; those individuals are then able to share their good fortune (shelter, hot water, food, or a secure home) with others, thus diminishing guilt-induced psychological disequilibrium.

Within days, this basic relief is replaced by dysphoria, fatigue, and frustration. As people begin the recovery effort, the incredible difficulty of tasks such as negotiating traffic without traffic signals, the absence of reliable supplies of food and water, the variability of ordinary services (sewers on one day, off the next), and the absence of news and information begin to tax patience and lead to grief and anger. People also begin to come to grips with the financial realities of job loss, insurance claims, and the immensity of the task of reconstructing their lives. At this stage people begin to deal with the emotional impact of the storm and to seek help from emergency services.

The sense of loss and sadness is pervasive. Everywhere people are displaced, homeless, and in psychologic shock. The presence of National Guard military units seems to exaggerate this feeling. Suddenly, the rubble in the streets, the homeowners searching through debris, the military in the background with fixed bayonets and automatic weapons are not on a newsreel from another country but are present in one's hometown. A sense of surrealism exacerbates the anxiety everyone experiences.

In South Carolina, the SCDMH has been the lead agency responsible for the delivery of crisis mental health services. The SCDMH establishes "Go-Teams" that include psychiatric aides, nurses, psychologists, physicians, and people with administrative expertise. These teams are equipped to do whatever is necessary to address the mental health needs of disaster victims, and are then sent on 3–5 day rotations into hurricane-ravaged areas. After a brief local orientation, Go-Teams are quickly disbursed to various shelters to begin dealing effectively with the needs of shelter residents. Go-Team members often help people in practical ways: baby sitting, getting medicines or food, providing information or referral. They can call in a mobile crisis group for true psychiatric emergencies. Go-Teams can also be invaluable in travelling through stricken areas to provide needs assessments, especially in more rural, isolated areas.

When a hurricane strikes one's own community, crisis team members, who may themselves be disaster victims, cannot be part of the Go-Team for their own area; instead, their role is to orient the Go-Team that arrives to help. During Hurricane Hugo, for instance, local mobile crisis staff helped orient the Go-Teams, and coordinated with them to ensure good communication with area disaster management teams and to provide continuity as the Go-Teams rotated through the area.

Local EPS personnel may interface not only with Go-Teams, but also with rotational teams of State Mental Health Agency public safety officers, whose presence may be extremely helpful. One officer may guard medicine supplies, another may accompany the mobile crisis team on calls occurring in the community. Even though mobile crisis teams routinely coordinate with local law enforcement officers when necessary for security reasons, local police may be unavailable after a hurricane, since they too are overwhelmed by increased demands. The postimpact area is often placed under martial law and a curfew is strictly imposed, increasing the apprehension of the populace. Military commands and volunteer police groups may not be familiar with mobile psychiatric emergency teams and their role in disaster recovery; the EPS director and State Department of Mental Health public safety police officers can provide the coordination needed to allow an MCP to deal with most psychiatric emergencies in an efficient, safe manner, and they can maintain the ongoing links between the EPS, local, state, and federal law enforcement, and military agencies.

As the emergency service responds to community calls, the most helpful initial intervention is supportive listening. Each person in crisis has a unique and often heroic story to tell. Traditional lines of professional practice must blur at times. Often, primary care and "real world" responsibilities have to be dealt with before psychiatric intervention. Unusual situations occur, for example, personnel must be aware of the severe shortage of alcoholic beverages and the real potential for life-threatening withdrawal syndromes. Medical staff should be refreshed on withdrawal protocols and should have appropriate medications on hand. Suicide calls also begin to increase in the weeks following the storm, as depression, PTSD, and frustration result in dysphoria and family discord.

The MCP team not only treats primary victims, but helping professionals too. This function is important as stress and exhaustion mount in the community, and tempers become short, exacting their toll on professional human services workers.

Resolution

Many of the mental health staff work daily for weeks. They too must be counseled to relieve their own stress by taking a break and removing themselves from the acute needs of the community. This is an important part of any postdisaster intervention. Crisis professionals are excellent at taking care of others' needs, but often are less able to care for themselves. A roster of psychiatrists and mental health volunteers is developed, so that crisis care responsibilities are gradually shared or shifted. Debriefing becomes an essential part of the crisis management scenario. Mental health professionals, police, EMS workers, and all other front-line service providers who may contribute extraordinary amounts of time and energy even in the face of personal tragedy and loss, must be helped to realize their own needs.

Gradually, the transition is made back to regular programs. Even so, the collective memory in a community will focus on pre- and postdisaster events. Hurricane Hugo occurred five years ago, yet clients of Charleston's EPS/MCP still refer to it as a pivotal point in their lives. It is important to recognize and acknowledge this phenomenon in treatment.

WHEN A HURRICANE AFFECTS ANOTHER COMMUNITY

Preparation and Administrative Sanction

Without organization, coordination, and communication, emergency mental health services will be delivered haphazardly and ineffectively. Mobile crisis teams entering a disaster area must have a coordinated, well-prepared, but flexible plan. They must be self-contained, prepared to "rough it" in every sense, and should have *official* permission to enter the area as well as a specific state or local mental health authority to contact. In the immediate postimpact phase, the needs of most victims center around basic life issues — obtaining shelter, food, clothing, medicines, financial assistance, communication with the outside world and with loved ones, surviving without water, electricity, and light, and issues of personal security and home repair. Psychologic and psychiatric issues are often postponed or neglected, and responses to trauma are frequently delayed until the second or third week postdisaster. After a hurricane, it often takes several days or longer for law enforcement, national guard, and military authorities to allow residents to reenter their homes and neighborhoods. During this phase, there is little coordination of services, and volunteers from outside the community may even be turned away.

Before entering a disaster area, an MCP should obtain necessary temporary licenses for practicing in another state or location and contact the appropriate state mental health authority in that region. Because an entire state will become, in effect, a "disaster victim," it is important to deal effectively with administrative tie-ups and snafus. For instance, one's own state medical or nursing board of licensure may need to communicate with the licensing board in another affected state to facilitate waiver of the usual licensure procedures on an emergency basis. The local mental health authority needs to authorize the crisis team's entrance into the area, so they can hook up with important community and administrative leaders. A consulting MCP should facilitate a close working alliance between a state mental health authority and a local mental health agency. This process assures smooth coordination and minimizes frustration and inefficiency. Without this structure, a volunteer crisis team may wind up adding to chaos, rather than ameliorating it. Identification tags, labeled vehicles, stickers, and/ or uniforms should be obtained for easy, safe access to affected areas.

Beginning Administrative Assistance

There should be a volunteer processing center, preferably located outside the impact area, to provide orientation and necessary identification to volunteers. Ideally, such a center should be staffed by representatives of a state's mental health authority with daily input from state and local mental health agencies in the impact area. Communication should occur frequently so that the coordination center knows about clinical and administrative needs, locations and functions of shelters (which open and close daily), and local supply needs. Coordinators should communicate directly via on-site visits in the impact area. Regular debriefing of volunteers can also be addressed at the coordination or impact sites by coordinators who enter the area. Debriefing should not be the responsibility of mental health professionals who live in the impact area, as they are already overwhelmed. Debriefing sessions also provide valuable information for planning and distributing clinical services.

Crisis teams should assess whether there are communication flaws between the coordination center and the local mental health agencies, and should help shore up communications in practical ways.

Contacts: Where's the Flow?

A mobile crisis team must first make sure it understands the lines of administrative power, and meet or speak with everyone in directorship positions from the state to the county or local levels. This will assure that everyone in the system sees the outside group as an ally working for the entire system. Disaster-related psychological trauma may temporarily make good friends become enemies. The mobile crisis team can act as impartial mediators or ambassadors of good will to help repair alliances that are critical to a coordinated disaster response. Informal debriefing of leaders helps consolidate administrative lines of care, diminish overall stress on key professionals, and consolidate the alliance between the victim "insiders" and visiting "outsiders." Never assume the role of service coordinators without invitation from all parties, and then only with great caution. Efforts to help reorganize the mental health community's normal communication and administration channels are essential in providing effective, organized care.

Ground Zero Home Base and Communications

The mobile team should ascertain the best place to set up their "home base" — in a local mental health center, a shelter, or a tent city. An alliance should be set up with the mental health representative in the local EOC headquarters, most often located within the impact zone. It is also helpful to introduce oneself to NIMH officials who are often in the area to help state and local mental health center personnel apply for disaster relief grants that fund community outreach counselors and programs in areas declared as federal disasters. It will then be important to find out who is in charge at the most local area and who coordinates local daily update meetings, which will include representatives appointed by the governor, the military, the Red Cross, federal law enforcement, etc.

If the disaster-affected community is supporting its victims through a series of shelters, the MCP can travel from one to another based on the needs communicated to the local EOC or via direct assessment visits. If the area's homeless victims are housed in "tent cities," the MCP may choose to set up its mental health headquarters on-site. Tent cities are often run by the military, or the Red Cross and other volunteer organizations. It is important for an MCP to establish contact with all these officials. Military officials can often provide supplies, such as lighting or electricity generators. Medical supplies for tent cities can often be obtained from Navy field hospitals. General clinical issues remain the same, i.e., brief crisis intervention, emergency evaluation, treatment, and referral.

CONCLUSIONS

In the wake of a natural disaster, people experience a numbness of thinking that is extremely disorienting. This affects disaster relief workers who may be victims, too. The breadth of destruction following hurricanes changes the cognitive-perceptual maps of victims overnight. Because of the associated anxiety and disorganization, it is difficult to organize disaster relief systems; the existence of an emergency plan is therefore critical. After emergency mental health services are set up and coordinated, administrative leadership can be gradually returned to those normally in charge.

During times of disaster, numerous community organizations need to work together to respond to the overwhelming physical and psychological trauma that results during and after catastrophes. It is important to have disaster preparedness plans so that numerous community agencies can quickly organize and work cooperatively. Police, fire departments, emergency medical services, and military officials, as well as county, state, and federal systems need to integrate and coordinate to deliver immediate services — including immediate mental health interventions — to those most in need.

Early visibility and intervention are critically important, as are disseminating mental health information to the public and providing assertive outreach to disaster victims. Immediately following hurricanes, psychiatrically ill people respond extremely well to relatively little support. With a hug, a dose of psychopharmacologic medicine, some hot coffee, a few words of encouragement, some patients with severe psychiatric illnesses are able to achieve a rapid state of remission. We were often impressed by the resiliency of the victims.

The experiences of the Emergency Psychiatry Service/Mobile Crisis Program after hurricanes validates much of the mental health literature regarding disasters. It has been reported that fear, anxiety, and extreme tension are often found among survivors of tornados, nuclear plant accidents, earthquakes, train wrecks, floods, and hurricanes. In addition to anxiety symptoms, depression and grief reactions frequently occur, as well as survival guilt, which adds to the distress of disaster survivors. Indeed, all these emotional responses were evident among hurricane victims.

The massive widespread destruction of a hurricane leaves victims in a daze, which often lasts several months. Communities are complex social entities that constitute symbolic objects of orientation for their residents and form the basis of cognitive maps for people who inhabit those communities. These mental maps render the local community familiar, safe, and readily accessible to its inhabitants. In addition, communities provide symbolic identification and become part of residents' personal identities. Extreme disruption of these cognitive and social frames, as in the aftermath of a disaster, evokes psychological pain and disorganization.

Researchers have noted two predominant interpretations in the field of disaster research. The first emphasizes a social view, that is, a disruption of interpersonal and social linkages and the importance of the social support system to determine disaster response. The second defines the extent to which disaster victims suffer from significant psychiatric disorders as a result of disaster stress. We found that it was necessary to attend to both factors in our post-hurricane crisis intervention. Often, finding social resources for people quickly calmed severe emotional symptoms. The quick action of community leaders and support from other communities allowed hope to prevail, preventing further trauma.

Because of our assertive approach to psychiatric emergencies and our previous experience in working as a mobile emergency unit within the community, we found that our services were utilized completely throughout all phases of hurricane disaster. Following a hurricane or other severe natural disaster, the immediate need for crisis intervention is apparent only if crisis teams venture out into the disaster areas. If one remains in the office, hospital, or clinic, a false impression may form that few psychiatric crises are occurring. We maintain that an assertive, outreach approach to crisis intervention is always indicated following a major disaster and that emergency psychiatry clinicians should assume leadership roles at these most difficult times of human suffering.

SUGGESTED READINGS

Bates, F. L., Fogelman, C. W., Partenon, V. J., et al. (1963). *The social and psychological consequences of a natural disaster: A longitudinal study of Hurricane Audrey* (Disaster Study No. 18). Washington, DC: National Academy of Sciences National Research Council.

Bolin, R. (1986). Disaster characteristics and psychosocial impacts. In B. L. Sowder, & M. Lystad (Eds.), *Disasters and mental health: Contemporary perspectives and innovative services to disaster victims* (pp. 11–35). Washington, DC: American Psychiatric Press.

Charney, D. S., Deutch, A. Y., Krystal, J. H., Southwick, S. M., & Davis, M. D. (1993). Psychobiologic mechanisms of posttraumatic stress disorder. *Archives of General Psychiatry, 50,* 294–305.

Erickson, K. T. (1976). *Everything in its path: Destruction in the community in the Buffalo Creek flood.* New York: Simon & Schuster.

Hunter, A. (1974). *Symbolic communities.* Chicago: University of Chicago Press.

Lifton, R. J., & Olson, E. (1976). The human meaning of total disaster: The Buffalo Creek experience. *Psychiatry, 39*(1), 1–18.

Smith, E. M., North, C. S., McCool, R. E., & Shea, J. M. (1990). Acute post-disaster psychiatric disorders: Identification of persons at risk. *American Journal of Psychiatry, 147,* 202–206.

Tichener, J. L., & Kapp, F. T. (1976). Family and character change at Buffalo Creek. *American Journal of Psychiatry, 133*(3), 295–299.

PART IV

CRASH COURSE IN MEDICAL PSYCHIATRY FOR THE NONPHYSICIAN

Chapter 19

INTRODUCTION TO THE BRAIN AND NERVOUS SYSTEM

Mean ought to know that from nothing else but the brain come
joys, delights, laughter and sports, and sorrows, griefs,
despondency, and lamentations.
— *Hippocrates (on the Sacred Disease)*

THE BRAIN—WHERE THE ACTION IS

IT IS SURPRISING, and sometimes even embarrassing, how little mental health professionals know about the nervous system and the brain. Imagine taking your car to a mechanic who never saw an engine or knew how it worked! You would certainly not entrust your valuable vehicle to such an expert. Yet, we often ask patients to entrust their very lives to us. We must, therefore, know as much as we can about the bio-psycho-social-spiritual approach to treating patients. The biological knowledge base is critically important, especially for professionals who are invested in treating the sickest patients who undergo the most extreme, severe crises.

In all severe psychiatric emergencies, patients are suffering from brain and nervous system dysfunction. The dysfunction can be caused by an inherited illness (e.g., schizophrenia or bipolar disorder), by exogenous substances or withdrawal from substances (e.g., alcohol), or by

We thank Shannon Tyson, M.D., for her contributions to this chapter.

Figure 19.1
A lateral (side) view of the brain.

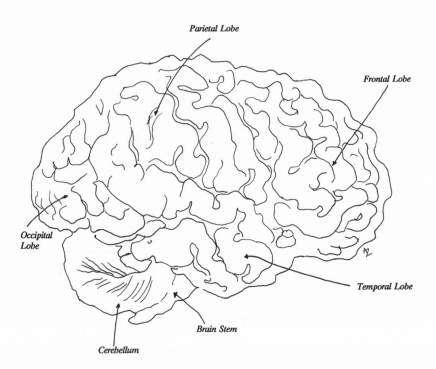

medical conditions that affect the mind and brain (e.g., brain tumors).

Some important structures of the brain and nervous system are described below and illustrated in Figure 19.1.

Frontal Lobe

A major function of the frontal lobe is movement of the body, or motor movements. Interestingly, the right frontal lobe controls the left side of the body, and vice versa. At the lower end of the left frontal lobe, near the temporal lobe, is an area called Broca's area, which is responsible for expression of speech. A stroke (or what is called a "CVA"— cerebrovascular accident) in that area will cause an expressive aphasia (the person cannot get words out but can understand them) and a right hemiplegia (paralysis on the right half of the body). The frontal lobe also controls higher cognitive function and integration of messages from other parts of the brain, and is involved in emotional expression. Before powerful psychiatric medications were discovered, people would sometimes undergo frontal lobotomy surgery, where the connections between the frontal lobe and the rest of the brain were severed. This procedure decreased a patient's aggressiveness, but also unfortunately decreased his or her ability to interact with others normally. Fortunately such psychosurgery is no longer practiced (surgery of the brain is sometimes indicated, however, for other reasons, such as severe, uncontrolled seizures). One dramatic anatomical difference that separates us from other animals is our large frontal lobe.

Parietal Lobe

This sits behind the frontal lobe and is separated by a deep groove in the brain, the central sulcus. The parietal lobe integrates sensation in the body. For instance, if you were to tickle someone's left foot, the nerve cells (neurons) in the right parietal lobe would pick up this activity. Note again that the right parietal lobe picks up sensory input from the opposite side of the body, and vice versa.

Occipital Lobe

This part of the brain is farthest to the back of the skull. The occipital lobe is where vision is integrated in the brain. A problem in the occipital lobe could lead to vision changes, blindness, and other visual disturbances.

Temporal Lobe

The temporal lobe sits below the parietal lobe and on each side of the brain. Much of the brain's emotions are stored and integrated here as well as by structures deep inside the temporal lobe, in the part of the brain known as the limbic system (see below). Many people have seizure disorders that come from this part of the brain, so-called complex-partial seizures or temporal lobe epilepsy. Such seizures can mimic unusual behaviors, such as strange repetitive movements, unusual body sensations, or unusual olfactory hallucinations (i.e., smelling malodorous things that are not there). The temporal lobe also integrates certain language and memory functions, as well as hearing.

Cerebellum

This lobe sits beneath the occipital lobe. It integrates complex motor movements. For instance, if a patient cannot touch his finger to his nose or to someone else's finger without his finger and hand moving rapidly back and forth (called an intention tremor), one might worry that he has a problem with his cerebellum.

Brainstem

This bundle of nerve fibers and structures leads to and from the brain. Its parts include the midbrain, the pons, and the medulla (which leads to the spinal cord). Most of the nerves that innervate the face and head (known as the cranial nerves) originate from here. Other nerves from the brainstem are involved in regulating all essential functions of life, such as the heartbeat or respiration.

Limbic System

The limbic system is a ring-like structure buried beneath the temporal lobe (*limbus* = ring) and is composed of structures involved with emotions and other important behavioral functions. For instance, the hippocampus is a seahorse-shaped structure that integrates short-term memory function. The amygdala is an almond-shaped structure that modulates aggression and anger.

Hypothalamus

This is the master control station for the body. Many functions are regulated and coordinated from the hypothalamus, which lies deep within the brain. Temperature, hormones, and sleep-wake cycles are a few examples. Chemicals from the hypothalamic nerves lead to the pituitary gland, directly below it, and tell that gland what to do. In turn, the pituitary gland sends out hormonal signals to many parts of the body, and thereby regulates how much hormone the body should produce. For example, the hypothalamus releases CRH (corticotropin releasing hormone) and signals the pituitary gland to release ACTH (adrenocorticotropic hormone). ACTH will signal the adrenal glands to secrete more cortisol, a hormone involved in states of stress. Thus, the nervous system and the hormone system are intimately connected. In states of depression, the HPA (hypothalamic-pituitary-adrenal) axis is often dysfunctional; because of its activity, depressed patients often have cortisol levels that are too high.

THE CHEMISTRY OF THE NERVOUS SYSTEM— A FEW DEFINITIONS

The brain is made up of millions of nerve cells called neurons. Each neuron is connected to thousands of others through areas of connection called synapses. At the synapse, nerves do not actually touch each other, but are separated by a tiny space called the synaptic cleft. Each nerve cell communicates with another via chemical messengers that cross the synaptic cleft and turn on or off a neighboring nerve cell. These messengers are known as neurotransmitters. The most notable ones are listed below.

- *Dopamine* is involved in schizophrenia. Antipsychotic drugs often block the receptor areas on nerve cells that pick up dopamine molecules.
- *Norepinephrine* is often involved in anxiety or depression. Some tricyclic antidepressant medications work on norepinephrine.
- *Serotonin* is involved in sleep and depression. Prozac and other newer antidepressant drugs are known as SSRI drugs, that is, serotonin specific reuptake inhibitors. These SSRI drugs often change the brain's serotonin chemical system.
- *Acetylcholine*. Many of the drugs prescribed in psychiatry affect and block this neurotransmitter's effects. These anticholinergic effects can cause a patient to experience blurring of vision, dry mouth, constipation, confusion, or difficulty with urination.

Hopefully, this overview has not been too painful. It's important for crisis clinicians to develop a familiarity with the language of neuroscience. Patients will often have many questions about their treatments and the effects of treatments on their overall well-being. It is important to have at least a working knowledge of a few basic concepts.

There is an information explosion in brain science. Readers are encouraged to keep up with the latest developments, so that information can be shared with patients.

SUGGESTED READINGS

Cooper, J. R., Bloom, F. E., & Roth, R. H. (1991). *The biochemical basis of neuropharmacology* (6th ed.). London: Oxford University Press.

Hyman, S. E., & Nestler, E. J. (1993). *The molecular foundations of psychiatry.* Washington, DC: American Psychiatric Press.

Kandel, E. R., & Schwartz, J. H. (Eds). (1985). *Principles of neural science* (2nd ed.). New York: Elsevier.

Konner, M. (1982). *The tangled wing: Biological constraints on the human spirit.* New York: Holt, Rinehart & Winston.

Chapter 20

THE ER PATIENT: MEDICAL HISTORY, MENTAL STATUS, AND LABORATORY ASSESSMENTS

So difficult a matter it is to trace and find out
the truth of anything by history.
—Plutarch, Lives (Pericles)

A NUMBER OF RECENT STUDIES suggest that many adult patients who present to the ER with new and severe psychiatric symptoms (e.g., agitation, hallucinations, violence) may have an organic etiology, that is, a *medical* cause, for the psychiatric symptoms. Such causes may include drugs or alcohol and their effects on the brain, infection, metabolic disturbances, or other acute medical, neurological, or surgical illnesses. Therefore, it is crucial to evaluate these patients medically before assuming a psychiatric diagnosis. Even in the clinic, home, or community setting, it is essential to have these concerns in mind. For instance, if a person walks into a clinic or is seen on a mobile call, and that patient possesses large, protruding eyes, a large mass in the front of the neck, a tremor of the hands, a rapid pulse, and intolerance to heat, a crisis clinician should at least be aware that the patient could be suffering from Grave's disease, the most common cause of hyperthyroidism. Hyperthyroid patients may present in crisis with symptoms of mania or extreme anxiety. Good crisis clinicians, however, should not feel that they must be physicians; yet a working knowledge of some illnesses, as well as the approach to a medical evaluation, alone with the types and indications for laboratory evaluation, may be helpful. If there is a strong suspicion of an acute or serious medical illness, the crisis clinician should suggest such interventions as a physical examination, a complete blood count and several other laboratory tests, an alcohol level, and a urine drug screen.

The information needed to be gathered when a patient is evaluated in an ER setting follows. Of course, basic history gathering and a thorough mental status examination will need to be performed on *every* patient, regardless of where they are seen—be it in an emergency department, in a home or shelter, or in a clinic setting.

THE PATIENT INTERVIEW: BASIC HISTORY GATHERING

1. Always begin by forming a treatment alliance, a rapport with the patient. NOTHING can be done for the patient (except to hospitalize him) unless you can establish a trusting relationship. If the patient is resistant, empathize with his situation. "I'm sorry you're having a hard time talking about things—I know it's hard to speak to a stranger" or "I know you've been waiting here a long time. Would you like something to drink or a snack perhaps?" These statements help the patient know that you intend to provide support and symbolic nurturance, and can begin a positive working alliance. Occasionally a patient may be too out of control to be interviewed. Explain that you'll come back later when he is feeling better, or that you'll return in a few minutes to see if he is feeling better able to speak with you. Sometimes patients won't talk because of psychotic thoughts or commands not to speak; such patients will often communicate with an examiner through writing.

2. Once an alliance is built, focus on the *main* problem that is troubling the patient. For instance, begin by asking, "Can you help me understand what brought you to the emergency room?" or if a patient cannot focus on a main problem (e.g., a disorganized, psychotic patient) and tells you about many things, it is sometimes helpful to ask, "Of all the difficult things you told me about so far, can you help me understand what the worst thing is for you?" People or families in crisis will feel very anxious or out of control due to anger or dysphoria, and often will not be able to focus their

thinking on the presenting problem. Structured questioning by the clinician will help assess the situation as well as diminish the anxiety of those in crisis. Remember, crisis intervention is always focused on the here and now, and on the main problem with which the patient is struggling.

3. The history of the current problem is also important. For instance, if a man is seen in the ER for a history of heavy alcohol usage over the past ten years, it is important to understand why that patient is in crisis *now*. He may be financially broke or homeless; his spouse may have threatened him with divorce if he did not seek immediate treatment; he may want disability and a lawyer recommended that he seek inpatient treatment; or he could have developed abdominal pain from pancreatitis (severe inflammation of the pancreas), making drinking impossible. Ask the patient, "How did the problem came about? Over what time course? Who are the people or circumstances involved? Have you ever had this problem before? What types of help did you seek, if any? What are your hopes for this visit to the ER?"

4. Finding out about a patient's past medical and psychiatric history is also important. For instance, if a patient has systemic lupus erythematosus (SLE), an autoimmune disease, but no history of prior psychiatric problems, it may be that the patient is having psychotic symptoms because of the medications he is taking for SLE (e.g., Prednisone, a steroid, is sometimes used to treat lupus, but it may have the side effect of causing irritability, psychosis, or manic-type symptoms), or it may be that the disease itself is causing a direct inflammation of the brain. If the patient has a long history of psychiatric disorder, ask, "Who have you been in treatment with? For what? What worked? How are things going in treatment? What kind of medicines, if any, are you on? What doses? Any side effects? How often are you attending treatment sessions? Any changes in treatment (e.g., is her therapist, doctor, or case manager leaving—a situation that often evokes a state of crisis)?"

5. Find out the time course of the patient's symptoms. Psychotic relapse often comes on over days to weeks or even months. Delirium comes on abruptly, in hours or days. Dementias present over months or years. An example is the sudden onset of psychotic symptoms in an elderly person with no psychiatric history. If a

clinician gathers history that suggests that this was a sudden change in the patient's mental state, and the patient has never had a psychiatric disorder, the clinical picture suggests an acute delirium secondary to a serious medical condition (patients who may be delirious will always require a thorough medical examination and appropriate laboratory examination).

6. Again, as you talk with a patient, find out what current medications he or she is taking and if any recent medication changes have occurred. Patients can experience crisis states if new medications aren't adequate to treat their illnesses (i.e., if a new medication has just been started and has not yet reached a "therapeutic level") or if they are experiencing withdrawal symptoms from suddenly stopping their long-term medicines. Abrupt discontinuation of benzodiazepine drugs such as Librium (chlordiazepoxide), Xanax (alprazolam), or Valium (diazepam) can lead to a withdrawal syndrome characterized by shaking, tremor, fast pulse (tachycardia), fever, delirium, seizures, and even death. This is also true of barbiturate drugs such as Donnatal (phenobarbital), or older sedative-hypnotic drugs such as Miltown or Placidyl. Certain beta-blockers such as Inderal (propranolol), which are often used to treat hypertension (high blood pressure) or chest pain from coronary heart disease (angina pectoris), may cause symptoms of depression in some people. Drug interactions can also come into play, so be sure you know all the medicines the patient uses.

7. Also ask about allergies to medicines. You would not want to recommend a drug to a patient if the patient is allergic to it. Ask the patient if he has ever taken a medicine that made him break out in a rash, or caused hives or difficulty breathing. If so, the patient is probably allergic to that medicine.

8. Be sure to inquire about the possibility of pregnancy prior to administering any psychiatric medications to women. Many psychiatric medicines have been implicated in causing possible birth defects when pregnant women have taken certain drugs, particularly in the first trimester of pregnancy (e.g., lithium has been implicated in causing an abnormality in the tricuspid valve of the fetal heart when taken during the first trimester of pregnancy).

9. Inquire about a patient's current living situation and social supports. "Who do you live with? Where do you live? Is everyone in the family getting along? Is there family discord or relationship

strife? Is the family aware of your distress? What do they think? If they are not aware of your problem, why aren't they?" Psychiatric disorders can often dehumanize patients, that is, they can stop bathing, become alcohol or drug addicted, or be chronically unemployed or homeless. Ask the patient if he works. If unemployed, when was the last time he did work? Work and self-esteem are very closely related. Does the patient need vocational rehabilitation? Is the patient receiving entitlement benefits? What are his strengths? Who are his supports?

10. A family history can be invaluable, particularly about issues of completed suicide and mental illness. Many illnesses, both medical and psychiatric, are genetically linked. New onset of severe psychiatric symptoms in a patient may be the result of a genetic medical disorder such as Huntington's Chorea (a degenerative movement disorder affecting the mind as well, causing personality and memory dysfunction). If the patient has a family history of completed suicide, he or she may have inherited a gene that leads to increased impulsivity toward self and others. Behavioral modeling within families is also of concern.

11. Always inquire about neurovegetative signs of depression: changes in sleep, concentration, appetite, and weight; hopelessness; helplessness; changes in libido; or diurnal changes in mood (i.e., patient feels better early or late in the day). These findings may imply the presence of a biological mood disorder.

12. Ask the patient about alcohol or drug use. Quantify how much, how often, what type, when the last use was, what symptoms, if any, the patient experiences if she stops using. Does the patient perceive her drug or alcohol use as a problem? Do others perceive it as problematic? If the patient has a history of intravenous drug abuse (IVDA), inquire about whether she's had a test for the presence of exposure to HIV.

13. It is good practice to ask a patient about headaches and seizures. Rarely, one may see a patient who presents with depression due to a slow-growing tumor of the brain. These patients will have daily, uncharacteristic headaches, often present upon awakening, and may experience a worsening of headache pain if they cough or sneeze because of slowly increasing intracerebral pressure from the "mass effect" of the tumor. A neurologist can be helpful as a consultant with a patient who has this history. Also, patients who

present after a seizure, in a postictal state, can be quite confused or even combative for as long as 12 to 24 hours. ER doctors must check these patients' levels of anticonvulsant medicines to test if they are reaching adequate blood levels to prevent seizures. For instance, patients on Dilantin (phenytoin) should have levels of 10 to 20. Patients can also have too much anticonvulsant medicine in their bloodstream, and these toxic levels can induce drowsiness, staggering, nystagmus (a rapid horizontal movement of the eyes when a patient looks to the side), and mental confusion. Occasionally, levels of anticonvulsant medicines can be too low (i.e., "subtherapeutic"), and this can contribute to marked irritability of the brain, causing psychiatric symptoms in seizure patients.

14. Finally, always attempt to confirm areas of concern or uncertainty in a patient's history by talking with others who are familiar with the patient's problems. This is particularly important if you are seeing anyone with organic brain impairment, for example, dementia, delirium, or psychosis. Sometimes patients may not be truthful due to fear or humiliation. Confirm histories as much as possible.

Table 20.1 summarizes the techniques of basic history gathering.

THE MENTAL STATUS EXAMINATION

General Comments

1. Let the patient's history guide the way you conduct your mental status examination. Again, if the patient is disoriented or psychotic, you should find a reliable historian to verify the patient's history, since obviously a patient who is disoriented or psychotic may not be capable of presenting a true or reliable sequence of events. It is always advisable to verify or validate important issues with other parties, for example, family members, concerned friends, police, EMS, therapists, or clinics. The mental status examination is like a doctor's physical examination. After a physician takes an extensive history, he uses his professional instruments (stethoscope, reflex hammer, blood pressure cuff) to define the specific illness with which a patient presents. Similarly, the mental status examination allows the crisis clinician to better define a patient's presenting psychiatric disorder.

Table 20.1
Techniques of Basic History Gathering

1. Always form a treatment alliance with the patient.

2. Once an alliance is formed, focus on the *main* problem troubling the patient.

3. Get the history of the current problem.

4. Get the patient's past medical and psychiatric history.

5. Find out the time course of the patient's symptoms.

6. Find out what medications the patient is taking and if any medication changes have recently occurred.

7. Ask about allergies to medications.

8. Ask female patients about the possibility of pregnancy.

9. Ask about the patient's current living situation and social supports.

10. Get a family history of medical and psychiatric illness and suicide.

11. Inquire about neurovegetative signs of depression or diurnal changes in mood.

12. Ask about alcohol and/or drug use.

13. Ask about headaches and seizures.

14. Confirm history as much as possible.

2. *Always* determine if a patient is having hallucinations, suicidal or homicidal ideas, or any cognitive changes. Document the presence or absence of these findings. If these findings are present, they must be investigated, and full documentation must support the clinical outcome. Be specific. For example, if the patient's record contains the statement "The patient is having suicidal (or homicidal) ideation," then follow-up notes such as "with no plan, means, or intent" must be documented if the patient is going to be treated as an outpatient. Always describe the patient's behaviors; do not write about them in global terms or jargon. It is more helpful to docu-

ment, "Patient was seeing green lizards coming through the floor and was trying to step on them, even though nothing was there," than to use the global statement, "Patient was hallucinating."

3. *Always* rule out medical causes of apparent psychotic syndromes. Psychosis is a symptom/sign which, like fever, can be caused by a multitude of etiologies. This will be discussed more in the section on delirium, but is an important point since delirium is a serious medical emergency which, if left untreated, often results in severe illness and, at times, death. Suspect a diagnosis of delirium if the patient is transiently disoriented, has visual hallucinations, has a "waxing and waning sensorium," or has diminished attentiveness or acute cognitive dysfunction. Delirious states come on abruptly, over several hours to days. A full laboratory evaluation should be performed on every patient with these signs.

Parts of the Mental Status Examination

Table 20.2 lists the specific parts of the mental status exam. Following are detailed descriptions.

Table 20.2
Parts of the Mental Status Examination

Appearance

Speech

Mood and affect

Thought content: What does the patient think about?

Thought process: What is the form of thought?

Perception: hallucinations

Suicidality/Homicidality

Insight and judgment

Cognitive function: orientation, memory, attention, concentration, calculation, drawing

Sensorium: level of arousal and consciousness

APPEARANCE

Comment on the patient's appearance with specifics. Is the patient showing signs of distress? Is the patient neatly dressed and groomed, slovenly or disheveled, with long or short or no hair, with unusual clothes, shirts, shoes, or tattoos?

· Manic patients may come in with wild or colorful clothing, or may be dressed like a historical figure.
· Patients with brain damage or dementia may have their clothes on backwards.
· Patients who are homeless often are disheveled. However, if they are temporarily residing in a shelter, they may have new clothes, since most shelters receive clothing donations from the public.
· Patients with schizophrenia or dementia may also appear disheveled.

SPEECH

Describe any abnormalities in the patient's speech.

· Mania produces rapid speech, at times almost impossible to keep up with. Manic patients will often need to be gently interrupted or redirected due to the pressure of their speech. Depressed people will often have soft, quiet speech and will often wait for a significant period of time before answering a question (this is often called prolonged speech latency).
· Patients with any injury to the speech centers (most often located on the left half of the brain, even in left-handed patients) can have an array of speech problems. Many of these patients have damage caused by a stroke (CVA) or closed head injury (e.g., from a motor vehicle accident). Some cannot articulate speech, but can comprehend it (Broca's aphasia). Others may speak gibberish or nonsense-sounding words, but the words, although incomprehensible, do flow (Wernicke's aphasia). Patients who may have damaged connections between speech centers may not be able to name items (anomic aphasia). Patients with neurologic disorders may have quick, scanning speech or difficulty articulating words (dysarthric speech).
· Drugs, alcohol, medications, or neurologic disorders can cause slurred speech.

MOOD AND AFFECT

Mood is what the patient describes. Often, clinicians may ask a patient to rate his or her mood on a scale from 1 to 10, 1 being most depressed, 10 representing the best mood possible. Moods can be happy, sad, depressed, angry, etc.

Affect is what the clinician observes.

- A patient who is severely depressed will have a limited range of emotional expression, so this might be described as a *blunted* mood.
- A patient with schizophrenia often exhibits a *flat* mood, where there is little to no emotional expression.
- A schizophrenic may also show *inappropriate* affect (e.g., the patient may smile when discussing her son's death).
- A patient with acute mania often portrays a *labile* or bouncy, erratic affect.
- A patient with a frontal lobe injury can also have a flat or labile affect.

THOUGHT CONTENT

Describe the predominance of ideas in the patient. What does the patient mostly think about? Is the content normal, or filled with fantastic or psychotic ideas? Does the patient dwell on beings from another planet who are out to take over his mind? Is the patient a disciple of God, here to save the world?

All the following abnormalities of thought content may be seen in psychotic disorders:

- A patient who thinks events are about him is experiencing *ideas of reference*. For example, a patient who lives in Durham, North Carolina has seen national newscast reports that a crime has been committed in California and believes he may have committed the crime, even though this is impossible.
- False beliefs that have no basis in reality are called *delusions*. For instance, a patient may believe that she has parasites in her body because her stomach is upset, and she is convinced her mother has put these parasites in her food. A fairly common delusion is that the patient can read the minds of others or that other people can read her mind.
- A patient who believes that others may place ideas inside his mind is experiencing *thought insertion*.

- Conversely, a patient who believes others have the ability to take thoughts out of her head is experiencing *thought withdrawal*.

THOUGHT PROCESS

Describe the patient's form of thought.

- If the patient goes slowly from one topic to another, then another, and much later returns to the original question and answers it, he is exhibiting *circumstantiality*. This can be normal or perhaps associated with anxiety.
- If the patient does not answer a question and slowly continues to talk, never returning to the subject, he is exhibiting *tangentiality of thinking*. This can be seen in mania or psychosis or dementia.
- *Prolonged speech latency* describes a prolonged delay in response to a question. This is common in profound states of depression.
- A patient's inability to answer a question due to his or her disorganization of thought is called *thought blocking*. This is seen in states of psychosis.
- A patient who rapidly shifts from one idea to another with some thin connection between ideas is exhibiting *flight of ideas*. For example, "I came here from South Carolina, nothing could be finer, yeah I'm fine how about you, you—you know nothing, I know all, All is a great detergent, I have dishpan hands, you have nice hands, do you sculpt, like Rodin or Renoir or Gauguin, Van Gogh lived with him 'til he cut off his ear, are you having trouble hearing me?" Flight of ideas is often seen in all types of manic states, including those induced by medical disorders or substances such as amphetamines or cocaine.
- When a patient skips from one thought to another, with no apparent logical connection between them, he is exhibiting *looseness of association*. For example, patients may say the following in response to a question: "I live in an apartment, do you like cheese, my fingernail hurts, will the sky fall tomorrow, in Russia they drink vodka, martians suck ties and confiscate ice cream sundaes."

PERCEPTION

Is the patient experiencing hallucinations? If so, what type?

- Audible voices heard inside or outside the head are called *auditory hallucinations*. Do not confuse this with a patient's acute awareness of her own thoughts. Ask the patient if she hears the voices out loud. When does she hear the voice? Voices heard only when the patient is falling asleep or waking up from sleep (i.e., hypnogogic or hypnopompic hallucinations) may be a nonspecific sign of stress and may not be indicative of a psychotic disorder. Auditory hallucinations can occur in any psychotic thought or mood disorder, or may result from a medical condition or substance abuse problem.

- *Visual hallucinations,* things a patient sees that are not there, are an important sign. If you observe a patient with florid visual hallucinations, and the patient is vigorously interacting with those hallucinations (e.g., talking to them, grabbing at them, fighting with them, etc.) then he may be delirious or suffering from the transient effects of a hallucinogen. Unlike delirious patients, those who are visually hallucinating from drugs will often not be disoriented and will generally not have fluctuating levels of consciousness. Sometimes patients with psychotic disorders (e.g., schizophrenia or psychotic depression) may see things, but they report these phenomena in the history and rarely react with these visually hallucinated phenomena.
- If the patient believes that invisible bugs or other things are crawling on his skin, he is experiencing *tactile hallucinations.* The sensation of ants crawling on his skin, is called *formication* (ants often secrete formic acid, which causes the pain of their bite). Tactile hallucinations are often found in states of delirium (e.g., DTs), or may be secondary to cocaine abuse ("cocaine bugs") or alcohol withdrawal delirium.
- Patients may often smell odors that are not really present, such as gasoline, or foul-smelling substances. These *olfactory hallucinations* are often found in patients with complex partial seizure disorders (temporal lobe epilepsy), since temporal lobe seizures cause excitation of the primitive brain centers where smell is integrated. Certain psychotic disorders may also produce olfactory hallucinations.

SUICIDALITY/HOMICIDALITY

Patients must always be asked if they are having suicidal or homicidal ideation. If the patient has neither, *document the absence* of these thoughts. If ideation is present, find out if the patient has any plan, means, or intent to carry out such ideas. This must be discussed in detail with the patient and in the consultation write-up. Clinicians should have a significant degree of worry when a patient says that suicide is running through his mind. However, if the patient has no plan, means, or desire to carry out such wishes, is able and willing to call if a loss of control seems imminent, and has a strong support system, often these patients can be treated as outpatients with appropriate rigorous and intense care.

INSIGHT AND JUDGMENT

Does the patient understand what is going on? Does the patient know why she is so upset? Ask some formal questions to gauge the patient's level of judgment. "What would you do if you found a stamped, addressed envelope lying on the street?"

Also assess the patient's actions prior to presentation. For instance, a patient who says, "I was hearing voices telling me to throw a rock through my neighbor's window, but I didn't want to, so I came to the ER for help," shows good judgment in comparison to a patient brought in by the police for throwing a rock through a neighbor's window in response to auditory hallucinations.

COGNITIVE FUNCTION

- *Orientation.* Ask the patient the month, date, year, and place.
- *Immediate memory.* Ask the patient to repeat numbers forward and backward. Most patients can repeat five to seven numbers forward, but this may not be true in states of anxiety or in disorders that can cause cognitive decline, such as delirium or dementia.
- *Short-term memory.* Name any three objects, such as "apple, bakery, car," and ask the patient to remember them; five minutes later, ask him to name them for you. In amnestic disorders, the patient may lose his short-term memory; if you leave the room for ten minutes, he may not recall having seen you.
- *Long-term memory.* Ask the patient to name the current president and the ones who preceded the current one. What is the patient's birthday? Use other questions to check memory function. Verify any answers. Do not ask a questions such as "What did you have for dinner last night?" unless it can be verified.
- *Attention.* This is the capacity to focus continuously on external stimuli. Your gross assessment of this variable will be based on the patient's ability to respond to your interview questions. The attention capacity is classically markedly abnormal in delirium.
- *Concentration.* Concentration is the capacity to focus continuously in one's thinking. Ask the patient to subtract 7 from 100 "in her

head" (i.e., not on paper), stating the remainders until she gets to zero (100, 93, 86, 79, etc.). If the patient is unable to perform the task, ask her to try subtracting 3 from 30 in the same way. Impaired concentration is sometimes associated with severe depression.

- *Drawing.* Ask the patient to draw a clock or simple house. Patients with dementias, strokes, or tumors will often have difficulty with this task. For example, a drawing of a wonderful clock but with all the numbers squashed into one side of the clock's face could indicate a nondominant hemisphere lesion in the brain (e.g., a stroke in the right parietal lobe). These constructional apraxias are common in a number of organic illnesses of the brain.

In dementias, you may find deficits or abnormalities in any or in all of the above cognitive functions. Some brief formal tests for dementia may be used in the ER to differentiate severe impairment from mild-to-moderate impairment.

SENSORIUM

Is the person's level of arousal and consciousness intact? Or is the sensorium abnormally depressed (e.g., a stuporous patient), or markedly elevated (e.g., an agitated, screaming, fighting patient)? Dramatic, unpredictable changes in sensorium are often found in states of delirium.

LABORATORY TESTING

In the ER setting, a patient's vital signs, such as pulse rate, blood pressure, and temperature, should *always* be taken; these simple clinical measures are neither costly nor time-consuming and can provide many diagnostic clues. For instance, if a patient is delirious and has an elevated temperature, consider infection or withdrawal states or other complicated medical syndromes such as meningitis. If the patient is on neuroleptic medications, and is extremely stiff and rigid, severely confused, and has an extremely high fever, consider the possibility of neuroleptic malignant syndrome as well as other serious acute illnesses. Elevated blood pressure and pulse in a patient who abuses alcohol may indicate withdrawal; the same signs in a patient who abuses cocaine may indicate recent cocaine use.

Laboratory tests should never be ordered routinely, but must be custom-designed to the patient's presentation. Some patients will require no laboratory tests; others will require a large number of diagnostic test evaluations. Specific laboratory testing should be ordered if the patient's history or physical examination suggests a particular acute medical problem, or if it is important to detect alcohol or drugs in the patient's system. Laboratory tests should be obtained only if the results will change the emergency treatment and disposition of that patient. The following guidelines should be used in ascertaining whether further laboratory studies are indicated in patients with psychiatric emergencies.

· Patients who are suffering from a delirium—that is, decreased attentiveness, disorientation, visual hallucinations, or altered sensorium (any one of these may be a cardinal symptom or sign of delirium)—should have a thorough physical examination and a complete laboratory evaluation. This would include:

1. *electrolytes* (i.e., sodium [Na], potassium [K], and chloride [Cl]), which are all critical for proper working of the neuromuscular system, and bicarbonate [HCO_3], which gives an indirect measure of the acidity of the blood—low if too acidic, high if too alkaline)
2. *glucose,* or blood sugar
3. *creatinine and blood urea nitrogen (BUN)*, which measure kidney function and the amount of nitrogen waste products in the blood
4. *calcium,* which is important in almost every metabolic process—it can cause confusion if it is too high
5. *Complete blood counts (CBC)*; a low red blood cell count may indicate anemia or internal bleeding or red blood cell destruction, and an elevated white blood cell (WBC) count can indicate an infection. A WBC *differential count* tells the types of WBCs seen in the peripheral circulating blood, and there is often a "left shift" with infection, that is, immature forms of WBCs are released to fight off infection.

Patients who appear to be delirious should also have their alcohol levels checked (often this will show no alcohol if the patient is in alcohol-withdrawal delirium), and a urine drug screen should be done. A urinalysis should also be performed to rule out urinary tract infection (UTI). UTI is a frequent cause of delirium, particularly in the elderly. Again, delirium is caused by a potentially catastrophic event that could be an acute medical or neurological illness, a condition requiring surgery, or a reaction to any medication or intoxicants or withdrawal from those substances. Delirious patients should *always* be admitted to an appropriate medical service.

- Any patient who presents with psychiatric symptoms and a history of progressive headaches should have a careful neurological evaluation and a complete fundoscopic examination (in which a doctor shines a bright light into the eyes to rule out papilledema, which could indicate increased pressure inside the brain). Frontal lobe brain tumors or chronic subdural hematomas (i.e., blood clots beneath the lining of the brain) may produce severe depressive disorders in patients, but can otherwise show no positive findings on neurological examination. Consideration should be given to complicated CT or MRI scans in only a select group of patients.

- Patients with a history of psychosis and polydipsia (i.e., drinking large amounts of fluids every day), who present with a sudden worsening of psychosis should be evaluated to rule out hyponatremia (a dilution of the sodium in their body). Normal levels of sodium are critical for the proper function of nerve cells in the brain. Some of these patients may drink 10 to 20 liters of fluid a day. Clues to this would include a history of polydipsia and a low specific gravity on urine testing (a measure of how dilute the urine is). Polydipsic patients often have specific gravities below 1.010 (which is extremely low) and a low serum sodium due to too much water in the body's circulation and tissues. A sodium level below 120 may be dangerous, especially if it has dropped quickly. These patients should be treated with fluid or water restriction and other modalities to prevent further psychosis, seizures, coma, and resultant death. In critical states of life-threatening hyponatremia (i.e., low sodium levels) admission to an intensive care unit is warranted.

- Urine drug testing to rule out the use of illicit drugs (e.g., marijuana, cocaine, LSD, PCP) need not be performed on every patient seen by a crisis service. For example, a patient may present to an ER and say that he is using cocaine and heroin, and therefore it would not be necessary to test for these substances if he presents with a valid history. On the other hand, patients with unexplained psychosis or delirium should receive urine drug screens to rule out the influence of intoxicating substances. The following guidelines should be considered in deciding whether to obtain a urine toxicology screen in the emergency room.

1. A urine drug screen in the emergency room should be done *only* if the results of that screen would change the emergency evaluation, treatment, or disposition of that patient's clinical problem.

2. If a patient is brought in on emergency evaluation papers and allegations have been made that the patient has been using substances and the patient denies it, then obtaining a urine drug screen could possibly validate a patient's negative history. On the other hand, a positive drug screen may allow you to break through such a patient's denial if indeed he or she is actively using chemical substances. Cocaine, via its metabolite, benzoyle-cgonine, can be detected for up to three days past use; heavy marijuana users have traces of cannabinoids in their urine for up to thirty days.

3. If the patient presents with a normal mental status except for, say, the possibility of depression or anxiety, and the patient's history of using drugs is negative, you might assume that obtaining the urine toxicology screen in the emergency situation may not be necessary. However, a significant number of patients seen in the ER with the chief complaint of severe depression or anxiety are simply feeling nervous or depressed from secretly using cocaine. Usually only half of the people who present in this fashion will be truthful about their drug use. Therefore, if you are suspicious about the surreptitious use of drugs, obtaining a urine drug screen may be indicated.

4. If the decision has already been made to hospitalize a patient, urine drug screening may be done on the inpatient unit after admission rather than in the emergency room or outpatient laboratory, where time may be more of the essence.

· Blood alcohol levels are often useful; approximately half of all psychiatric emergency patients seen today abuse alcohol and/or drugs. Psychiatric examinations may often not be valid if a patient's alcohol (ethyl alcohol, ETOH) level is >0.100–0.150 (depending on the patient's history of use). A patient's alcohol level may decrease by 0.030 units per hour in heavy users, and 0.012 units per hour in occasional drinkers. So, in heavy users of alcohol, a good rule of thumb is that they will drop a total of 0.100 points in three hours (e.g., it will take three hours for a patient to go from an alcohol level of 0.300 to 0.200, and another three hours to go from 0.200 to 0.100). Remember that extremely heavy users of ethanol may be in full-blown withdrawal states, even with high alcohol levels. Some heavy users of alcohol will be completely coherent at high levels of alcohol in their blood, which implies a high tolerance of alcohol and a large degree of physiologic alcohol dependence.

· If patients are intoxicated and having suicidal ideation, you may, at times need to wait until their ETOH levels are ≤0.100 before performing your complete psychiatric evaluation. In most patients, suicidal ideation will abate as the alcohol level comes down below 0.100. Those patients who have ongoing suicidal ideation after reaching a fair degree of sobriety will probably need inpatient treatment.

· A word of advice to crisis clinicians: You will see a large number of alcohol dependent patients. Watch out for delirium from ETOH withdrawal. Also, always ask ER staff to give alcoholic patients an intramuscular shot (i.m. injection) of vitamin B_1 (thiamine) due to the relative depletion of vitamin B_1 that most alcoholics experience. Vitamin B_1 is a water soluble vitamin, and is rapidly depleted in people who have poor nutrition. A fifth of liquor will almost have all the calories needed to fulfill a patient's daily caloric intake requirements. Therefore, a number of alcoholics will be severely deficient in vitamin B_1 (and other vitamins, too). Such deficiencies can lead to serious damage to the nervous system (e.g., Wernicke's encephalopathy may develop in thiamine-depleted patients; see chapter 21).

· Following are some ideas about laboratory work-ups in patients who have taken drug overdoses:

1. *Tylenol (acetaminophen) overdoses.* Acetaminophen is found in numerous medications sold over the counter. It is therefore important to check on the ingredients of any medication a patient has taken in an overdose attempt. If the patient has taken an overdose containing acetaminophen, it is *essential* to obtain an acetaminophen blood level at least 4 hours after the overdose. If the level at 4 hours is less than 140, this usually means that the overdose is not in the toxic range. Levels of 140 or higher will require treatment with N-acetylcysteine to prevent liver damage and possible death. Usually after a significant acetaminophen overdose, a patient will feel fine. However, if the patient has taken a toxic overdose and has not received treatment, liver damage may

occur 24–72 hours *after* drug ingestion. A potentially toxic dose is approximately 140 mg/kg of body weight, or approximately 20 extra-strength Tylenol tablets in a 150-pound person. Therefore, a relatively small overdose of pills can result in a lethal outcome.

2. *Aspirin (acetylsalicylic acid) overdose.* For the most part, with emergency treatment, small aspirin overdoses are not lethal. A patient's salicylate levels should be checked and electrolytes should be drawn. If the patient's salicylate level is nontoxic and his or her HCO_3 (bicarbonate) level is normal (signifying that the patient is not experiencing toxic acid levels in the blood), then admission to a medical unit is usually not necessary. However, toxic salicylate levels, markedly diminished HCO_3, or other metabolic abnormalities should be taken extremely seriously.

3. *Tricyclic antidepressant (TCA) overdose.* If a TCA overdose is suspected, time is of the essence! The potential for lethality is extremely high with a toxic dose of tricyclic antidepressant, due to its deleterious effects on the heart. A crisis clinician should never make the mistake of making a mobile call to psychiatrically evaluate a patient who has taken a serious drug overdose. Have EMS (and police, if necessary) immediately take the patient to be evaluated by a physician in an emergency medical facility.

A final note. In general, laboratory tests are very costly, and should *never* be done routinely on every patient. Use the data from ordered lab tests very carefully, and do not ignore these results if they are found to be positive. For instance, if a patient appears delirious and his white blood cell count is high (e.g., 19,000), assume that the abnormal laboratory finding has something to do with the patient's psychiatric status. Do not make the mistake of ignoring such a finding.

SUGGESTED READINGS

Forster, P. (Ed). (1994). Emergency psychiatry [Special issue]. *Psychiatric Annals*, 24(11).

Henneman, P. L., Mendoza, R., & Lewis, R. J. (1994). Prospective evaluation of emergency medical clearance. *Annals of Emergency Medicine*, 24(4), 672–677.

Lieberman, P. B., & Baker, F. M. (1985). The reliability of psychiatric diagnosis in the emergency room. *Hospital and Community Psychiatry*, 36(3), 291–293.

Riba, M., & Hale, M. (1990). Medical clearance: Fact or fiction in the hospital emergency room. *Psychosomatics*, 31, 400–404.

Chapter 21

INTRODUCTION TO THE DSM-IV CLASSIFICATION SYSTEM

Diseased Nature oftentimes breaks forth in strange eruptions.
— *William Shakespeare (King Henry IV)*

THROUGHOUT THE HISTORY of medicine, there has been general agreement about the need for a classification of mental disorders. However, there has been little agreement on the optimal method for their organization. This is due in large measure to the absence of biological markers for individual disease categories.

In 1952, the American Psychiatric Association published a Diagnostic and Statistical Manual (DSM-I) of Mental Disorders, and a revision (DSM-II) soon followed. DSM-III was published in 1980, introducing more explicit diagnostic criteria, a multiaxial system, and a more descriptive approach that described the phenomenology of mental disorders but contained few psychological theories as to their cause. The DSM-IV was published in 1994 as an updated version. The DSM system of classification codes divides mental disorders into types based on criteria sets with defining features, with each category assigned a separate coding number. This naming of categories is the traditional method of organizing and transmitting information and has been the fundamental approach used in all systems of medical diagnosis.

The DSM multiaxial system involves an assessment on several dimensions (axes), each referring to a different domain of information:

- axis I: clinical disorders
- axis II: personality disorders and mental retardation
- axis III: general medical conditions
- axis IV: psychosocial and environmental problems (standardized scale)
- axis V: global assessment of functioning (standardized scale)

It is important to understand three things:

1. No category of mental disorder is a completely separate entity with absolute boundaries dividing it from other mental disorders or from no mental disorder.
2. Not all individuals described as having the same mental disorder are alike in all important ways.
3. A classification of mental disorders does not classify people — rather, it classifies disorders that people have. Therefore, crisis clinicians are discouraged from using terms such as "a 34-year-old schizophrenic male," and encouraged to use, instead, terms such as "a 34-year-old male with a previous diagnosis of schizophrenia."

The DSM system is meant to be used by individuals with appropriate clinical training and experience in diagnosis. In this chapter we will review this system. This review will be brief, and is meant to serve only as an introductory guide to the crisis clinician. We recommend referring to the DSM-IV and other psychiatric textbooks for a more complete listing of disorders and their criteria.

AXIS I: CLINICAL DISORDERS

Cognitive Disorders: Delirium, Dementia, and Amnestic Disorder

DELIRIUM

The crisis clinician must constantly be wary of patients who present with delirium. When the brain manifests a clinical picture of delirium, something serious, potentially catastrophic and lethal, is occurring within the body. Delirious patients should always be admitted to a medical unit from an ER. While medications (antipsychotics and benzodiazepines) can help control a patient's agitation and symptoms, the underlying cause must be uncovered and treated.

1. Symptoms
   * An acute change in mental status in which the hallmark symptom is a disturbance of consciousness (reduced clarity of awareness of the environment) with reduced ability to focus, sustain, or shift attention
   * Impairments in cognition (memory deficit, disorientation, language disturbance, or confusion)
   * A perceptual disturbance (florid visual or tactile or even auditory hallucinations, and behavioral interactions with the hallucinated material)
   * Abnormalities in mood regulation (patients may rapidly alternate among anger, rage, unwarranted fear, apathy, depression, or euphoria)
   * Unstable fluctuations in vital signs
   * Marked problems with attention (e.g., they won't be able to do serial subtractions by 7s from 100, or they may not be able to spell "world" backwards)

   Delirium has a sudden onset (hours or days) and a tendency to fluctuate during the course of the day (with episodes of increased agitation interspersed with periods of quiet confusional states).
2. Causes
   * Any serious medical, neurological, or surgical illnesses
   * Intoxication from medications (such as lithium) or toxic agents (such as alcohol, cocaine, PCP)
   * Withdrawal (often seen with alcoholics or patients who abuse benzodiazepines or other sedatives, especially barbiturates)
   * Multiple etiologies, for example, a patient who is taking cimetidine (Tagamet) intravenously (which can cause hallucinations and delirium in some patients), and who is also in alcohol withdrawal delirium
3. Risk factors
   * Advanced age is a major risk factor for development of delirium.
   * Very young age, preexisting brain damage, history of delirium, alcohol dependence, diabetes, cancer, sensory impairment, and malnutrition are other risk factors.

DEMENTIA

1. Distinguish dementia from delirium.
   - In contrast to the sudden onset of delirium, the onset of dementia is usually insidious (except for some types of vascular dementia where there may be a sudden worsening of cognitive deficits).
   - A patient with dementia is usually alert; a patient with delirium may have episodes of decreased consciousness.
   - Cognitive impairment in dementia is usually more stable over time and does not often fluctuate rapidly.

2. Symptoms
   - Memory impairment
   - Lack of orientation (e.g., patient may get lost)
   - Language impairment (aphasia)
   - Personality changes
   - Impaired ability to carry out motor activities (apraxia)
   - Failure to recognize or identify objects (agnosia)
   - Psychosis
   - Depression
   - Anxiety
   - Agitation

   Dementia may be progressive or static, permanent or reversible. It is essentially a disease of the aged, although it may present in younger patients. Patients with Down's syndrome often develop an Alzheimer's-like dementia in their 40s. Seventy-five percent of all cases of dementia are Alzheimer's type or vascular dementia. Alzheimer's disease affects the entire brain. Vascular dementia is caused by cerebral vascular disease and, particularly, severe, uncontrolled high blood pressure.

3. Causes
   - A significant number of patients with AIDS develop a dementing illness. HIV patients who show signs of dementia should always receive a thorough physical and neurological examination, including an EEG, CAT scan, or MRI, and a lumbar puncture (spinal tap) to exclude other infectious illnesses (e.g., toxoplasmosis of the brain, an opportunistic infection which usually affects only patients who are severely immunocompromised).
   - Head trauma may lead to a dementia.
   - Parkinson's disease can cause profound dementia.

- Severe depression commonly leads to a state so severe that it appears the patient is demented—this is the syndrome called "pseudodementia," which is treated with antidepressants and will resolve as the depression improves. Patients with pseudodementia often reply "I don't know" to questions or avoid them completely due to their anxiety, as opposed to patients with true dementia who cannot perform, but often attempt cognitive tests.
- Huntington's disease is a hereditary illness that often affects one's personality and cognition. Patients also develop a severe choreiform (jerky) tremor.
- Pick's disease primarily affects the frontal and temporal lobes.
- Creutzfeldt-Jakob disease causes a rapid onset of dementia. This uncommon illness is probably caused by prions, proteinaceous particles that can be spread by exposure to infected organs of the nervous system. One sees myoclonus (sudden jumping of the muscles) and a characteristic EEG (triphasic waves).
- Substance-induced persisting dementia is most commonly secondary to alcohol, but sometimes secondary to huffing gasoline or other inhalants or to heavy PCP use.

A significant number of patients who present with dementia have a reversible underlying cause that can be detected with a comprehensive laboratory work-up, including CBC, electrolytes, thyroid function tests, vitamin B_{12} levels, urine analysis, CT scan, EEG, lumbar puncture for spinal fluid analysis (to rule out an infection of the nervous system), urine test for heavy metal toxicity, and ventral disease research laboratories (VDRL) to exclude syphilis infection. A patient's history must always be confirmed by a reliable historian. Crisis clinicians should also remember that demented patients can also develop delirium states, which can cause a dramatic worsening of dementia signs and symptoms.

AMNESTIC DISORDERS

1. Distinguish amnestic disorders from dementia.
   - Unlike patients with dementia, the amnestic patient only has a deficit in memory, not in overall cognitive ability and functioning.
2. Causes
   - Medical conditions or substance use; amnesia is most commonly found in alcohol use disorders and head injury.
   - Cerebrovascular diseases (strokes).
   - Multiple sclerosis.

- Korsakoff's syndrome, which is caused by thiamine deficiency, most commonly associated with the poor nutritional habits of persons with chronic alcohol abuse. In this tragic syndrome, patients have deficient short-term memories but intact long-term memories. They don't have a future or recent past.
- Alcoholic blackouts, which are temporary losses of memory associated with high levels of alcohol. (*Note:* Some patients can be very aggressive, disinhibited, or suicidal during an alcoholic blackout.)

Mental Disorders Due to a General Medical Condition

Any number of medical conditions can induce a change in overall mental well-being, including:

- Degenerative disorders, such as Parkinson's disease
- Epilepsy
- Brain tumor
- Head trauma
- Demyelinating disorders, such as multiple sclerosis
- Infectious diseases, such as certain types of encephalitis
- Immune disorders, such as SLE (lupus)
- Endocrine disorders, such as thyroid problems
- Metabolic disorders, such as hypercalcemia from a lung tumor
- Nutritional disorders, such as deficiencies of niacin, thiamine (vitamin B_1), and cobalamin (vitamin B_{12})
- Poisoning from certain toxins, such as mercury

A general medical condition can also cause a personality change where the individual shows a persistent personality disturbance that is a change from his or her previous characteristic personality pattern. For example, a mild-mannered individual becomes periodically explosive starting one year following a severe head injury.

Substance-Related Disorders

ALCOHOL-RELATED DISORDERS

Alcohol abuse and dependence are by far the most common substance-related disorders.

1. *Alcohol abuse* is defined by 1 or more of the following symptoms occurring within 1 year:
   - Recurrent use that results in a failure to fulfill major role obligations at work, school, or home (e.g., absences, poor performance, neglect of children)
   - Recurrent use in situations where it is physically hazardous (e.g., driving a car or operating machinery)
   - Recurrent alcohol-related legal problems (e.g., arrests)
   - Continued use despite social or interpersonal problems caused or exacerbated by effects of the substance (e.g., arguments with spouse, physical fights)
2. *Alcohol dependence* is defined by 3 or more of the following symptoms occurring within 1 year:
   - A need for increasing amounts of alcohol to achieve intoxication or diminished effect with continued use of the same amount
   - Withdrawal symptoms
   - Frequent consumption of alcohol in larger amounts or over a longer period than was intended
   - A desire or unsuccessful efforts to cut down or control alcohol use
   - Much time spent in activities necessary to obtain alcohol, use it, or recover from its effects
   - Important social, occupational, or recreational activities given up or reduced because of alcohol use
   - Continued substance use despite the knowledge of having a persistent or recurrent physical or psychological problem likely to have been caused or made worse by alcohol

   In crisis, alcohol-dependent patients may present with serious signs of withdrawal. Appropriate medical treatment or detoxification is indicated. All patients with alcohol dependence should receive thiamine in the crisis situation due to their frequent deficiencies in this vitamin.
3. *Alcohol intoxication* can lead to coma, respiratory depression, and death. The severity of symptoms correlates roughly with the blood concentration of alcohol, which reflects the alcohol concentration in the brain.
4. *Alcohol intoxication delirium* and *alcohol-induced psychotic disorder* are seen with extremely high levels of alcohol. They resolve with detoxification and sobriety.

5. *Alcohol-induced persisting dementia* most often occurs in chronically dependent and addicted heavy drinkers.

6. *Alcohol-induced persisting amnestic disorder* is a disturbance in
short-term memory caused by the prolonged heavy use of alcohol.
   - Wernicke's syndrome is the acute and reversible form. It is present when an alcoholic patient presents with the triad of ataxia
   (stumbling gait), ophthalmoplegia (paralysis of some of the eye
   muscles), and confusion. Injections of thiamine are often cura-
   tive of Wernicke's syndrome and can prevent the onset of alcohol-induced persisting amnestic disorder.
   - Korsakoff's syndrome is the chronic form. Both forms are
   caused by thiamine deficiency.

7. *Alcohol-induced mood disorder.* People who drink heavily can develop profound depression, others develop depression first, and
then secondarily begin to drink alcohol to get relief. The former
describes the alcohol-induced mood disorder. Substance abuse
treatment and detoxification are probably indicated. Most of these
patients will no longer be depressed once they've achieved significant sobriety. However, those with primary depression (the latter
category) will often need antidepressant treatment as well as substance abuse counseling.

8. *Alcohol-induced anxiety disorder* is rarely seen with alcohol per se,
but is more common with other substances that are abused, such
as amphetamines and other stimulants, cocaine, and cannabis.

9. *Alcohol-induced sexual dysfunction,* usually impotence, is often
caused by heavy alcohol use.

10. *Alcohol-induced sleep disorder* is possible, as alcohol interferes with
the sleep cycle, leading to chronic fatigue and insomnia.

11. *Alcohol withdrawal.* Symptoms include:
    - Tremulousness (shakes or jitters).
    - Hallucinations, seizures, and delirium tremens (DTs) can occur
    in untreated withdrawal.

12. *Alcohol withdrawal delirium* occurs within one week after the person stops or reduces alcohol intake. The most severe form of the
withdrawal delirium syndrome is known as DTs. Symptoms include:
    - The feeling of bugs (tactile hallucinations) or ants (formication)
    crawling over the the skin
    - Confusion

- Extremely frightening visual hallucinations
- Violence
- Agitation
- Extremely high pulse rates
- Fever
- Dangerously elevated blood pressure

This is a medical emergency that can result in death. Treatment includes medical hospitalization, benzodiazepines, antipsychotics, nutritional support, intravenous fluids, and a secure environment.

COCAINE-RELATED DISORDERS

Cocaine is one of the most addictive, commonly abused, and dangerous substances. It has been associated with sudden death and seizures. Patients sometimes mix it with heroin and "shoot it up" in the form of "speedballs." This is an extremely addicting form of drug habit and can be particularly risky to the addict (e.g., the late John Belushi died from speedballs).

Crack is an extremely potent, freebase form of cocaine, highly addictive, and anecdotally associated with extremes of violent behavior. Its use is endemic in certain parts of every American community.

Mixing alcohol and cocaine may produce a compound in the body that may be especially dangerous, since the liver metabolizes cocaine plus alcohol to form cocaethylene, which lasts much longer in the body and may explain the dangerous cardiac effects of cocaine. Users of cocaine in combination with alcohol may have a risk of sudden death 21.5 times higher than those who use only cocaine.

1. *Cocaine dependence* manifests the same diagnostic criteria as alcohol dependence (see above).
2. *Cocaine abuse* manifests the same issues as alcohol abuse (see above).
3. *Cocaine intoxication* occurs with recent use of cocaine. Behavioral signs are:
   - Agitation
   - Irritability
   - Impaired judgment
   - Impulsive sexual behavior
   - Aggression
   - Increased psychomotor activity
   - Mania

Physical symptoms are:
- Tachycardia (rapid heartbeat)
- Hypertension (high blood pressure)
- Mydriasis (dilated pupils)

4. *Cocaine intoxication delirium* is most common with high doses of cocaine; when the cocaine has been used over a short period, resulting in a rapid increase in blood concentration; or when cocaine is mixed with other psychoactive substances. Previous episodes of cocaine intoxication increase the risk for cocaine intoxication delirium.

5. *Cocaine-induced psychotic disorder* presents with paranoid delusions and varies with dose, duration of use, gender (more common in males), and individual sensitivity. It is most common with IV users and crack users. Its presentation can be quite dramatic but the disorder usually responds well to neuroleptic (antipsychotic) medications.

6. *Cocaine-induced mood disorder* displays hypomanic/manic symptoms, with depressive symptoms associated with withdrawal.

7. *Cocaine-induced anxiety disorder* shows brief obsessive-compulsive symptoms, panic symptoms, and phobias.

8. *Cocaine-induced sexual dysfunction,* usually impotence, results from repeated use.

9. *Cocaine-induced sleep disorder* can be caused by intoxication (insomnia) or withdrawal (disrupted sleep or excessively long sleep [hypersomnolence]).

10. *Cocaine withdrawal* reveals:
- Postintoxication depression (crash) with dysphoric mood and fatigue
- Vivid bad dreams
- Sleeplessness or heavy sleep
- Increased appetite
- Psychomotor retardation or agitation

In a patient who has been using cocaine heavily, withdrawal symptoms may last up to a week and can be associated with suicidal ideation.

Many patients who abuse cocaine will not admit to its use because of shame, fear of the law, or denial. Differentiating clinically between substance use and other disorders is often difficult. For example, a patient's history for cocaine use is often similar to that of someone with a bipolar disorder. Highs from cocaine feel "incredible" or "orgasmic"; patients spend inordinate sums of money to buy the drug; it makes them paranoid or delusional, or causes them to hallucinate when high or when coming down; and they feel depressed, despondent, tearful, and sometimes suicidal when they are "crashing" down from the cocaine's high. Such a history can lead to a mistaken diagnose of bipolar disorder. Always look for surreptitious drug use, and rule it out as the cause of other presenting symptoms. Crack cocaine use is also a common cause of a symptom picture that closely resembles major depression. However, in major depression, antidepressant therapy and psychotherapy are the indicated treatments. On the other hand, with cocaine-induced mood disorders, being drug free and receiving substance abuse counseling and NA (Narcotics Anonymous) involvement are probably the main treatments of choice.

OTHER SUBSTANCE-RELATED DISORDERS*

In addition to cocaine, there are numerous other drugs that may be abused. You should be familiar with these compounds and their clinical effects:

1. *Amphetamines* (speed, uppers) can cause:
   • Weight loss
   • Transient paranoid psychotic states
   Treat with short-term antipsychotics if necessary and refer the patient to substance abuse treatment.
2. *Caffeine* can:
   • Cause anxiety symptoms
   • Worsen panic disorder
   Withdrawal can cause severe headaches.
3. *Cannabis* (THC, reefer, grass, joints). Chronic use can lead to:
   • Malaise
   • Indifference
   • Lassitude
   • Depression

---

* Note: All other substance-related disorders have the same criteria for abuse, dependence, and substance-induced disorders as do alcohol- or cocaine-related disorders as defined in the above sections.

Cannabinoids (cannabis and its byproducts) can also induce anxiety and panic. Watch out for "wet willies" (marijuana dipped in PCP!); any form of PCP can cause extreme agitation and violence in a patient.

4. *Hallucinogens* (LSD, peyote). LSD causes:
   - Acute, vivid visual hallucinations
   - Synesthesias (a mixing of sensory phenomena, such as hearing colors, smelling sounds)
   - Occasionally, chronic, long-lasting flashback hallucinations. Rarely, these can be worsened by use of drugs such as fluoxetine (Prozac) or others.

   Bad trips, where patients become frightened or paranoid from LSD, can usually be handled by having the patient relax in a quiet room with dim lights and occasional use of lorazepam or haloperidol if needed. Unfortunately, LSD use among teenagers appears to be on the rise.

5. *Inhalants* (glue, gas, typewriter correction fluid, paints). Young people may enjoy the highs from acute intoxication from inhalants. Patients who present in emergency situations often have residual inhalant upon their body or clothing and therefore smell of the volatile substance. Intoxication causes:
   - Confusion
   - Agitation
   - Aggression
   - Irritability

   Freon gas and other inhalants can cause respiratory arrest and death.

   Chronic use of inhalants can lead to:
   - Depressive states
   - Suicidality
   - Inhalant-induced persisting dementia

   Patients need substance abuse treatment and, depending upon the severity of their habit, hospitalization.

6. *Opiates.* Heroin addiction is probably the most severe form of opiate addiction that the crisis clinician encounters. Heroin addiction is still common in a number of urban areas. As previously mentioned, speedballs (intravenous cocaine plus heroin) are sometimes used by addicts, since the heroin diminishes the anxiety and dysphoria that people feel as the cocaine levels decrease. Most opiate-related emergencies will present in *overdose* states; symptoms include:

- Small "pinpoint" pupils
- Respiratory depression or arrest
- Sometimes, coma

Symptoms of *withdrawal* include:

- Demands for more opiates
- Runny nose
- Watery eyes
- Sniffs, sneezes
- Cramps or diarrhea
- Goose pimples (piloerection)
- Enlarged pupils

Opiate *overdose* can be treated with intravenous naloxone (Narcan), an opiate antagonist that quickly reverses the effect of opiates. Opiate *withdrawal* can be treated with clonidine (Catapres), which diminishes the outflow of norepinephrine from the nervous system. A patient's blood pressure should be monitored during clonidine treatment. A typical starting dose might be 0.1 mg t.i.d. The drug may be slowly withdrawn over a period of several days to weeks.

Patients who live with chronic pain may be at some risk of opiate addiction because they require increasing amounts of medication to live with the chronic pain. These patients should be referred to pain management centers for a holistic approach to their severe problems.

7. *Phencyclidine* (PCP, angel dust, dusted, wet willy [a marijuana "joint" soaked in PCP]). PCP is easily cooked up in bathtubs and for this reason can be sold cheaply. It probably acts in the brain through what are called excitatory NMDA receptors, and can cause severe violence and agitation. Symptoms include:

- Violence
- Inability to feel pain
- Horizontal and vertical nystagmus (the eyes "jump" from side to side and up or down when the patient is asked to follow an examiner's finger)
- Hypertension
- Tachycardia (fast pulse)
- Paranoia
- Dramatic states of psychosis

These patients may require careful restraint, antipsychotics, benzo-diazepines for sedation, and, often, hospitalization.

8. *Sedatives* (tension-reducing drugs), *hypnotics* (sleep-inducing drugs), and *anxiolytics* (anxiety-reducing drugs). These include:
   - Benzodiazepines
   - Older medicines that are generally no longer prescribed, such as meprobamate (Miltown)
   - Barbiturates (e.g., phenobarbital)

   These drugs are potentially addictive and when mixed with alcohol in overdose quite dangerous. A significant withdrawal syndrome may develop with a rapid reduction in usage; the syndrome is similar to the withdrawal from alcohol, but can begin at a longer time out from the last dose of drug (e.g., those who are addicted to diazepam [Valium] may potentially go into withdrawal five or more days after stopping the drug; this is due to the drug's long half-life).

The majority of men and women with a diagnosis of substance abuse or dependence have an additional psychiatric diagnosis. The diagnosis of two or more psychiatric disorders in a single patient is called comorbidity or dual diagnosis. In general, the most potent and dangerous substances have the highest comorbidity rates (for example, comorbidity is more common for opiate and cocaine use than for marijuana use).

Anxiety Disorders

PANIC DISORDER

1. Symptoms

   Panic disorder (PD) is characterized by the spontaneous, unexpected occurrence of panic attacks. Panic attacks are relatively short periods (usually less than one hour) of intense anxiety or fear, accompanied by a set of the following symptoms:
   - Palpitations
   - Pounding heart or accelerated heart rate
   - Sweating
   - Trembling or shaking
   - Sensations of shortness of breath or smothering
   - Feeling of choking
   - Chest pain or discomfort
   - Nausea or abdominal distress

- Dizziness, lightheadedness, or faintness
- Feelings of unreality or detachment from oneself
- Fear of losing control or going crazy
- Fear of dying
- Parathesias (numbness or tingling)
- Chills or hot flushes.

Patients often have recurrent panic attacks and are persistently anxious about having these additional attacks. Such fear and anxiety often lead to avoidant behavior, such as agoraphobia.

Patients experiencing a panic attack often come to an ER and present symptoms of medical illness. They settle down quickly as the attack subsides and are often told that they have "anxiety," "hyperventilation syndrome," or that they are just acting "hysterical." Panic attacks are probably caused by a dysfunction within a patient's autonomic nervous system.

2. Treatment
   - Benzodiazepines are very effective.
   - Antidepressants are also effective, but usually do not work as quickly as benzodiazepines.

   Antidepressant treatment may initially increase a patient's anxiety, so doses should be started at a low level and increased gradually. Most antidepressants treat panic; bupropion (Wellbutrin) may be an exception.

3. Panic disorder with agoraphobia

   Sometimes patients feel anxiety about being in places or situations from which escape might be difficult or embarrassing, or in which help might not be available if a panic attack occurs. In the most extreme case, patients can be totally housebound. Agoraphobic fears commonly involve situations that include being outside the home alone, being in a crowd or standing in line, being on a bridge, and traveling in a vehicle. Panic with agoraphobia often requires pharmacologic treatment to block the panic attacks and behavioral treatment (systematic desensitization) to treat the agoraphobia.

PHOBIAS

1. *Specific phobias* are the most common mental disorders among women and the second most common among men. Phobias are characterized by persistent excessive or unreasonable fear in response to the presence or anticipation of a specific object or situation. These most frequently center on animals, storms, heights, illness, injury,

and death. Exposure to the phobic stimulus provokes an immediate anxiety response, and the person avoids the phobic situation to the point of interference with normal routine. Patients with specific phobias will rarely present in crisis unless there is a complicating psychiatric problem.

2. *Social phobia* is like specific phobia, but the fear is of social or performance situations involving unfamiliar people or scrutiny by others. These patients will not usually present in crisis unless there is an additional factor involved, such as alcohol abuse to decrease symptoms.

OBSESSIVE-COMPULSIVE DISORDER (OCD)

An obsession is a recurrent and intrusive thought; a compulsion is a conscious, standardized, recurrent thought or behavior, such as counting, checking, or avoiding. Obsessions tend to increase anxiety, whereas carrying out compulsions reduces anxiety. The obsessions or compulsions cause marked distress, are time-consuming and significantly interfere with the person's normal routine or functioning.

Most patients with OCD lead lives of private suffering; however, recently introduced drug treatments are quite effective. Drugs such as fluoxetine (Prozac), often at high doses (e.g., 80 mg/day), chlorimipramine (Anafranil), and fluvoxamine (Luvox) are quite successful in the treatment of OCD.

POSTTRAUMATIC STRESS DISORDER (PTSD)

Patients with PTSD have experienced an emotional stress of a magnitude that would have been traumatic for almost anyone. PTSD is very common among war veterans, victims of crime, natural catastrophes, serious accidents, etc. The disorder consists of:

- Reexperiencing the trauma in dreams and waking thoughts (including flashbacks)
- Persistent avoidance of reminders of the trauma and numbing of responsiveness to the reminders
- Persistent hyperarousal

Common associated symptoms include:

- Depression
- Anxiety
- Cognitive difficulties (such as poor concentration)

Symptoms must have been present for at least one month to meet criteria for this disorder. In crisis, patients may present with complications of PTSD, such as alcohol dependence, depression, or dissociation.

Treatment includes:

- Supportive therapy and occasional short-term use of benzodiazepines
- Antidepressant therapy and relaxation treatments with more chronic forms of PTSD

GENERALIZED ANXIETY DISORDER (GAD)

This disorder is characterized by an excessive and pervasive worry that is accompanied by a variety of somatic symptoms and causes significant distress and impairment in social or occupational functioning. Patients rarely come for crisis treatments for pure symptoms of GAD. However, comorbid problems may develop, such as alcohol dependence, that can lead to crisis states.

Somatoform Disorders

This is a group of disorders that manifests physical symptoms for which there is no adequate medical explanation. It is not the result of malingering. Rule out depression, delusions, psychosis, suicidality, or primary anxiety disorders, and then refer the patient to a general physician and psychiatrist.

1. In *somatization disorder,* the patient has many physical complaints affecting many organ systems (onset before age 30).
2. In *conversion disorder,* there are one or two neurological complaints (such as paralysis, blindness, or mutism) that cannot be explained after a careful physical and neurological examination. Conversion can be associated with depression, and most often occurs in a time of great stress.
3. In *pain disorder,* there are symptoms of pain related to psychological factors. Patients often have long histories of medical and surgical care, visiting many doctors and requesting many medications. These patients often present with persistent, sometimes irate demands for opiates and pain medications. Refer these patients to

ongoing care in a pain management center. In the crisis setting, rule out depression, potential for suicidality and opiate withdrawal.
4. In *hypochondriasis,* patients believe that they have some specific disease. Give these patients reassurance and advice on follow-up; rule out underlying depression, psychosis, or anxiety disorders. Anti-obsessional medicines (Prozac, Anafranil, or Luvox) can sometimes help.

Factitious Disorders

Some patients are known to intentionally produce signs of medical or mental disorders and misrepresent their histories and symptoms. This is an uncommon presentation in crisis settings. The only apparent objective of the behavior is to assume the role of a patient. Thus, the patient feigns mental illness due to his inner psychological distress and needs. This is in contrast to malingering, where a patient feigns psychiatric illness for discrete secondary gain, such as getting out of jail after arrest.

Mood Disorders

CLINICAL DEPRESSION (MAJOR DEPRESSIVE EPISODE)

1. Symptoms

   The diagnosis of clinical depression requires approximately two weeks of a number of the following symptoms:
   • Depressed mood
   • Decreased interest
   • Increased or decreased weight
   • Increased or decreased sleep
   • Fatigue
   • Feelings of worthlessness or guilt
   • Decreased concentration
   • Thoughts of death
   • Hearing voices saying the patient is worthless, evil, or should commit suicide (i.e., psychotic depression)

2. Treatment

   Patients who meet criteria for a major depressive episode are commonly seen in crisis settings. It is important to bring quick relief and hope to the patient. Treatment should begin as soon as possible.

- Effective and safe antidepressants are now available (e.g., the SSRIs, such as Prozac, Paxil, or Zoloft), and may be initiated in the crisis setting if appropriate follow-up systems are in place.
- Always consider alcohol or drug dependence as well as underlying medical or endocrinologic causes of major depression.
- Always look for a history of mania in depressed patients. These individuals should be on a mood stabilizer (e.g., lithium, Tegretol, or Depakote) as well as an antidepressant, since antidepressants alone may precipitate a manic response.

DYSTHYMIC DISORDER

Dysthymic disorder is characterized by longstanding presence of a depressed mood, but less severe symptoms than major depressive disorder. This is a chronic disorder with a steady presence of symptoms that sometimes last for years. Dysthymia responds well to antidepressant treatments.

BIPOLAR DISORDERS

1. *Bipolar I disorder* manifests with extreme mood swings from clinical depression (as above) to manic episodes, which show symptoms of:
   - Elevated mood or irritability
   - Decreased sleep
   - Pressured speech
   - Flight of ideas
   - Distractibility
   - Agitation
   - Excessive hedonism or paranoia
2. *Bipolar II disorder* manifests as depressive symptoms interspersed with episodes of *mild* manic symptoms (hypomania) rather than full mania.
3. *Cyclothymic disorder* is a much milder form of bipolar II disorder.

Bipolar patients are frequently seen in emergency and crisis settings. These often creative and energetic patients pose true dilemmas for treatment. They can be as happy as comics or as aggressive as warriors.

Mood states can shift from minute to minute. Structure, limit setting, and use of medication (i.e., mood stabilizers) can be very helpful. Often, involuntary hospitalization may be indicated with severe states of mania. Depressed bipolar patients need special care and vigilance. Any onset of suicidal ideation must be closely monitored.

Remember that mood disorders can be caused by general medical conditions such as endocrine and neurological disorders or structural damage to the brain. Examples include hyperthyroidism as a cause of mania and Cushing's disease as a cause of depression (i.e., abnormally high amounts of cortisol in the body). When patients present with severe mood disorders, they should be evaluated to rule out an underlying medical cause. A substance-induced mood disorder may be caused by medications, especially antihypertensives; by accidental and perhaps unknowing exposure to neurotoxic chemicals; or by recreational drugs, such as cocaine. Alcohol-induced mood disorder is common. Always differentiate this possibility by getting a good history from the patient. What came first, depression or drinking? Did the patient ever feel depressed when he had been alcohol- or drug-free for a period of time? Has he ever had a significant period of sobriety? How did he feel then?

Schizophrenia and Other Psychotic Disorders

SCHIZOPHRENIA

The diagnosis of schizophrenia requires at least a 6-month prodrome (difficulty with learning and social interactions). The active phase of symptoms must be at least 1 week long, with 1 of the following:

- Delusions
- Prominent hallucinations
- Incoherence or marked loosening of associations
- Changed affect (e.g., flat or inappropriate)

There is a progressive decrease in function (note that a psychotic mood disorder may present a similar picture, so this must always be ruled out).

There are several schizophrenia "clusters":

1. The *paranoid* cluster presents with preoccupation with one or more delusions (often of persecution) or frequent auditory hallucinations. It does *not* show prominent disorganized speech, disorganized or catatonic behavior, or flat/inappropriate affect. These patients are typically tense, suspicious, guarded, and reserved. They may be hostile or aggressive.
2. The *disorganized* cluster presents predominantly as disorganized speech, with prominent disinhibited, primitive, and/or unorganized behavior, and flat or inappropriate affect.
3. The *catatonic* cluster exhibits marked disturbance of motor function such as catalepsy (waxy flexibility) or stupor, and excessive, apparently purposeless motor activity. There is extreme negativism or mutism, as well as peculiarities of voluntary movement (assuming strange postures, prominent mannerisms, or grimacing), and echolalia or echopraxia (repeating words or sentences).
4. The *undifferentiated* cluster meets criteria for schizophrenia, but can't be easily fitted into one of the subtypes.
5. The *residual* cluster has no prominent active symptoms, but reveals evidence of the schizophrenic disturbance, such as emotional blunting, social withdrawal, eccentric behavior, illogical thinking, and mild loosening of associations.

SCHIZOPHRENIFORM DISORDER

Schizophreniform disorder is identical in every respect to schizophrenia except that the disorder lasts at least 1 month, *but less than 6 months.*

SCHIZOAFFECTIVE DISORDER

A patient with a schizoaffective disorder meets criteria for a mood disorder while concurrently meeting criteria for schizophrenia. The patient's active symptoms (delusions or hallucinations) are present in the history for at least 2 weeks in the absence of prominent mood disorder symptoms.

Patients with schizophrenia will require antipsychotic medications and careful psychosocial management. Relapse of psychotic symptoms must be treated aggressively with antipsychotic medicines. Often, vigorous drug treatment can forestall or even prevent relapse (see chapter 22).

The Differential Diagnosis of Bipolar, Schizoaffective, and Schizophrenic Disorders

Unlike a patient with bipolar disorder, the patient with schizophrenia does not go into a state of complete remission and will have great difficulty with role functioning compared to the premorbid state (the state that the patient was in prior to the onset of illness). It is important to remember that in a crisis situation, schizophrenia, mania with psychotic features, and schizoaffective disorder may all look the same. In all three disorders, patients can present with psychosis and agitation. The longitudinal history, signs of mood disorder, and return to premorbid state after the acute illness goes into remission will help with this diagnosis.

- Patients with a bipolar disorder should return to a state of normality after the acute illness is controlled.
- Patients with a schizoaffective disorder will have manic or depressed features and psychotic features during their illness, but will not return to a complete premorbid state of function.
- Patients with schizophrenia, when well, will have few symptoms of mood instability and will not return to a completely normal premorbid state of function.

Delusional disorder differs from schizophrenia in that delusions are "nonbizarre"—that is, they are possible in real life, for example "being followed by the FBI" as opposed to "being controlled by Martians." Delusions must endure for over 1 month. Delusions occur in the absence of other symptoms of schizophrenia, including bizarre behavior, catatonia, and flat affect. The functional impairments are much milder than in schizophrenia.

The term *brief psychotic disorder* is reserved for individuals presenting with a major psychotic symptom (delusions, hallucinations, disorganized speech, or disorganized/catatonic behavior) but short duration (1–30 days) with eventual full return to previous level of functioning. (Be sure the disturbance is not better accounted for by a mood disorder, substance-related disorder, or psychotic disorder due to a general medical condition.)

Shared psychotic disorder, a rare condition better known as *folie à deux* develops during a long-term relationship with another person who shares a similar psychotic syndrome. It commonly involves two people: a dominant person who is the primary patient and a submissive person who has the shared psychotic disorder. The dominant person develops a delusional system and then progressively imposes that delusional system onto the other person. Treatment will involve antipsychotic medication for the dominant patient and a period of separation for the couple in order to perform reality testing to the pair.

Dissociative Disorders

A mentally healthy person has a unitary sense of self as a single human being with a single basic personality; a person with a dissociative disorder has lost that unitary state of consciousness and feels the lack of such an identity, confusion around his or her identity, or has multiple identities. Dissociation occurs in patients who have a history of psychological trauma. Amnesia (memory loss) occurs in almost all dissociative disorders.

DISSOCIATIVE AMNESIA AND DISSOCIATIVE FUGUES

1. *Dissociative amnesia* is an inability to recall information related to a stressful or traumatic event that is not explained by ordinary forgetfulness, and for which there is no evidence of an underlying brain disorder. The common form involves amnesia for one's personal identity, but intact memory for general information.

   It is uncommon for patients with amnesia secondary to an organic illness or injury to forget their own identity. If a patient can remember certain facts but not their own identity, this may imply a dissociative amnesia (formerly called psychogenic amnesia).

2. *Dissociative fugues* are sudden, unexpected travel away from home or work, failure to recall one's past, and confusion about personal identity or assumption of a new one.

DISSOCIATIVE IDENTITY DISORDER

Dissociative identity disorder, more commonly called "multiple personality disorder," is a chronic disorder that almost always involves childhood physical or sexual abuse. Usually two or more distinct personalities recurrently take control of the person's behavior and attitudes. Patients may need brief hospitalization around crises of self-harm behaviors or true suicidal or homicidal urges. In crisis, the clinician must focus on the "chief" or "organizing" persona to evaluate if the patient is in control. A secure environment is needed if this "main alter" cannot guarantee the patient's safety.

DEPERSONALIZATION DISORDER

Depersonalization disorder involves persistent or recurrent alterations in self-perception to the extent that a patient loses the sense of her own reality and may think that she is mechanical, in a dream, or detached from her body. Be sure to investigate the possibility of a complex partial seizure disorder with an EEG in patients who present with recurrent dissociative spells or severe depersonalization. Mild depersonalization and derealization (i.e., things seem unreal around the patient) can also exist in panic disorder and depression.

Eating Disorders

ANOREXIA NERVOSA

A patient with anorexia nervosa:

- Refuses to maintain body weight at or above a minimally normal weight for age and height
- Intensely fears gaining weight or becoming fat, even though she is underweight
- Has a disturbed body image (the patient feels fat or misshapen while denying her thinness)
- May miss consecutive menstrual cycles

BULIMIA NERVOSA

A patient with bulimia nervosa has recurrent episodes of eating large amounts of food accompanied by a feeling of being out of control and recurrent compensatory behaviors (purging, fasting, excessive exercise) to prevent weight gain. Self-evaluation is based on body shape and weight. Patients may maintain a normal body weight.

In crisis situations involving patients with eating disorder patients, clinicians should rule out severe metabolic emergencies. Patients can lose large amounts of sodium and potassium from recurrent binge-eating or vomiting, which can also cause severe changes in the acid-base balance of their bodies. Severely anorectic patients may experience unusual and severe metabolic complications as well as cardiovascular and hepatic damage. SSRI drugs, particularly fluoxetine (Prozac), can be effective in the treatment of eating disorders.

Sleep Disorders

Sleep disturbance is a symptom of many psychiatric illnesses, such as depression, anxiety and mania. Patients with sleep disorders (in the absence of other psychiatric illness) do not present in crisis, but we include them here as a general review. Patients suspected of having sleep disorders should be referred to sleep laboratories for sleep study analyses.

1. *Primary insomnia* is difficulty falling asleep or maintaining sleep; it is sometimes a symptom of depression, anxiety, or mania.
2. *Primary hypersomnia* is excessive amounts of sleep and excessive daytime sleepiness (somnolence); may be associated with major depressive disorder.
3. *Narcolepsy* involves:
   - Irresistible attacks of sleep occurring daily for at least 3 months
   - Hypnopompic or hypnogogic hallucinations (hallucinations when waking or falling asleep)
   - Sleep paralysis (feeling paralyzed when waking or falling asleep)
   - Cataplexy (loss of muscle tone with intense emotional experience)
4. *Breathing-related sleep disorders* include sleep apnea, where there is loud snoring due to blockage or cessation of air flow within the respiratory tract, or inadequate respiratory rates during sleep due to central nervous system dysfunction. These patients may develop chronic headaches, depressed mood, forgetfulness, hypertension, and other complications.
5. *Parasomnias* are unusual or undesirable phenomenon that appear suddenly during sleep or at the threshold between sleeping and waking. For example:
   - *Sleep terror disorder* features arousal in the first third of the night during deep non-REM sleep, inaugurated by a piercing scream or cry and accompanied by intense anxiety. It is common in childhood. Patients with sleep terrors often don't recall a complex, frightening, elaborate story during sleep, which would be more consistent with a nightmare — which also occurs during REM

sleep. Sleep terror should also be distinguished from nocturnal panic attacks, which occur in a different phase of the sleep cycle. It is not uncommon for patients with panic disorder to wake up from a sound sleep with a panic attack.

- *Sleepwalking disorder*, also known as somnambulism, involves repeated episodes of getting out of bed during sleep and walking about; it is relatively rare.

Impulse-Control Disorders

Patients with these disorders fail to resist an impulse, drive, or temptation to perform some action that is harmful to themselves or others, feel increased tension or arousal before committing the act, and feel pleasure, gratification, or release while committing the act. In *intermittent explosive disorder* there are several discrete episodes of failure to resist aggressive impulses that result in serious assaultive acts or destruction of property. The degree of aggressiveness during episodes is grossly out of proportion to any precipitating stressors. The disorder can be treated effectively with mood stabilizers; in rare circumstances of extremely violent behaviors, high doses of beta-blocker drugs (e.g., propranolol [Inderal]) are effective. Antiaggression drugs are currently being investigated in experimental laboratories. Depression, mania, personality disorders, substance abuse, or psychosis can also lead to aggression.

Adjustment Disorders

An adjustment disorder is characterized by a short-term maladaptive reaction to what a layperson might call a personal misfortune (psychosocial stressor). Symptoms appear within three months of the onset of the stressor; the patient:

- Exhibits marked distress beyond what might be expected (depressed mood, tearfulness, and hopelessness)
- Manifests anxiety with palpitations, jitteriness, agitation
- May violate the rights of others or disregard age-appropriate norms, such as truancy, vandalism, reckless driving, fighting
- Has significant impairment in social, vocational, or academic functioning

Once the stressor has terminated, symptoms don't persist for more than an additional six months. These disorders are common in the crisis setting and can lead to extremes in behavior, which are generally short-lived.

AXIS II: PERSONALITY DISORDERS

Diagnostically, personality disorders are defined as enduring patterns of inner experience and behavior that deviate markedly from the expectations of the individual's culture. "Inner experience and behavior" includes such areas as:

- Cognition (ways of perceiving and interpreting self, other people, and events)
- Affect (the range, intensity, lability, and appropriateness of emotional response)
- Interpersonal functioning
- Impulse control

The patient's personality structure is inflexible and pervasive across a broad range of personal and social situations and is of long duration (can be traced back at least to adolescence or early adulthood) and leads to clinically significant distress or impairment in social, occupational, or other important areas of functioning.

With the exception of the avoidant personality (see below), most people who suffer with personality disorders often don't see the problem within themselves. More often, especially when these patients are in crisis, they can only see the problems in their life as resulting from the actions of others. These patients are often prone to impulsiveness, reckless behaviors, suicide attempts, self-harm, aggression, agitation, and extreme dysphoria and moodiness.

Patients with these disorders can be very difficult for novice clinicians. While most "normal" people have ambivalence and can see the world in terms of "grays," patients with personality disorders often deal with the world in terms of "black and white." This clash between the "normal" reactions of a clinician and the more extreme reactions of the patient often creates much anxiety for a clinician. These patients can discharge uncomfortable thoughts and feelings, such as rage and helplessness, onto others in a way that can stir up anger, guilt, helplessness, and anxiety in the crisis clinician. It is critically important that clinicians do not act out their negative feelings toward the patient (counter-transference). When clinicians feel rage or hatred or fear toward the patient, they can misuse their influence with disastrous consequences.

Empathy, limit setting, structure, resources, and sometimes, medications, can help resolve the crisis. If dangerous ideation persists, brief hospitalization or securing a "holding bed" for the patient is often required.

Paranoid Personality Disorder

1. Symptoms

   The essential feature of paranoid personality disorder is a pervasive and unwarranted tendency to interpret other people's actions as deliberately demeaning or threatening. For example, patients:
   * May suspect others of harming, exploiting, or deceiving them
   * May be preoccupied with unjustified doubts about loyalty or trustworthiness of friends or associates
   * May be reluctant to confide in others for fear that the information will be used against them
   * May read hidden demeaning or threatening meanings into benign remarks or events
   * Are often pathologically jealous

2. Causes

   Paranoid personalities enter crisis states when there is a change in their relationship with a loved one (e.g., a husband with a paranoid personality may enter a crisis state after his physically abused wife finally decides to leave him) or with someone who may have power over them, as in an employer-employee or teacher-student relationship. These patients often feel others are laughing about them or plotting against them. They live on the edge of losing their sense of reality but do not become overtly psychotic unless there is a comorbid axis I problem. It is always important to assess paranoid patients for homicidal ideation, especially when their romantic relationships are in danger of breaking up.

3. Treatment
   * Empathy and reassurance are very important to help bring patients in crisis back to a state of better emotional control.
   * Often, small amounts of benzodiazepine medications for diminishing anxiety (e.g., lorazepam) or a small dose of low-potency

antipsychotic agents to diminish paranoid feelings (e.g., low-dose Mellaril [thioridazine] or low-dose Serentil [mesoridazine]) can help the patient feel better.

- Support groups for men and women who are physically abusive can be very helpful. Such groups can enhance the reality testing of patients, and gentle confrontation of paranoid defenses can sometimes be accomplished in a group setting.
- Rule out dysthymic disorders, since depressed patients may appear chronically suspicious.
- Also rule out other causes for which a patient can present in a state of paranoia, such as chronic cocaine abuse, bipolar disorder, schizophrenia, psychotic depression, amphetamine-induced psychosis, or a central nervous system infection (e.g, syphilis).

Schizoid Personality Disorder

Individuals with schizoid personality disorder:

- Take pleasure in few if any activities
- Lack close friends or confidants
- Appear indifferent to the praise or criticism of others
- Show emotional coldness, detachment, or flattened affect
- Prefer to be alone and do not wish for friends
- Often gravitate toward jobs where they can be alone

People with this disorder will occasionally marry, but often leave much emotional space between themselves and their spouse.

These patients usually experience a crisis state in the midst of an overwhelming stressor and return to baseline rather quickly. They usually do not seek treatment because of their indifference to others unless they develop an axis I disorder or experience another overwhelming stressor in their life.

Schizotypal Personality Disorder

Individuals with schizotypal personality disorder:

- Are characterized by strikingly odd or strange thinking, behavior, and speech
- Experience acute discomfort with, and reduced capacity for, close relationships

- Exhibit cognitive or perceptual distortions and eccentricities (such as ideas of reference, odd beliefs or magical thinking, unusual perceptual experiences including bodily illusions, suspiciousness, inappropriate or constricted affect, excessive social anxiety)
- Often have a family history of schizophrenia

These patients often present with problems related to the world's not tolerating their odd or unusual behaviors. A number of these patients can also present in a state of depression. Most are not dangerous, but will have eccentric and bizarre ways of doing things. Once out of crisis, they will not usually stay in long-term mental health treatment. Suggestions, support, and referral to community resources can often be extremely helpful. Low-dose antipsychotics can be helpful during the crisis phase.

Antisocial Personality Disorder

1. Symptoms

   People with antisocial personalities:
   - Are unable to conform to social norms
   - Continually engage in antisocial or criminal acts
   - May present a normal, even charming, exterior, but actually are deceitful, lie repeatedly, use aliases, and con others for profit or pleasure
   - Are impulsive
   - Are consistently irresponsible
   - Lack genuine remorse
   - Have no self-esteem

   In most cases, they are also using substances, such as alcohol or cocaine.

2. Causes

   Antisocial personalities are most often seen in crisis when:
   - A romantic relationship ends
   - A support system is unavailable
   - The patient is in trouble with the criminal justice system.

3. Treatment

   In crisis, these patients can be impulsive, manipulative, violent, and dangerous.

- Limit setting is a must.
- Be sure these patients will not harm themselves or anyone else.
- If necessary, use security or police with sociopaths who are threatening.
- Restore self-esteem to these patients, who commonly present from jail with suicidal ideation after arrest. After arrest, these patients often feel they have "lost face," and are very humiliated. Empathy or a show of respect will often resolve their feelings of dysphoria.
- Verify the sociopath's history whenever possible and be vigilant for inconsistent information, as these patients frequently lie and malinger for secondary gain.

Borderline Personality Disorder

1. Symptoms

People with borderline personality disorder almost always appear to be in crisis. Their behavior can be highly unpredictable as they engage in frantic efforts to avoid real or imagined abandonment. Characteristics include:
- A life history of unstable and intense personal relationships
- A persistently unstable self-image or identity
- Impulsivity in self-destructive areas (spending, sex, substance abuse, reckless driving, binge-eating)
- Recurrent suicidal behavior, gestures, threats, or self-mutilation
- Intense mood swings
- Chronic feelings of emptiness
- Inappropriate intense anger or difficulty controlling anger
- Short-lived stress-related psychotic symptoms

2. Treatment

Patients with this disorder are at times impulsive, chaotic, and frightening due to their acute suicidal and homicidal states.
- For agitation in the crisis setting, medicine (e.g., lorazepam) and limit setting are helpful.
- For psychotic states, which are usually short-lived, antipsychotic drugs can be very helpful.
- Supportive, well-structured, non-regressive therapy techniques are beneficial.

- It is important to get borderline patients into meaningful treatment, with both psychopharmacologic medications and psychotherapeutic techniques. Either in isolation is probably ineffective.

Case managers and therapists must coordinate with crisis programs regarding the management of these patients, and must also clearly explain the plan to the patient. Plans are often complicated, so they should always be written down (preferably typed), updated, and shared among the patient, crisis professionals, and (with the patient's permission) others in the helping professions (e.g., hospital ERs or police and EMS). Once a treatment plan has been set, the patient will test the limits of the plan. Therefore, crisis clinicians should give helpful input to case managers and therapists, especially if the emergency clinicians will be expected to carry out the plan.

Traditional telephone counseling is usually ineffective with borderline patients, unless it is structured into a treatment plan (e.g., one 15-minute call per weekend day until the case manager returns on the following Monday). If a therapist advises a patient with a borderline disorder to call a crisis line, the patient should be given clear guidelines and expectations. Borderline patients who are in crisis and who feel suicidal should be told to call local emergency mental health personnel. If the patient is still unsafe after a *brief* conversation with a crisis counselor, the patient should be seen. During crisis interviews, it is important to rule out psychosis, suicidality, and homicidality. These patients frequently desire to cut or injure themselves when in crisis; low-dose antipsychotics or IM lorazepam can sometimes curb these feelings.

Histrionic Personality Disorder

1. Symptoms
   - Excessive emotionality and attention seeking
   - Inappropriate sexually seductive or provocative behavior
   - Discomfort when not the center of attention
   - Inability to maintain deep, long-lasting attachments
   - Rapidly shifting and shallow emotions
   - Speech style that is impressionistic and lacks detail
   - Self-dramatizing, theatrical behavior (e.g., fainting, making dramatic suicide attempts, or overtly lying to form fantastic stories)

- Easily influenced by others or by circumstances
- Exaggerated expression of emotions
- In crisis, lying to manipulate people

2. Treatment
   - Relationship difficulties most often induce crisis states in histrionic patients.
   - Limit setting, crisis hospitalization, empathy, and structure can be very helpful.
   - Low-dose anxiolytic agents (e.g., lorazepam) can be useful.
   - Mood stabilizer agents can sometimes help histrionic personalities who frequently enter into severe states of crisis.
   - Rule out the presence of other causes of dramatic mood changes and behavior, such as bipolar disorder.

Narcissistic Personality Disorder

1. Symptoms
   - Grandiose sense of self-importance
   - Preoccupation with fantasies of unlimited success, power, brilliance, beauty, or ideal love
   - Require excessive admiration
   - Extreme sense of entitlement (patients expect favorable treatment or automatic compliance with their expectations)
   - Belief that they are special and unique and should only associate with other special or high-status persons
   - Lack of empathy
   - Exploitation of others to achieve their own ends
   - Envy of others or belief that others envy them
   - Arrogance and haughty attitudes or behaviors

In crisis, narcissistic persons will feel depressed, enraged, or suicidal. They will seek out someone who will help them and will often seek to idealize a crisis clinician. The opposite pattern may also be seen, that is, the narcissistic patient in crisis is enraged, and may devalue or belittle the therapist who is trying to help. By putting down someone else, a narcissistic patient may indirectly help himself feel better.

2. Treatment
   - Rule out the possibility of a bipolar disorder. Manic patients will frequently overestimate their power and worth due to the euphoric moods they experience.

- In general, narcissistic patients will respond quickly to crisis intervention techniques, but may not stay in treatment for long periods of time.

Avoidant Personality Disorder

1. Symptoms
   - Extreme sensitivity to rejection
   - Timidity
   - Avoidance of occupational activities that involve significant interpersonal contact because of fears of criticism, disapproval, or rejection
   - Unwillingness to get involved with people unless certain of being liked
   - Restraint in intimate relationships because of fear of being shamed or ridiculed
   - Preoccupation with criticism or rejection in social situations
   - Inhibition in new interpersonal situations
   - Feelings of social ineptness and inferioriority
   - Reluctance to take risks or engage in new activities

2. Treatment

   Individuals with avoidant personality disorder wish they could interact more with others, but are often fearful and anxious about this (unlike schizoid personalities who are indifferent to close relationships and friends). They occasionally come into crisis if they are forced to interact with others (e.g., giving a presentation or going through a test or oral examination). Patients often also suffer from anxiety disorders, such as panic and social phobia; the anxiety problem is often etiologic (causative) in their avoidance. Treatment of the anxiety disorder will often improve the avoidant lifestyle. Occasionally these patients suffer from alcohol or sedative-hypnotic abuse as a way to "self-medicate" their anxiety.

Dependent Personality Disorder

1. Symptoms
   - Dependent and submissive behavior
   - Difficulty making decisions
   - Difficulty expressing disagreement with others

- Need for others to assume responsibility for most major areas of life
- Fear of being left to take care of him- or herself; uncomfortable being alone
- Urgency to replace a close relationship that ends

People with dependent personality disorder will often have relationship crises. They gravitate toward those who will take charge, make decisions for them, and allow them to live "in the shadow of another." These patients' partners often are substance abusers or physically abusive because individuals with dependent personality disorder do not believe they deserve better and feel powerless to assert themselves in a relationship.

2. Treatment
    - Referral to psychotherapy (or shelters for the battered or abused) and to other resources, e.g., Al-Anon, groups for "Women (or Men) Who Love Too Much," etc., is often helpful. It is difficult for people with dependent personalities to assert themselves with others or to extricate themselves from abusive relationships. They often cycle through one crisis after another until they are able to assert their autonomy. Their perceived "weakness" can evoke a negative reaction in the crisis clinician.
    - With patients in an abusive relationship where the level of violence is escalating, insist that they go to a safe place. Involve law enforcement if necessary. Remember, dependent people have often come from backgrounds where they were beaten, abused, or suffered severe emotional deprivation. They may truly feel that they "don't deserve any better."
    - Always be a reality voice.

Obsessive-Compulsive Personality Disorder

1. Symptoms
    - Pervasive pattern of perfectionism and inflexibility
    - Preoccupation with details, rules, lists, order, organization, or schedules to the extent that the major point of the activity is lost
    - Perfectionism that interferes with task completion
    - Excessive devotion to work and productivity to the exclusion of leisure activity and friendships
    - Overconscientious, scrupulous, and inflexible about morals, ethics, or values
    - Rigid and stubborn behavior

2. Treatment

People with obsessive-compulsive disorders may go into crisis when their personality style conflicts with those around them, when "the universe fails to cooperate with their plans," or when a lover "leaves mysteriously with no reason." These patients are exceptionally driven (e.g., type A people in professions) and are often quite successful. They respond well to logic, reassurance, support, suggestion, and planning.

Passive-Aggressive Personality Disorder
(Negativistic Personality Disorder)

Individuals with this disorder often create havoc and are often unaware of this. They vent their frustration indirectly and are often unaware of having normal angry feelings. Other people may become frustrated and enraged with persons who have a passive-aggressive disorder, who often have no idea why the world is so annoyed. Psychotherapy is frequently helpful.

A WORD OF CAUTION

Be cautious about using axis II diagnostic labels to explain behaviors that are really caused by axis I disorders. For example, patients with major depression can often present with suicidal behaviors and marked irritability due to the mood disorder and its resultant biological dysregulation of the nervous system. One could mistakenly see such behaviors as coming from a patient who is "borderline." However, a personality disorder would imply a longstanding, fixed character structure and series of dysfunctional behaviors. Patients with major depression will have a discrete change in their normal personality structure, and will usually have an illness that responds to appropriate treatments.

Bipolar patients may present with narcissistic traits due to their overly inflated sense of importance, their rage, and their idealization or devaluation of others. A crisis clinician would not want to misdiagnose a bipolar patient as having a narcissistic personality disorder. Bipolar patients can occasionally appear "borderline" until their first bona fide mania appears. Look for the family history of bipolar disorder as a clue.

Of course, axis I and axis II disorders may coexist in patients, so that some borderlines may develop major depression and bipolar patients may have narcissistic personality disorders or avoidant personality disorders at baseline. As in every situation, it is important to take a good history and determine what symptoms developed first, if the symptoms went away, how long the problem has existed, whether it is chronic, and whether the symptoms are caused by drugs, alcohol, or medical illness.

COMORBIDITY: AXIS I AND II INTERACTIONS

There is a certain level of comorbidity with the axis I and axis II disorders. For example, a person with avoidant personality disorder may have developed that axis II disorder because of an associated anxiety disorder, such as panic disorder (with phobic avoidance) or social phobia. Treatment of the underlying anxiety disorder may result in improvement or disappearance of the patient's overall avoidance. A patient with cyclothymic, dysthymic, or bipolar II disorder may appear to suffer from extraordinary mood swings similar to a "borderline" patient, but will improve with biological treatments and/or psychotherapy for their mood disorder.

CLINICAL EXAMPLES

The following examples are given to provide an approach to diagnostic formulation. Diagnoses are important, as they orient the clinician to the appropriately indicated treatments.

Axis I Crises

A 23-year-old man is brought into the ER by police for fighting in a Waffle House Restaurant. He is angry, verbally abusive, very irritable, and exhibits rapid pressured speech and flight of ideas. When the crisis clinician goes to interview the patient he fondles himself and asks the clinician for sex. When he tries to break the door down, he is placed into four-point, leather restraints. The patient's parents say he has not slept for the past four days. They've never seen him this way. According to the parents, the patient has no history of alcohol or drug abuse, no medical problems, and no recent stresses in his life. He is a senior in college and hopes to begin a Ph.D. program in literature next week. He attends school full-time and is employed at a gas station. In the ER his laboratory tests are normal and his urine drug screen is negative. His vital signs are normal.
Axis I: bipolar I disorder

Axis II: none
Axis III: none

A 40-year-old woman is seen in her home after calling the crisis line to say she thought she might kill herself. She had suicidal thoughts only, and promised she would not act on them if she could get help. She tells the clinician she has been feeling more overwhelmed and distraught because of a crack cocaine habit that has been worsening for two years. During the last year she resorted to prostitution in order to pay for her crack cocaine. She is using ten or more "rocks" per day, at $20 per rock. Two months ago a doctor checked her blood and told her she is HIV positive. She denies any active symptoms suggestive of AIDS. She is depressed, sad, tearful, and having some trouble sleeping. She thinks that there is nothing left to live for unless she can get "detoxed" and treated.

Axis I: cocaine-induced mood disorder
Axis II: none
Axis III: HIV positive

Martha, a 36-year-old mother of two, tried to hang herself while under the influence of alcohol. She has been feeling depressed for most days over the past five years, but her depression worsened during the previous month, when she developed feelings of hopelessness, helplessness, crying spells, vivid suicidal thoughts of shooting herself, and lost 15 pounds of body weight. Tonight she wrote a suicide note to her husband and children, telling her husband to take good care of the kids. She waited until they left to go to a baseball game. She never drinks, but tonight she had half a bottle of vodka in order to "get up the courage to do it." She stood on a chair, strung a rope up to a chandelier, placed the rope around her neck, and jumped off the chair. By mere coincidence, her husband returned because he had left his wallet at home. He found her and cut her down. She was initially blue around her face, but soon was breathing normally. EMS brought her into the hospital ER. She is on insulin for diabetes but otherwise is in good health. Her alcohol level in the ER was 0.287. She had no other drugs in her system.

Axis I: alcohol intoxication; major depressive episode; dysthymic disorder
Axis II: none
Axis III: insulin-dependent diabetes mellitus

Axis II Crises

A borderline patient began to make further demands on her therapist, including demands for unscheduled visits and meetings during the therapist's lunch break. She began waiting in her truck across the street from the mental health clinic in hopes of seeing her therapist, calling him at home during evenings and weekends, etc. Unfortunately, the therapist gave in to several of the patient's demands. After reviewing the calls, the therapist's supervisor told the patient that she would be transferred to a new therapist. The patient left, then snuck back into the clinic the next day and waited for the supervisor, the therapist, and the clinic's psychiatrist. The patient had armed herself with a shotgun and multiple rounds of ammunition. Fortunately she was discovered before anyone was harmed. In a letter to her therapist, she noted that she had been wrong, but "if she had been given the structure she needed, none of the aforementioned behaviors would have occurred."

This vignette illustrates the need for firm limits and structure in the borderline patient's treatment.

A patient with a narcissistic personality disorder calls the crisis line and says he wants to get help. The crisis counselor knows the patient's history and has talked with the patient several times before. The patient says, "I don't want to talk to you, you're stupid!" "I'm sorry you feel that way, Mr. Jones," the counselor replies. "I *am* here to try to help, so please tell me what I can do to be of help to you."

Narcissistic patients can project negative feelings or thoughts. Like patients with borderline disorders, they also can see clinicians and others as "all good" or "all bad," (i.e., splitting). Clinicians need to take a reassuring but firm approach and focus on the reality of the interaction in the here and now.

A man is brought into an emergency room on involuntary evaluation papers due to his crack cocaine addiction. He has been in and out of jail and mental health treatment settings for most of his life. The crisis clinician speaks to the patient's wife who initiated the legal papers. "I'm worried about him. I'm worried he'll die or be hurt by the drug dealers. I love him and he needs help. Every time I try to help him he hits me. If I don't give him money, he'll threaten me. He spends $2000 per week on drugs, and doesn't see this as a problem." The patient's wife is nice, concerned, and her story seems accurate and believable. The clinician interviews the patient. "It's my goddamn wife's fault," he says. "She won't stop harassing me. All she does is make me look bad in front of my friends. It's been that way for years. I'll stop using cocaine if she divorces me. I'm using it to get back at her. She's such a bitch."

On further exploration, it becomes clear that this man has a history of an antisocial personality disorder. Unfortunately, he cannot see his wife's concern, and completely denies his need to stop using cocaine. In his mind, the wife is the one with the problem!

SUGGESTED READINGS

American Psychiatric Association. (1994). *Diagnostic and statistical manual of mental disorders* (4th ed.). Washington, DC: Author.

Kaplan, H. I., Sadock, B. J., & Grebb, J. A. (1994). *Kaplan and Sadock's synopsis of psychiatry* (7th ed.). Baltimore: Williams & Wilkins.

Frankel, F. H. (1995). Discovering new memories in psychotherapy: Childhood revisited, fantasy, or both? *New England Journal of Medicine, 333*(9), 591–594.

Chapter 22

PSYCHOPHARMACOLOGIC TREATMENT: AN OVERVIEW

Better use medicines at the outset than at the last moment.
— *Publilius Syrus (Maxim 865)*

THE RECENT EXPLOSION in knowledge resulting from the past several decades of research in the neurosciences and pharmacology has led to new and improved medicines to treat the major psychiatric disorders. These drugs are bringing new levels of hope for individuals afflicted with psychiatric syndromes. This chapter will outline the major types and classes of drugs, and some of the important issues with which every crisis clinician should be familiar.

A BRIEF HISTORICAL NOTE

Prior to the use of chlorpromazine (Thorazine) in the early 1950s, few pharmacologic agents were available to treat the most severe forms of psychiatric illness. Bromides, barbiturates, electric shock, and lobotomies were often used, since no other agents seemed effective in treating severe states of psychosis or depression. Thus, the treatments of psychiatric illness were often negative, poorly controlled, and rather diabolical in the public's view. Even today, such views may carry over although the current medications are safe and effective if used properly.

Pharmacologic intervention is complicated and requires considerable expertise since the brain and nervous system are very sensitive

We thank Ryan Finkenbine, M.D., Timothy J. Paolone, M.D., and Shannon Tyson, M.D., for their contributions to this chapter.

organs. Specific agents are now available to treat specific syndromes. Crisis clinicians must help patients understand that the brain becomes dysfunctional in severe states of crisis, and medications are designed to return the patient's biochemistry back to a state of wellness and normality.

ANTIPSYCHOTICS

Clinical Uses

All antipsychotics do the same thing: They diminish signs and symptoms of psychosis. However, they all differ in their side effects. Thus, good crisis clinicians will become familiar with the range of side effects exhibited by antipsychotics. Side effects are one of the most common reasons that patients stop using these medicines.

Chlorpromazine is the prototype of antipsychotic drugs. It is a member of the drug class called *phenothiazines*. Others of this class include **thioridazine** (Mellaril), **mesoridazine** (Serentil), **perphenazine** (Trilafon), **trifluoperazine** (Stelazine) and **fluphenazine** (Prolixin).

Another class of medications frequently used in the crisis or emergency setting is the *butyrophenones*, which include **haloperidol** (Haldol) and **droperidol** (Inapsine).

There are many other antipsychotics, including **molindone** (Moban), **thiothixene** (Navane), and **loxapine** (Loxitane), among others.

Generally, in the emergency setting, *high-potency* antipsychotics are used to treat patients who may be experiencing severe psychotic symptoms. The high-potency drugs include **haloperidol** (Haldol), **fluphenazine hydrochloride** (Prolixin HCl) and **droperidol** (Inapsine). For agitated psychotic patients, or for patients who need immediate control of their psychoses (e.g., those with command hallucinations to hurt themselves), an intramuscular injection of 5.0 mg of **droperidol** (Inapsine) or the mixture of **haloperidol** (Haldol) and **lorazepam** (Ativan, an antianxiety drug), 5.0 mg and 2.0 mg respectively, will bring the patient's psychotic agitation under control within a few minutes. **Droperidol** has an advantage because it is not a *benzodiazepine* (Ativan is), and so will not potentially cause respiratory compromise in a patient with a great deal of alcohol in his bloodstream.

Haldol or Prolixin HCl can be given orally, either in tablet or liquid concentrate form, to patients who are cooperative. The usual dose is 5.0 to 10.0 mg for acute exacerbations of a psychotic illness. A typical starting dose for the patient who is not going to be hospitalized is about 5.0 mg b.i.d (twice a day).

Certain preparations of Haldol and Prolixin can be given to patients in an injectable form so they can maintain a sustained long-term anti-psychotic blood level. These are the so-called decanoate forms of these drugs. Haldol decanoate can be given to patients every four weeks, and Prolixin decanoate can be administered every two weeks. These medication forms can help patients who have difficulty taking oral medicine or who metabolize these drugs too quickly within their livers. (All oral medicines are absorbed through the stomach and must then pass through the liver. This is termed "first pass metabolism." Many drugs are quickly "chewed up" metabolically as they pass through the liver. Decanoate drugs are absorbed directly from the muscle into the bloodstream, thus bypassing the liver, resulting at times in more effec-tive blood levels of the drug). Once the patient is stabilized on these long-term antipsychotics, they often will not need to take antipsychot-ics in oral forms

Side Effects

Almost all antipsychotics cause several major classes of side effects.

EXTRAPYRAMIDAL SIDE EFFECTS (EPS)

EPS often result from the effects of blocking dopamine receptors in the brain's nerve cells. Such side effects may be classified as acute, subacute, and long-term.

1. *Acute side effects* occur within hours to days after starting an anti-psychotic drug, and include a dystonic reaction or an oculogyric crisis.
   - A *dystonic reaction* is a painful, abrupt onset of muscle contrac-tion. A patient may appear to be unable to swallow or breathe; he or she may have a tightly clenched jaw (trismus); the tongue may appear to protrude; the neck and head may be twisted to one side (torticollis); the arms or legs may twist around; and the spine may arch over backward in a stiff inverse direction (opisthotonos). Anticholinergic drugs can be injected into the patient's muscle for quick relief (e.g., **benztropine** [Cogentin], 2.0 mg i.m., or **di-phenhydramine** [Benadryl], 25 mg i.m.). The injection must al-

ways be followed by oral tablets of these anticholinergic agents because the injectable drugs used to treat the dystonic reactions are quickly utilized by the body. Patients will return to the emergency setting if oral medicine is not given to supplement the effects of the fast-acting injectable agent.

These reactions are common in young people who begin treatment with antipsychotics, particularly the high-potency Haldol or Prolixin, and therefore anticholinergic drugs are given along with them to prevent dystonic reactions and other EPS.

· Another frightening acute side effect of antipsychotics, particularly high-potency ones, is the *oculogyric crisis*. A patient's eyes may suddenly and painfully appear to be "stuck" in the tops of the eye sockets. Often only the whites of a patient's eyes can be seen. This hurts, and also frightens patients. Injections of Cogentin or Benadryl will stop the crisis. Patients should also be started on oral medication to prevent a recurrence of an oculogyric crisis, since drugs given by intramuscular injection to stop this side effect are usually short-lived.

2. *Subacute EPS* occur within days to weeks after beginning an antipsychotic drug, and can manifest as akathisia or parkinsonism.
   · *Akathisia* may be one of the most frequent causes of patients' noncompliance with antipsychotic medication. Akathisia is a profound sense of restlessness. Sometimes people with this side effect are seen walking ceaselessly, moving, standing, sitting, sauntering. Akathisia can be a cause of insomnia. After a few moments in bed, the akathisic patient will get up and move around. She cannot sit still or feel at rest. Sometimes the effect is not visible, but is more internal, that is, a subjective state of restlessness. Decreasing the dose of the antipsychotic or administering a low dose of an *anticholinergic*, an *anxiolytic* (e.g., **benzodiazepine**), or a *beta-blocker*, such as **propranolol** (Inderal), will stop the restlessness. Increasing the dose of antipsychotic medicine will only make akathisia worse.
   · Antipsychotics can make patients appear to be suffering from Parkinson's disease (a condition known as *parkinsonism*). Characteristics include akinesia (lack of movements), masked facies (the patient's face lacks emotion, like a mask), rigidity (patient may walk stiffly or have cogwheeling rigidity, where the patient's arm

or wrist may feel like a cogwheel when the clinician passively flexes the patient's wrist or arm), shuffling gait or walk, diminished movement of the arms when walking, and a slow rhythmic tremor of the hand or arm (parkinsonian tremor), which is usually present at rest (this can be the "pill rolling" tremor, where the patient's thumb rolls over the index finger as if there was a pill between the fingers, or a small circular movement of the whole hand, arm, or leg at rest). These side effects can be treated with the oral use of *anticholinergic* drugs.

3. *Long-term effects* can be seen within months to years after starting an antipsychotic medicine.
   • *Tardive dyskinesia (TD)*, the most common long-term side effect, is sometimes irreversible and can occur any time after taking an antipsychotic for more than three months. It presents as sudden, jerky movements of the body, which come and go, such as sudden eye blinking or oral-buccal-lingual movements (puckering movements of the lips, puffing movements of the cheeks, or flicking movements of the tongue). The extremities may also be involved.
     TD occurs in about 20 percent of patients on long-term antipsychotic therapy. There is evidence to suggest that the cumulative dose of antipsychotic is what puts a patient at risk for developing TD. Therefore, in the long-term maintenance treatment of a psychotic illness, "less is more"—one should keep the antipsychotic at the minimally effective dose to avoid TD. Every time a patient is seen, ask him to open his mouth, keeping the tongue in; watch for "vermiform" movements of the tongue (rapid, darting, worm-like tongue movements)—this is often an early warning sign of the development of TD.

ANTICHOLINERGIC SIDE EFFECTS

Anticholinergic side effects often occur when antipsychotic drugs block muscarinic receptors, areas that bind the neurotransmitter acetylcholine, and include dry mouth, blurred vision, fast heart rate (tachycardia), constipation, difficulty urinating, and (in severe cases) confusion and delirium.

These side effects can be particularly severe in elderly patients, who have a low tolerance for anticholinergic side effects. These occur most commonly with the low-potency antipsychotics, such as **thioridazine**

(Mellaril). The high-potency drugs, such as Prolixin HCl and Haldol, have the least anticholinergic side effects. These high-potency medicines are therefore often used for geriatric patients who require antipsychotic treatments.

HYPOTENSION

Antipsychotic agents can cause transient drops in blood pressure, called orthostatic hypotension, particularly when a patient goes from a lying or sitting position to a standing position. It is found most commonly with the low-potency antipsychotics, particularly with **chlorpromazine** (Thorazine). Hypotension is another reason why the high-potency antipsychotic drugs are used with older patients, who may easily fall and fracture their hips or other bones if they become dizzy from a drop in blood pressure.

SEDATION

The low-potency antipsychotics are most sedating, another reason these compounds are not frequently used in elderly patients who can fall from drowsiness and sedation.

MISCELLANEOUS SIDE EFFECTS

Antipsychotics can cause literally dozens of other side effects. We will list a few more.

1. Galactorrhea

   Dopamine connections from neurons in the hypothalamus inhibit the production of human milk. This normal inhibition of lactation is reversed by antipsychotic drugs and can thereby cause the abnormal secretion of milk, or galactorrhea. Decreasing the dose or changing to another form of antipsychotic drug will sometimes resolve the problem.

2. Impotence

   This side effect is most frequent with the lower potency antipsychotics, particularly with Mellaril, which can rarely cause problems with ejaculation. Clinicians should always ask their male patients on long-term drug therapy whether they are having any abnormal sexual side effects. Many patients are shy about discussing this issue. It can certainly be a significant cause of medication noncompliance.

3. Seizures

Antipsychotics (especially low-potency ones) can lower the seizure
threshold and may increase seizure activity in some patients with a
seizure disorder.

4. Neuroleptic malignant syndrome (NMS)

NMS is rare, but may be fatal in more than 10% of cases. The
syndrome presents with one or more of the following signs:
  · Fever, sometimes low-grade, sometimes extreme
  · Rigidity, which can be dramatic; the patient's arms and legs can
    be as stiff as a "lead pipe"
  · Delirium or confusion
  · Dysautonomia, (that is erratic pulse and blood pressure)
Lab tests can help diagnose this condition. Extreme muscle rigidity
and breakdown of muscle tissue can cause elevated CPK enzymes
and WBC, as well as a release of myoglobin, another muscle tissue
component, which can be found in the patient's urine (myoglobinu-
ria can also lead to kidney failure). It is important to recognize
NMS, as it is an unusual occurrence, and it will then be imperative
to discontinue the antipsychotic medicine immediately.

This is a potentially life-threatening syndrome. The patient must
be hospitalized on an internal medicine ward or, if the symptoms
are severe, in the intensive care unit. Medicines such as **bromocriptine** and **dantrolene** are used to treat the physical effects; **benzodiazepines** can be used to treat muscle relaxation. In addition, cooling
blankets and intravenous hydration are necessary in cases of extreme fever. Patients who have had NMS should *never* again be
given the specific antipsychotic agent thought to have caused the
syndrome, as rechallenge with that drug will probably precipitate
the NMS once again.

ATYPICAL ANTIPSYCHOTICS

Clozapine (Clozaril) is effective in approximately one-third of patients
who have treatment-resistant schizophrenia. Clozapine may also not
cause TD and, in some instances, may provide a treatment for refrac-
tory TD. Clozapine also is effective in treating some of the negative
effects of schizophrenia, such as social withdrawal, lack of motivation,
lack of interest, etc. Clozapine may, however, cause a significant and

potentially fatal side effect called agranulocytosis (lack of granulocytes, the white blood cells that fight off bacterial and other infections). Thus, every patient who takes clozapine must undergo a weekly blood count. Crisis clinicians must be aware of the potential for agranulocytosis and should obtain a blood count on any patient who presents with a fever, sore throat, malaise (significant fatigue), or signs of infection. If the dose is too high, clozapine can cause seizures; thus, patients must not receive more than 900 mg per day (most patients are in the 400–700 mg range). Finally, patients on clozapine should not take *benzodiazepines* to avoid a possible sudden respiratory failure and death. If a patient stops taking clozapine for a significant amount of time, he or she should only begin again at the lowest dose and gradually build back up to the previous dose level over days or weeks.

Risperidone (Risperdal) is the latest antipsychotic on the market. Like clozapine, it treats both positive and negative symptoms of schizophrenia; unlike clozapine, it does not lead to agranulocytosis and has a mild side effect profile.

ANTIANXIETY AGENTS (ANXIOLYTICS)

Clinical Uses

A number of medicines are effective in diminishing anxiety. The safest and fastest-acting are the *benzodiazepines*. The prototype drugs of this class are **chlordiazepoxide** (Librium) and **diazepam** (Valium). Some of these medications are metabolized primarily in the liver and require extensive metabolic work by the body to excrete them. A problem can occur if the patient has significant liver disease and these medicines accumulate to high levels. **Oxazepam** (Serax) and **lorazepam** (Ativan) do not require such extensive degradation and are therefore safe in patients with or without liver disease.

As mentioned in earlier sections, **lorazepam** (Ativan) is an ideal drug for use in the crisis or emergency setting. It can be given in five ways: by mouth (p.o.), intramuscular injection (i.m.), intravenous injection (i.v.), under the tongue (s.l.), and per rectum (p.r.). Most benzodiazepines are not well absorbed through muscle tissue, so lorazepam is an exception. This makes it quite useful in treating emergency patients with high degrees of agitation or anxiety. A markedly agitated patient can be helped to calm down quickly with 2.0 mg Ativan, i.m. or p.o. Lorazepam can also be mixed with a high-potency antipsychotic to quickly diminish psychotic agitation states. It may also have a moderate antimanic property. Most patients will be calm, and many will be asleep following an injection of lorazepam.

Another injectable benzodiazepine is **midazolam** (Versed). This drug is not used routinely due to its potential adverse effects on respiration.

Ativan or any of the benzodiazepines can also be used to treat alcohol withdrawal. Psychiatrists sometimes use benzodiazepines with oral doses of antipsychotics in the long-term management of schizophrenia. Certain benzodiazepines are useful in the treatment of panic disorder, especially **clonazepam** (Klonopin) and **alprazolam** (Xanax).

The crisis clinician should be familiar with all the benzodiazepines. A drug named **buspirone** (BuSpar) is also used to treat generalized anxiety, but often takes days or weeks to curtail a patient's high levels of nervousness. BuSpar has the advantage of not reacting with alcohol the way benzodiazepines do (see below).

Side Effects of Benzodiazepines

In general, the benzodiazepines are very safe drugs, but a few side effects should be kept in mind.

SEDATION

Too much benzodiazepine can cause drowsiness or impair task performance (e.g., driving, reading). Patients must be warned not to mix these drugs with alcohol as they act synergistically to depress the function of the nervous system and, in high dose, may cause serious respiratory depression. The intravenous antagonist drug, **flumazenil** (Remazicon), can almost instantly reverse decreased consciousness or decreased respirations caused by too much benzodiazepine (e.g., a Valium overdose).

ADDICTION

A minority of patients may become addicted to benzodiazepines. (This should not preclude the use of these drugs for the short-term management of agitation in the emergency setting). Caution must be exercised in prescribing benzodiazepines for outpatients with a history of addiction or alcoholism. Watch out especially for the patient who feels euphoric from the drug, is using higher and higher doses, or mysteriously "loses prescriptions."

WITHDRAWAL

If benzodiazepines are terminated abruptly in patients who have been taking them for a long time, a withdrawal syndrome may develop. Patients may experience tremors and shakiness, fever, racing pulse, high blood pressure, confusion, anxiety, hallucinations (often visual), seizures, delirium, and even death. This syndrome can begin from 24 hours to 10 days following the cessation of the drug (depending on the drug used). Patients in benzodiazepine withdrawal delirium require medical hospitalization.

DISINHIBITION (PARADOXICAL EXCITATION)

Usually an injection of Ativan will relax a person and help him calm down and fall asleep. Uncommonly, a patient may experience the opposite effect and become excited and more agitated. This paradoxical excitation may occur in patients with a history of significant organic brain injuries, infections of the nervous system, or dementia.

ANTIDEPRESSANTS

Clinical Uses

Antidepressants are used in treating depression, panic disorder, obsessive compulsive disorder, bulimia, and many other psychiatric syndromes.

Classical Tricyclics

These were the main treatments of choice until the 1980s when other antidepressants appeared. *Tricyclic antidepressants* (TCAs) include **imipramine** (Tofranil), **desipramine** (Norpramin), **nortriptyline** (Pamelor), and **amitriptyline** (Elavil), among many others.

TCAs are very effective, but do have significant side effects. Often it is necessary to have a patient on a maximum dose (often up to 300 mg per day) for at least three weeks before the drug can be deemed ineffective. If the dose or blood level is too high or is out of the therapeutic range (e.g., nortriptyline must be in the 50–150 blood level range to be considered effective), then the patient may show signs of toxicity or poor antidepressant effect. Tricyclics often have significant anticholinergic side effects (blurred vision, dry mouth, rapid heart beat, constipation, urinary retention, confusion), produce orthostatic hypotension, and, in high doses, may produce seizures or disturbances in heart rate. They are very effective drugs, however, and are often required to treat severe states of depression.

As mentioned in chapter 20, crisis clinicians should worry about any patient who takes a TCA overdose. Only 1.0 gram (i.e., 1000 mg, or 20 50-mg tablets) can cause death. These overdoses are very frightening to emergency room physicians. Many ER doctors can recall the patient who has taken a TCA overdose, walked into an ER, and died in less than one hour. A patient who has taken such an overdose must rush to an ER for medical emergency treatment. TCA overdoses may cause lethal cardiac conduction abnormalities that will eventually stop the heart. Intravenous sodium bicarbonate can sometimes diminish the toxicity on the heart. Patients in crisis should never be given more than half a gram (500 mg) total of a TCA on the first visit until a firm therapeutic alliance with a therapist is formed. If a depressed patient attempts suicide, 500 mg will not kill the patient; 1000 mg or more, however, may.

A patient who has taken a TCA overdose should be admitted to a medicine service (often on a "monitored bed" to evaluate their heart rhythms) if any of the following are found during a six-hour observation period after the overdose:

- A change in mental status (no matter how slight), such as sedation, decreased concentration, or confusion
- A change in the patient's cardiogram, no matter how insignificant the EKG abnormality is!
- A toxic blood level or toxic dose (> 1.0 grams) of the TCA

Monoamine Oxidase Inhibitors (MAOIs)

Phenelzine (Nardil) and **tranylcypromine** (Parnate) are the two MAOIs most frequently used. These agents act by inhibiting the monoamine oxidase enzyme, which is partially responsible for the metabolic breakdown of certain neurotransmitters. There are two potential side effects to be anticipated with the MAOIs: orthostatic hypotension and the hypertensive crisis. The hypotension often responds to a dose reduction or, if severe, will mandate a change to another drug. A patient switching to another type of antidepressant must wait *at least* 14 days before beginning the new drug. Otherwise, the new medicine may cause a hypertensive crisis. It takes about 14 days for the MAO enzyme to regain its full metabolic function.

Certain foods or drugs can interact with MAOIs, resulting in a hypertensive crisis and causing a stroke or death. Patients must be warned to stay away from foods high in tyramine content, such as blue cheese, aged cheeses, wine and beer, smoked meats and fish, food additives, among others. They must avoid medicines such as antihistamines, epinephrine (often found in local anesthetics), Demerol (a pain medicine), or other antidepressants. Patients who are taking MAOIs should probably carry a card or Medalert bracelet stating that they are on an MAOI drug, as well as 10-mg **nifedipine** (Procardia) tablets, to place under the tongue in case of an inadvertent hypertensive reaction. Signs of such high blood pressure would include severe head and neck ache, dizziness, numbness or tingling, faintness, nausea, and other unusual signs. Patients with such symptoms must report to an ER for a blood pressure check. Patients on MAOIs should also carry a list of all the foods and medicines to be avoided. These lists can be obtained from psychopharmacologic texts, pharmacists, and the PDR (*Physician's Desk Reference*).

MAOIs can be very effective in treating atypical depression, where the depressed patient has increased somnolence, is sensitive to interpersonal rejection, craves carbohydrates, and is often quite anxious. MAOIs are also effective in treating panic disorder.

Some Other Antidepressants

Amoxapine (Asendin) is used mainly in the treatment of psychotic depression. It is closely related to the antipsychotic **loxapine** (Loxitane). Amoxapine has caused several cases of TD and, in overdose, causes severe seizures and cardiac problems.

Maprotiline (Ludiomil) ushered in a new phase of tetracyclic compounds; it can cause seizures and cardiac problems in overdose.

Bupropion (Wellbutrin) may slightly increase the incidence of seizures in certain patients — those with a history of eating disorder or primary seizure disorder. Bupropion probably is ineffective in treating panic disorder, whereas all other antidepressants are probably effective in blocking panic attacks. Recent investigations suggest that patients with bipolar II disorder who are on bupropion may experience fewer episodes of antidepressant-induced manic spells relative to other antidepressants. (As mentioned in chapter 21, every depressed patient must be asked questions to rule out a bipolar disorder. If you are treating a depressed bipolar patient, a mood stabilizing drug should be used in conjunction with an antidepressant, otherwise the antidepressant drug can induce a manic episode.)

Trazodone (Desyrel) is often used in small doses (50 mg) to help patients sleep. There have been rare reports of trazodone causing priapism in male patients. Priapism is a prolonged, painful erection—a urologic emergency often resulting in impotence. This risk must be kept in mind when prescribing the drug in young men.

SSRIs and Beyond

The SSRI (serotonin specific reuptake inhibitor) drugs act on the serotonin system of neurons. **Fluoxetine** (Prozac) is the prototype drug. It was followed by **sertraline** (Zoloft) and **paroxetine** (Paxil). A new type of compound that predominantly affects the serotonin and noradrenergic neurotransmitter systems is called **venlafaxine** (Effexor). In early 1995, **fluvoxamine** (Luvox), a new antidepressant effective against obsessive compulsive disorder, arrived on the market. **Nefazodone** (Serzone) is also a newly marketed antidepressant.

SSRIs are very safe drugs with milder side effects (headache, nausea, diarrhea) than the TCAs or MAOIs. Some patients can develop increases in blood pressure on high-dose Effexor, so patients' blood pressures should be monitored on this medicine. SSRI drugs are safe even in overdose (unless mixed with large quantities of other drugs or alcohol). Therefore, unlike TCAs, SSRIs can be started in a crisis situation for treatment of major depression with neurovegetative signs if the patient will be appropriately followed up until he or she is "locked into" more definitive outpatient care. Again, this makes the SSRIs ideal agents to be used by crisis programs, due to the low risk of cardiac toxicity in overdose.

MOOD STABILIZERS AND ANTICONVULSANTS

Lithium was first discovered as a drug in the late 1940s but didn't come into widespread use until the 1970s. Lithium is primarily used as a mood stabilizer, but is also used in the treatment of depression, often in conjunction with antidepressants. The therapeutic range for lithium is usually 0.8 to 1.2 mEq/liter. If the blood level is maintained below that range, lithium may not be effective in preventing recurrence of mania. On the other hand, if the blood level begins to increase significantly, the patient will show signs of lithium toxicity. Severe dehydration or certain diuretics or anti-inflammation medicines such as **ibuprofen** (Motrin) can cause an increased blood level of lithium. Potential signs of toxicity include frequent urination, tremor of the hands, nausea, vomiting, diarrhea and confusion. In the emergency situation, it is always useful to check a lithium level in a patient on lithium who presents with agitation and signs of confusion and mania. Occasionally, a patient with lithium toxicity can present with symptoms that exactly mimic mania. Patients with lithium toxicity should be admitted to a medicine unit for intravenous hydration and observation. In severe cases, patients may require dialysis (usually with levels of lithium >2.0 to 3.0, or above).

Typical starting doses of lithium carbonate would be 900 to 1200 mg per day. Lithium is often given in b.i.d. or t.i.d. dosage (twice a day or three times a day, respectively). Lithium can also produce some disturbing long-term side effects such as psoriasis, polyuria (frequent urination), hypothyroidism, and cognitive dulling.

Carbamazepine (Tegretol) is an anticonvulsant used to treat complex partial seizures. In addition, it is useful in the treatment of bipolar disorder, particularly in patients who have a rapid cycling form of illness (four or more episodes of illness per year). Rapid cyclers may be resistant to lithium, and there is some evidence that those patients may respond better to anticonvulsants. The usual starting dose is 200 mg once or twice a day, building up over several days to a dose of 400 mg or more, administered b.i.d. The dose range will often need to be increased beyond this range, as carbamazepine will "auto-oxidize," that is, induce the liver to form enzymes that will break down and metabolize the drug faster. Therefore, a patient's blood level should be monitored, to stay in the range of approximately 8 to 12 mcg/ml. Doses below that range may be ineffective, whereas above that range a patient may experience signs of drug toxicity, such as dizziness, staggering gait, and sedation.

Two potential side effects are of note with carbamazepine. One is aplastic anemia, a potentially fatal decrease in the bone marrow's production of all blood cells. Fortunately, this is rare. However, if the patient reports any serious bleeding or infection, an immediate CBC (complete blood count) should be performed. Another side effect, which often complicates the initiation of treatment with carbamazepine, is the development of SIADH (syndrome of inappropriate antidiuretic hormone), which results in the dilution of the body's sodium level. Patients may present with confusion, weakness, lethargy, seizures, or a worsening of their psychiatric syndrome. A serum sodium test will diagnose this. Often the dose of carbamazepine must be diminished and then increased more slowly, and the patient may require fluid restriction until the serum sodium level returns to normal.

Carbamazepine has also been used to treat alcohol withdrawal and appears to be as safe and effective as some of the benzodiazepines. Finally, clinicians should remember that carbamazepine can reduce a patient's blood level of haloperidol. This may explain why a psychotic patient maintained on Haldol worsens when carbamazepine is added to the medication regimen. The haloperidol dose should be monitored accordingly.

Valproic acid (Depakene) or its salt, **sodium valproate** (Depakote), is another anticonvulsant used for the treatment of bipolar disorder. It may be best for the treatment of dysphoric mania, where the manic patient has simultaneous feelings of depression or irritability. Valproate is usually begun at a dose of 250 mg t.i.d. and can be increased to bring the patient's blood level into a range of 50 to 100 mcg/ml or higher, depending on the patient's clinical condition. Side effects can include nausea, tremor, sedation, or liver inflammation (rare in adults, common in children). Periodic liver function tests and blood levels should be monitored in patients. Enteric-coated valproate appears to be easier on a patient's stomach, and may cause less nausea.

Current studies are looking at "valproate loading" to treat acute mania. There is evidence that this technique (using 20 mg/kg of body weight over 24 hours, or about 1500 mg/day in a 70 kg [150 lb] person) can break manic symptoms quickly, perhaps better than the traditional modes of treatment. A parenteral (intravenous) form of valproate is currently being investigated.

All the mood stabilizer drugs can be used to treat bipolar disorder, as well as episodic agitation and violence, which may be associated with head injuries, seizures, mental retardation, or other organic illnesses. Sometimes, combinations of agents must be used, for example, valproate + lithium, etc., if symptoms are only partially controlled.

A FEW OTHER MEDICATIONS OF NOTE

- **Clondine** (Catapres), originally marketed as a drug to treat high blood pressure, is used to treat Tourette's disorder (a movement disorder manifested by motor tics and other phenomena such as coprolalia [involuntary cursing]), attention-deficit/hyperactivity disorder (ADHD), and withdrawal from opiates. It can be useful for opiate addicts in withdrawal in the ER. Blood pressure must be carefully checked. Clonidine can be taken orally or absorbed through the skin via a skin patch. The latter is particularly effective in patients with ADHD. Clonidine can sometimes be helpful when stimulants (Ritalin, Cylert) or antidepressant trials are ineffective in the treatment of ADHD.
- **Disulfiram** (Antabuse), when taken with alcohol, will cause a patient to become violently ill (flushing, chills, nausea, vomiting). Alcoholic patients sometimes use this medication to help them to avoid drinking.
- **Zolpidem** (Ambien) is a relatively new drug used to treat insomnia.
- **Naltrexone** (ReVia) is a long-acting opiate antagonist, initially marketed under the name of Trexan, and first developed for the treatment of opiate addiction. The drug may be used in combination with other effective psychosocial treatments to prevent relapse binge drinking in alcoholics.

Pharmacologic treatments in psychiatry change on a rapid basis. New ideas and techniques of intervention occur almost weekly. The explosion of knowledge in the neurosciences has allowed researchers to develop a vast array of effective, safe treatments for people who suffer from severe mental disorders.

This chapter is only a general overview that summarizes some of the important medicines with which every crisis clinician should be familiar. The clinician should frequently consult the *Physician's Desk Reference* and speak with physicians, nurses, and pharmacists. Most of all, the patient must be consulted. Simplicity of treatment regimens and lack of side effects predict successful treatment. Complicated drug treatments can increase the likelihood of noncompliance, side effects, and drug-drug interactions. These potential complications can make the difference between successful treatment or a recurrent series of crises and emergencies. Treatment of psychiatric illness is often empirical—antidepressants can be effective with depression, OCD, panic, or established symptoms of PTSD. The astute crisis clinician will want to read broadly and widely. These drugs work, sometimes dramatically. They can form a powerful tool and knowledge base for the emergency mental health clinical specialist.

SUGGESTED READINGS

Arana, G. W., & Hyman, S. E. (1991). *Handbook of psychiatric drug therapy* (2nd ed.). Boston: Little, Brown.

Maxmen, J. S., & Ward, N. G. (1995). *Psychotropic drugs: Fast facts* (2nd ed.). New York: Norton.

CONCLUSION: RESEARCH
AND THE FUTURE

O brave new world . . .
— *William Shakespeare (The Tempest)*

THE FIELD OF EMERGENCY psychiatry will increase in importance as health care dollars become scarce and as greater emphasis is placed on alternatives to costly hospitalization of patients. Managed care is already in full-swing. Thus, high-quality research should assist health care policymakers in determining cost-effectiveness strategies for treating psychiatric crises in the most clinically meaningful, yet efficient fashion.

Unfortunately, much of the literature in emergency psychiatry is dated, nonrandomized, and often poorly controlled. Recently, some improved studies have been performed, but in general, the field of emergency psychiatry research is wide open. Further research is needed into cost-effective, comprehensive clinical and service interventions in the field of crisis/emergency management and services. Future research might include the following studies:

- *Needs assessment*, to characterize the population served in terms of demographics relevant to predicting the need for services: area population size, age, income, utilization of existing services. Such studies would form the basis for the initial planning of an emergency service.
- *Utilization studies*, to characterize the population who actually use

275

a particular emergency service either in terms of demographic variables such as age, sex, race, and income, or clinical variables such as diagnosis, repeated use of the emergency service, and presenting complaint.

- *Service description,* to study costs, costs per unit of service, staffing patterns, staff recruitment, stress, and job satisfaction.
- *Quality assurance,* to evaluate whether the quality of treatment meets certain standards; quality assurance studies look at process rather than outcome.
- *Outcome measurement,* including hospitalization, return to the emergency service, completed or attempted suicide or assault, symptom change, compliance with follow-up treatment recommendations, and client satisfaction.
- *Controlled comparisons,* to compare outcomes before and after alterations in the service.
- *Cost effectiveness.* Can one program or intervention produce results equal to another at lower cost in terms of dollars or staff time?
- *Diagnostic research,* to define a clinical entity, address the utility of various diagnostic categories, and identify risk factors and predictors of outcome. Particularly relevant to the emergency setting is the study of posttraumatic stress reactions, suicides, delirium, acute psychoses, and responses to disasters. For example, there still is no biological test or psychological marker that can be used to truly predict a patient's suicide.
- *Severity index.* It would be very helpful to have a measure by which to "triage" or prioritize psychiatric emergencies. There are few, if any, standardized behavioral indices which are routinely used in the crisis/emergency setting.
- *Intervention,* to evaluate the response to particular treatment intervention. Ideally, such studies should be double-blind (for instance, neither the patient nor the clinician knows who is receiving a medication and who is receiving a placebo), randomized, and controlled comparisons of a particular intervention against the standard treatment and/or no treatment. New forms of rapid tranquilization, pharmacologic treatment, and psychosocial interventions must be studied in rigorous ways.

The field of emergency psychiatry is truly in its infancy. Perhaps in the next decade we will be using techniques that can instantly measure or identify the patient's illness or predict the outcome of certain treatments. Wouldn't it be wonderful to have a hand-held PET scanner or quantitative MRI scanner that could immediately identify and differentiate acute mania or schizophrenia? This may seem far-fetched, but the technology is virtually here. Good images of the brain can now be accomplished in seconds by chemical imaging techniques. Such technologic advances would give more credibility to the illness concept (i.e., if you can see and measure the pathology in the brain, then there is something wrong) and would make for more fascinating research.

Training also needs to be advanced. Wouldn't virtual reality and computerized multimedia training be ideal for crisis clinicians? Newer drugs and medication techniques may be discovered and used to help patients improve more dramatically. Brain research will lead us to these new advances. Soon, a parenteral form of valproic acid will be available. Could this be used to "break" mania in an ER or holding bed area, the way that an ER can often "break" a patient's asthma attack?

Better psychosocial advances need development. We need to systematically study what the best forms of therapeutic intervention are to motivate substance abusers for treatment. Should AA or NA representatives be available to every ER and crisis setting? Should all substance abusers see a film on chemical dependency prior to ER discharge? Should case managers take an alcohol-dependent patient home and, with the patient's permission, remove all alcohol from the patient's home? What are the risks and advantages of such an idea?

What about comorbidity? Should everyone brought to the ER setting be screened for panic, PTSD, OCD, or other disorders? Are prevalence rates of a certain disorder low in psychiatric emergency populations, or are they low because we do not routinely screen for these disorders?

Should crisis interventions be mobile, ER-based, or clinic-based? Which is more costly? Which is more effective? What works when crisis services are called to help the police? What is contraindicated? How do you cover large rural geographic spaces? Should rural clinics and ERs have telemedicine hookups with experts in mental health emergency services? Should police in the field or EMS also have that capability? Should crisis clinicians be trained like "mental health paramedics" to administer emergency psychopharmacologic medicines to people in the field?

We wish you well in your future endeavors as you teach, learn, and research more in the area of crisis and mental health emergency work. There is no field in psychiatry as difficult, as challenging, or as rewarding.

SUGGESTED READINGS

Arana, G. W., & Hyman, S. E. (1991). *Handbook of psychiatric drug therapy* (2nd ed.). Boston: Little, Brown.

Bengelsdorf, H., Levy, L. E., Emerson, R. L., & Barile, F. A. (1984). A crisis triage rating scale: Brief dispositional assessment of patients at risk for hospitalization. *The Journal of Nervous and Mental Disease, 172*(7), 424–430.

Curry, J. L. (1993). The care of psychiatric patients in the emergency department. *Journal of Emergency Nursing, 19*(5), 396–407.

Ellison, J, M., Hughes, D. H., & White, K. A. (1994). An emergency psychiatry update. *Hospital and Community Psychiatry, 40*(3), 250–260.

Gutheil, T. G. (1990). Ethical issues in confidentiality. *Psychiatric Annals, 20*(10), 605–611.

Hillard, J. R. (Ed). (1990). *Manual of emergency clinical psychiatry.* Washington, DC: American Psychiatric Press.

Hillard, J. R. (1994). The past and future of psychiatric emergency services in the U.S. *Hospital and Community Psychiatry, 45*(6), 541–543.

Hyman, S. E., & Tesar, G. E. (1994). *Manual of psychiatric emergencies* (3rd ed.). Boston: Little, Brown.

Kalogerakis, M. G. (1992). Emergency evaluation of adolescents. *Hospital and Community Psychiatry, 43*(6), 617–621.

Kaplan, H. I., Saddock, B. J., & Grebb, J. A. (1994). *Synopsis of psychiatry,* Baltimore: Williams & Wilkins.

Puryear, D. A. (1992). Proposed standards in emergency psychiatry. *Hospital and Community Psychiatry, 43*(1), 14–15.

Stroul, B. A. (1991). *Profiles of psychiatric crisis response systems.* Rockville, MD: National Institute of Mental Health.

Zealberg, J. J., Christie, S. D., Puckett, J. A., McAlhaney, D. M., & Durban, M. (1992). Mobile crisis program collaboration between emergency services and police. *Hospital and Community Psychiatry, 43*, 612–615.

Zealberg, J. J., Santos, A. B., & Fisher, R. K. (1993). Benefits of mobile crisis program. *Hospital and Community Psychiatry, 44*, 16–17.

Zealberg, J. J., Santos, A. B., Hiers, T., Ballenger, J. C., Puckett, J., & Christie, S. (1990). From the benches to the trenches: Training residents to provide emergency outreach services—A public academic project. *Academic Psychiatry, 14*(4), 211.

INDEX

accessibility
  of emergency psychiatric services, 39
  to inpatient care, 41–42
access to care, through a crisis team, 19
acetaminophen (Tylenol), overdose of, 216–17
acetylcholine, 197
N-acetylcysteine, for acetaminophen poisoning, 216–17
acetylsalicylic acid (aspirin), overdose of, 217
addiction
  to benzodiazepines, 266
  genetic components of, 135
adjustment disorders, 243–44
administration, of shelters, 179
adolescents, 123–37
adrenocorticotropic hormone, 197
advocacy
  for adolescents with conduct disorders, 133
  by the mental health clinician, 3–8
affect
  assessing, in a mental status exam, 208
  in mentally retarded patients, 151
aggression
  by media representatives, 166–67
  in mentally retarded patients, 152
agitation
  in homeless patients, 144–45
  management of, 105–11
  in mentally retarded patients, 151
agoraphobia, 153–54
  and panic attacks, 232
  in a retarded woman (case example), 150
agranulocytosis, as a side effect of clozapine, 265

AIDS
  dementia associated with, 221
  among prisoners, 147
akathisia, from antipsychotics, 261
alcohol
  and amnesia, alcoholic blackouts, 223
  and cocaine, interactions, 226
  and depression, 24–27
  disorders related to, 223–26
  and suicidal ideation, 117–18
  testing for, 213
  and validity of psychiatric examinations, 215–16
allergies, to drugs, 202
alliance with crisis patients, 24–29, 107, 163
  case examples, 169
  and their families, 127
  see also treatment alliance
alprazolam (Xanax)
  for panic disorder, 266
  withdrawal syndrome, 202
Alzheimer's dementia, 221–22
Ambien, see zolpidem
amitriptyline (Elavil), 267
amnesia, dissociative, 240–41
amnestic disorders, 222–23
amoxapine (Asendin), for psychotic depression, 269
amphetamines, disorders associated with, 228
Anafranil, see chlorimipramine
anorexia nervosa, 241
Antabuse, see disulfiram
anticholinergic drugs, for the elderly, 140
anticholinergic side effects, of antipsychotics, 262–63

anticonvulsants, interactions with other drugs, 152
antidepressants, 267–70
    for adolescents, 130
    for children, 122
    for clinical depression, 236
    for panic disorders, 232
antipsychotics, 259–64
    atypical, 264–65
    dystonic reaction to, 260–64
    for elderly patients, 140–41
    side effects of, 260–64
antisocial personality disorder, 247–48
anxiety
    alcohol-induced, 225
    cocaine-induced, 227
    of law enforcement personnel, 160
    norepinephrine in, 197
anxiety disorders, 231–34
anxiolytics, 231, 265–67
aplastic anemia, as a side effect of carbamazepine, 271
arrest, crises following, 146–48
Asendin, see amoxapine
aspirin (acetylsalicylic acid), overdose of, 217
assessment
    absolute indications for hospitalization, 35–36
    by a crisis team, accuracy of, 19–20, 123–26
    of elderly patients, 138
    in the emergency room, 199–217
    of imminent danger to self or others, 31–33
    mental status examination, 204–12
    personal, before civil commitment, 96
    of prisoners, 145–46
    quick, of violent patients, 110
    of retarded patients, 150–52
    of risk of suicide, 114–16
    tips on interviewing, 74–75
    of willingness to comply with recommendations, 33–34
Ativan, see lorazepam
attention-deficit/hyperactivity disorder
    in aggressive adolescents, 134
    clonidine for, 273
authority, lines of, in disaster relief, 186
autonomy, of rational adults, 88
avoidant personality disorder, 251

barbiturates, withdrawal syndrome, 202
barricade situations, 157
behavior, controlling violent patients, 107–10
behavioral modeling, of family dysfunction, 203

Benadryl, see diphenhydramine
benzodiazepines
    for akathisia, 261
    for anxiety, 232, 265
        in natural disasters, 177
        in paranoid personality disorder, 245–46
    interaction with clozapine, 265
    for neuroleptic malignant syndrome, 264
    side effects of, 266–67
    withdrawal syndrome, 202
benztropine (Cogentin), 7
    for dystonic reaction to antipsychotics, 260–64
    emergency supply of, 58
beta-blockers
    for aggressive mentally retarded patients, 152
    for akathisia, 261
    depression as a side effect of, 202
    for intermittent explosive disorder, 243
biopsychosocial interventions, xiv, 29
bipolar disorder, 236–37
    in adolescents, 123–24, 135
    case examples, 155–56, 168
    differentiating from cocaine abuse, 228
Blumenthal, S. J., 114
borderline personality disorder, 248–49
brain, 193–98
    effects of injury to, on speech, 207
brainstem, 196
breathing-related sleep disorders, 242
brief psychotic disorder, 239
Broca's aphasia, 207
Broca's area, 194–95
bromocriptine, for neuroleptic malignant syndrome, 264
bulimia nervosa, 241–42
bupropion (Wellbutrin), 232
    side effects of, 269–70
BuSpar, see buspirone
buspirone (BuSpar), 266
    for aggressive mentally retarded patients, 152
butyrophenones, antipsychotics used in a crisis setting, 259

caffeine, disorders associated with, 228
callback system, safety provisions in, 70–71
Campbell, Mary, 67
cannabis, disorders associated with, 228–29
carbamazepine (Tegretol)
    for adolescents with psychiatric disorders, 134
    for bipolar disorder, 271–72
    for depression, 236

caregivers, interviewing children in the presence of, 121–22
Carter, Nancy, 173
case examples
  alcohol use, in an adolescent, 124–25
  antisocial personality disorder, 256–57
  axis I disorders, 254, 255
  axis II disorder, 255–56
  bipolar disorder
    political considerations in threats of, 155
    son of a VIP, 155
  borderline personality disorder, young woman, 27–29
  child, parent's fear of, 120
  cocaine-induced disorders, 255
  communication, with a suicidal patient, 169
  crisis situation, contact with precipitating individuals, 169–70
  depression
    in an adolescent, 130
    in a child, 122
    crisis situation, 168–69
    emergency room visit, 24–27
  emergency room, anger of patient in, 91
  homelessness, 144–45
  manic-depressive woman, in care of family, 4
  narcissistic personality disorder, 256
  panic attacks, in a retarded woman, 150
  paranoia, crisis situation, 170
  schizophrenia
    chronically ill man, 9–12
    ethics in mobile crisis response, 91–92
  suicide
    crisis situation, 168
    failure of system communication, 40
  terminally ill suicidal patient, 92–93
  violent behavior, 106–7
case management, responsibility for, 44
CAT approach, to violent or agitated patients, 106
Catapres, *see* clonidine
CDCMHC, *see* Charleston/Dorchester Community Mental Health Center
central nervous system, acute effects of alcohol on, 117–18
cerebellum, 196
cerebrovascular accident, aphasia following, 194–95
Charleston/Dorchester Community Mental Health Center (CDCMHC), 174–75
children, special problems in managing, 120–22

chlordiazepoxide (Librium), 265
  withdrawal syndrome, 202
chlorimipramine (Anafranil), for obsessive-compulsive disorder, 233
chlorpromazine (Thorazine), 258, 259
  hypotension as a side effect of, 263
Christie, Scott, 88
cimetidine (Tagamet), delirium as a side effect of, 220
civil commitment, 95–97
clinical disorders, DSM-IV classification, 219–23
clinic-based client interviews, space for, 54–55
clinicians
  feelings toward patients with personality disorders, 244–45
  managing difficult situations, 65
clonazepam (Klonopin)
  for agoraphobic patients, 153
  for panic disorders, 266
clonidine (Catapres)
  for aggressive retarded patents, 152
  for opiate withdrawal, 230
  for Tourette's disorder, 273
clozapine (Clozaril), for schizophrenia, 264–65
Clozaril, *see* clozapine
cocaine, disorders related to, 226–28
Cogentin, *see* benztropine
cognitive function, changes in an emergency room patient, 205
cognitive maps, disruption in disaster, 188
communication
  with chronic or manipulative callers, 63–65
  in a crisis situation, 158, 163–64
  in emergency psychiatric services, 40
  equipment for, 56–57
  fostering within the crisis team, 50–51
  with law enforcement personnel, continuing, 79
  after a natural disaster, 181
  by telephone, guidelines for, 159–60
    addressing crisis patients, 61–62
    thanking collaborators, crisis situations, 166
community
  disaster preparedness in, 175–84
  expectations of, and limitations of crisis teams, 22
community-based care, 37–45
  advantages of, 41
  for the elderly, 138–39
  planning for, in case of disaster, 176

comorbidity
    of DSM axis I and axis II disorders, 254
    in substance abuse, 231
complex-partial seizures, in the temporal
        lobe, 195–96
conduct disorders, in aggressive adolescents,
        133–34
confidentiality
    in crisis situations, 166–67
    ethical considerations in, 89–90
    legal considerations in, 93–95
confirmation of patient histories, 204
consultation, during a crisis situation, 163
control, in a crisis situation, 161–62, 164
conversion disorder, 234
Cooper, P., 129
Corcoran v. United Healthcare, 100
corticotropin releasing hormone, 196–97
cost-effectiveness
    of crisis teams, 20–21
    of psychiatric emergency programs, 38
court order, for psychiatric evaluation, 170
crack cocaine, 27–29, 226–28
Creutzfeldt-Jakob disease, dementia in, 222
crisis prevention, 38–39
crisis services, 160–63
    advantages and disadvantages of, 16–22
    triaging access to, 21–22
crisis teams
    communication within, 50–51
    cost effectiveness of, 20–21
    debriefing of, 167
    efficiency of, 20
    equipment for, 56–57, 159–160
        natural disaster checklist, 178
    identification of, tags for, 55
    meetings among supervisors, 42
    mobile, entering a disaster area, 184–89
    personal qualities of members, 49–50
    role in natural disasters, 183
    support for suicidal adolescent, 132
    vehicles for, identification of, 57
critical situations, collaborating with law en-
        forcement personnel in, 157–70
culture
    changes in, and adolescent management,
        125–26
    sensitivity to
        and ethical values, 90
        in interviewing, 75
Cushing's disease, 237
cyclothymic disorder, 236

dantrolene, for treating neuroleptic malig-
        nant syndrome, 264

debriefing
    after a crisis situation is resolved, 158, 167
    during recovery from natural disasters,
        184
    for volunteers in disaster relief, 186
    in work with law enforcement personnel,
        79
decanoate drugs, 260
defiance, in adolescents, 132–34
delirium
    causes of, 21, 206, 219–20
    from cocaine intoxication, 227
    evaluating
        in the emergency room, 201–2
        tests for, 213
    as an indication for hospitalization, 36
    tactile hallucinations associated with, 210
delusional disorder, 239
dementia
    in elderly patients, 139–40
    evaluating, 221–22
Depakene, see valproic acid
Depakote, see sodium valproate
Department of Mental Health, coordination
        of disaster work through, 175
Department of Social Services
    integrating services with, 45
    referral to, of elderly patients, 139
dependent personality disorder, 251–52
depersonalization disorder, 241
depression
    in adolescents, 124, 129–30, 135
    affect in, 208
    case examples, 24–27, 168–69
        child, 122, 130
    in children, 122
    clinical, 235–36
    hypothalamic-pituitary-adrenal axis, dys-
        function in, 197
    impaired concentration associated with,
        212
    involvement of serotonin in, 197
    neurovegetative signs of, 203
    norepinephrine in, 197
    pseudodementia in, 222
    in retarded patients, 152
    speech patterns in, 207
desensitization, for panic disorder, 154
desipramine (Norpramin), 267
Desyrel, see trazodone
developmental changes, stress from, 37–45
developmental crises
    in adolescents, 126
    in the mentally retarded, 149
diabetes, agitated behavior in, 106–7

Diagnostic and Statistical Manual of Mental Disorders (DSM-IV), 218–57
diazepam (Valium), 265
  addiction to, and withdrawal, 231
  withdrawal syndrome from discontinuation of, 202
differential diagnosis, of bipolar, schizoaffective, and schizophrenic disorders, 239–40
Dilantin, *see* phenytoin
diphenhydramine (Benadryl)
  for dystonic reaction to antipsychotics, 260
  emergency supply of, 58
disaster, natural, 173–89
disorientation, following disaster, 187–88
dissociative disorders, 240–41
disulfiram (Antabuse), 273
documentation
  in emergency psychiatric services, 40, 97–98
    barricade situations, 158, 159
  of emergency room consultation, 87
  on returning a "suicidal" patient to jail, 148–49
  securing records in anticipation of disaster, 177
  see also log sheet
Donnatal, *see* phenobarbital
dopamine, 197
Down's syndrome, dementia developing in middle age, 221–22
droperidol (Inapsine), 259–60
  for agitated retarded patients, 151
  emergency supply of, 58
DSM-IV, *see* Diagnostic and Statistical Manual of Mental Disorders
due process, 96
DuRand, C. J., 145
Durban, Maria, 77, 119, 157
duty to protect, 94–95
duty to warn, 91
dysarthric speech, 207
dysthymic disorder, 236

eating disorders, 241–42
Effexor, *see* venlafaxine
Elavil, *see* amitriptyline
elderly patients, 120, 137–39
emergency, defining in terms of immediate danger, 6
emergency medical services, collaboration with, 83
emergency psychiatric services
  availability of, 39

integration in the community, 39–40
integration in the mental health system, 43–45
multidisciplinary approach, 40
emergency room
  assessment in, 199–217
  consultation, 85–86
  defining a safe area in, 54–55
  defining services from and to, 45
  handcuffing violent prisoners in, 149
  maintenance of mental health areas, 55
  managing violent and agitated patients, 105–111
  personnel, 82–84
  priority in natural disaster, 174
  protocol for work in, 81–87
  referral to, after a crisis standoff, 166–67
  triaging a patient to, 69
    for intoxicant clearance, 146
    safety considerations, 105
empathy, with a chronic or manipulative caller, 63–65
entitlement, sense of, in mentally ill homeless people, 144–45
epidemiology, of suicide risk, 31–33, 114
EPS, *see* extrapyramidal side effects
ethical issues, 89–93
  confidentiality, and the duty to protect, 94–95
  confidentiality, of patients in crisis situations, 166–67
evacuation plan, for shelters, 177
evaluation, *see* assessment
extrapyramidal side effects (EPS) of antipsychotics, 260

factitious disorders, 235
family
  of adolescents, 128–29
  cost-effective reduction of burden on, 20
  crisis in, and adolescent assessment, 123
  interviewing separately, 74–75
  response to emergency situation, 5–6
  separation of arguing members of, 127–28
  therapy for, 43, 136
    multisystemic, 133
family system
  and adolescent crises, 124
  and adolescent depression, 131
Federal Emergency Management Agency (FEMA), 175
Federal Employee Retirement Security Act, 100
feedback, to a violent patient, 108

FEMA, *see* Federal Emergency Manage-
    ment Agency
field work, protocol for, 67–76
financing, concern of mental health pro-
    grams, 42–43
Finkenbine, Ryan, 88, 258
Fisher, Richard K., 16
flumazenil (Remazicon), for treating benzo-
    diazepine overdose, 266
fluoxetine (Prozac), 197, 270
    for eating disorders, 242
    for obsessive-compulsive disorder, 233
    side effect of, with hallucinogen use,
        229
fluphenazine (Prolixin), 259
    emergency supply of, 58
fluvoxamine (Luvox), for obsessive-
    compulsive disorder, 233
follow-up, 75–76
    for prisoners, 147, 149
formication, 210
freon, respiratory arrest from inhaling, 229
frontal lobe, 194–95
    injury to, effect on affect, 208
frontal lobotomy, 195
fugues, dissociative, 240

generalized anxiety disorder, 234
goals
    of an emergency room consultation, 84–
        87
    of a mobile crisis program, 42
    of a mobile visit, 67–68
    for supervisors, 51–52
Goodyer, I., 129
Go-Teams, for disaster response, 182–83
Grave's disease, 199

Haldol, *see* haloperidol
hallucinations
    auditory, 209–10
    documenting, 205–6
    olfactory, 210
    tactile, 210
    visual, 210
hallucinogens, disorders associated with, 229
haloperidol (Haldol), 7, 106
    as an antipsychotic, 259–60
    emergency supply of, 58
    for hallucinogen treatment, 229
Hardesty, Susan J., 77, 157, 173
headache, history of, 203–4
health insurance, xiii
heroin, disorders associated with, 229–30
history
    in barricade situations, 159

family, to identify links with genetic ill-
    nesses, 203
    guidelines for gathering, 205
    of headache or seizures, 203–4
    interviewing family and friends, crisis situ-
        ation, 162
    of mental illness, 37–38
    pertinent to the current problem, 126–27,
        201
    pertinent to the drug abuse, 136
    of violence, as a predictor, 111
histrionic personality disorder, 249–50
homeless patients, 142–45
home visit, for a child in crisis, 121
homicidal intent, 205, 210–11
hospitalization
    for adolescents, 136–37
    indications for, 30–36
    involuntary
        in bipolar disorders, 237
        schizophrenic man, 10–11
        in personality disorder, 245
        in phencyclidine-caused disorders, 230
        in refusal of an emergency room visit, 5
        of a suicidal patient, 116–17
Hughes, Mary, 67
Huntington's chorea, 203, 222
hypersomnia, primary, 242
hyperthyroid patients, 199, 237
hypnotics, disorders associated with, 231
hypochondriasis, 235
hyponatremia, identifying in the emergency
    room, 214
hypotension side effect
    of antipsychotics, 263
    of monoamine oxidase inhibitors, 268–69
hypothalamus, 196–97

ibuprofen (Motrin), interaction with lith-
    ium, 271
imipramine (Tofranil), as an antidepressant,
    267
impulse-control disorders, 243
    in adolescents, 134
Inapsine, *see* droperidol
incidents, critical, 79
Inderal, *see* propranolol
infectious disease precautions, 72
information, telephone calls seeking, 69
informed consent
    ethical basis of, 90, 92
    language as a barrier to, 90
inhalants, disorders associated with, 229
inpatient care, xiii
    accessibility to, 41–42
    community-based, 8

limitations of, 12
  see also hospitalization
insomnia, primary, 242
intensive care settings, accessibility to, 41–42
intermittent explosive disorder, 243
interviewing a patient, 74–75
  adolescent, 127–29
  in the emergency room, 200–204
  special considerations with children, 121–22
intoxication
  alcohol, lethal effects of, 224
  cocaine, 227
  and suicidal ideation, 117–18
introductions, 72–73, 107–8
involuntary treatment
  ethical consideration in, 90
  justice and fairness issues in, 89

jail clearance, 145–46
  guidelines for, 148–49
jails, liaison with, 43
juvenile justice system, 133–34

Klonopin, *see* clonazepam
Korsakoff's syndrome, 223, 225
Kulbok, P. A., 113
Kupfer, D. J., 114

laboratory testing
  to identify causes of dementia, 222
  offering from the emergency room, 212–17
law enforcement personnel
  collaboration with, 77–80, 83–84
  cost-effectiveness of working with, 20
  defining crisis services with, 44–45
  help from, 69–70
    in managing violent patients, 105, 127–28
  response to an emergency request, 4–5
  safety responsibilities of, 7, 157–70
learning disability, in aggressive adolescents, 134
least restrictive settings, 18
  ethical considerations in preference for, 90
legal issues, 93–101
  on entering a residence, 72
  in sexual or physical abuse, 134
legal system
  involuntary hospitalization, 89
  juvenile justice system, 133–34
Lesch-Nyhan syndrome, and self-injurious behavior, 151

liaison
  between the crisis team and community resources, 21, 41, 44
  with jails, 43
Librium, *see* chlordiazepoxide
licensing, temporary, for disaster relief teams, 185
limbic system, 196
limit setting
  for adolescents, 125
    depressed, 129–30
  in antisocial personality disorder, 247–48
  for chronic telephone callers, 64
  in a prison setting, 146
lithium, 7, 270–71
  for adolescents with psychiatric disorders, 134
  for depression, with a history of mania, 236
  effects on a fetus, 202
  side effects of, 271
location, of crisis evaluation, 71–72
log sheet, 14–15
  preparation by the clinician, 6, 65–66
  see also documentation
lorazepam (Ativan), 7, 28, 265
  paradoxical excitation, as reaction to, 267
  for agitated retarded patients, 151
  emergency supply of, 58
  hallucinogen treatment with, 229
  for histrionic personality disorder, 250
  for paranoid personality disorder, 245–46
loxapine (Loxitane), 259, 269
Loxitane, *see* loxapine
Ludiomil, *see* maprotiline
Luvox, *see* fluvoxamine

McAlhany, Deborah, 77, 157
McBride, Dona, 67
McCabe v. the City of Lynn, 96–97
malingering, by prisoners, 146–47
malpractice insurance, and law violation, 97
managed care, and hospitalization, 100–101
management
  structure in disaster relief, 185–86
  supportive, for crisis teams, 42, 43
management plan, involving the crisis service in, 63–65
mania
  affect in, 208
  in a crisis situation, 162
  in depressed patients, 236
  speech patterns in, 207
MAOIs, *see* monoamine oxidase inhibitors
maprotiline (Ludiomil), side effects of, 269
marijuana, disorders associated with, 228–29

media
    communication with, 166–67
    cooperation with
        in a crisis situation, 164
        in a disaster, 176
medical problems
    alcohol withdrawal delirium, 225–26
    evaluating
        in prescribing antidepressants, 122
        in retarded patients, 152
    excluding
        in emergency room patients, 199, 206
        in aggressive adolescents, 134–35
        in agitated patients, 106–7, 110, 144,
            152
        in agoraphobic patients, 153
        in amnesia, 222–23
        in elderly patients, 138–39
        in patients with mood disorders, 237
    trained volunteers to deal with, in disas-
        ters, 176–77
    treating, in prisoners, 147
medical staff, collaborating with, in emer-
    gency evaluations, 82
Medical University of South Carolina
    (MUSC), 175
medication
    adequacy of, in a crisis, 32–33
    for depressed patients with a history of
        mania, 236
    history of, 202
    interactions among, 152
    overdose of, and mobile team calls, 217
    securing supplies of, in a disaster, 177
Mellaril, see thioridazine
memoranda of agreement (MOAs)
    among community resource centers, 41,
        99–100
    with emergency room management, 82
mental health center
    communication with, 45
    follow-up treatment at, 11
mentally retarded patients, 135, 149–52
mental status examination, 204–12
    appearance, 207
    cognitive function, 211–12
    insight and judgment, 211
    mood and affect, 208
    perception, 209–10
    sensorium, 212
    speech, 207, 209
    suicidality/homicidality, 210–11
    thought content, 208
    thought process, 209–10
mesoridazine (Serentil), 259
    for paranoid personality disorder, 246

midazolam (Versed), 266
Miltown, withdrawal syndrome from discon-
    tinuation of, 202
MOAs, see memoranda of agreement
Moban, see molindone
molindone (Moban), 259
monoamine oxidase inhibitors (MAOIs),
    268–69
mood disorders, 235–37
    in adolescents, 135
    alcohol-induced, 225
    cocaine-induced, 227
mood lability, in a crisis situation, 162
mood stabilizers, 236, 270–72
Motrin, see ibuprofen
multidisciplinary approach, of emergency
    psychiatric services, 40
multiple sclerosis, amnesia associated with,
    222–23
MUSC, see Medical University of South Car-
    olina

naloxone (Narcan), for opiate overdose, 230
naltrexone (ReVia), for opiate addiction, 273
Narcan, see naloxone
narcissistic personality disorder, 250–51
narcolepsy, 242
Nardil, see phenelzine
National Institute of Mental Health, commu-
    nication with representatives of, in a
    disaster, 186–87
natural disasters, 173–89
    Hurricane Hugo, 179–84
    Hurricane Andrew, 184–87
Navane, see thiothixene
negotiation in a crisis situation
    with armed patients, 165
    failure of, 167–70
nervous system, 197–98
neuroleptic malignant syndrome (NMS),
    212, 264
neuroleptic medication
    for cocaine-induced psychotic disorder, 227
    side effects of, 212
neurologic examination, of emergency room
    patients, 214
neurons, 197
Newman, Rebecca, 119
nifedipine (Procardia), 269
NMS, see neuroleptic malignant syndrome
norepinephrine, 197
Norpramin, see desipramine
nortriptyline (Pamelor), 267
nurse manager, emergency room, collabora-
    tion with, 83
nursing care facilities, for the elderly, 139

obsessive-compulsive disorder (OCD), 233, 252–53
occipital lobe, 195
OCD, *see* obsessive-compulsive disorder
oculogyric crisis, response to antipsychotics, 261
opiates, disorders associated with, 229–30
outcomes, program, defining, 42
outpatient care, following crisis intervention, 7
outreach
  to agoraphobic patients, 153–54
  assertive, to disaster victims, 188, 189
  by clinicians, 42
  to homeless patients, 143
overhead costs, of mobile versus hospital-based services, 20–21
oxazepam (Serax), 265

pain disorder, 234–35
Pamelor, *see* nortriptyline
panic disorders, 231–32
  agoraphobia, 153–54
Paolone, Timothy J., 258
paranoia, in a crisis situation, 162, 170
paranoid personality disorder, 245–46
parasomnias, 242
parens patriae, 96
parietal lobe, 195
parkinsonism, as a side effect of antipsychotics, 261–62
Parkinson's disease, dementia associated with, 221
Parnate, *see* tranylcypromine
paroxetine (Paxil), 270
passive-aggressive personality disorder, 253
paternalism, 89
patient's rights
  to refuse treatment, 96
  and risk of imminent harm, 34
Paxil, *see* paroxetine
PCP, *see* phencyclidine
perphenazine (Trilafon), 259
personality change, medical conditions related to, 223
personality disorders, 244–54
  in chronic and manipulative telephone callers, 63–65
phencyclidine (PCP), 230
phenelzine (Nardil), 268
phenobarbital (Donnatal), withdrawal syndrome from discontinuation of, 202
phenothiazines, 259
phenytoin (Dilantin), testing levels of, in seizure patients, 204
phobias, 232–33

physical abuse, and defiant or aggressive behavior, 134
physical restraint, before approaching a violent or agitated patient, 108–9
Pick's disease, 222
Placidyl, withdrawal syndrome from discontinuation of, 202
polydipsia, assessing in an emergency room patient, 214
posttraumatic stress disorder (PTSD), 233–34
  in crisis clinicians, response to client injury, 167
  in response to natural disaster, 173
prediction of behavior, for the near future, 33
Prednisone, side effects of, 201
pregnancy, and prescription of medications, 202
presenting problems, of adolescents, 129–36
prisoners, working with, 145–49
problem, establishing the nature of, 126–27, 200–201
problem solving, with a telephone caller, 61
Procardia, *see* nifedipine
professional training
  in biopsychosocial techniques, 41
  place of mobile crisis services in, 17–18
  for staff, 49–52
profile, of the suicidal patient, limitations of, 113–18
Prolixin, *see* fluphenazine
propranolol (Inderal)
  depression as a side effect of, 202
  for intermittent explosive disorder, 243
protocols
  for collaborating with police department, 77–80
  for disaster work, 175
  for emergency room work, 81–87
  for field work, 67–76
Prozac, *see* fluoxetine
pseudodementia
  accompanying severe depression, 222
  in the elderly, 139
psychiatric disorders
  in defiant, aggressive adolescents, 133–34
  in the homeless population, 142–43
  resulting from disaster stress, 188
psychopharmacologic supplies, 57–59
psychopharmacologic treatment, 258–74
psychosis
  in adolescents, 134–35
  cocaine-induced, 227

psychosocial referral, for elderly patients in crisis, 139
psychotherapy, for adolescent depression, 130
PTSD, see posttraumatic stress disorder

rape, in prison, counseling for, 147
referral sources, interfacing with, 22
relationships, outside the family, relevance to adolescent patients, 124
relaxation techniques, for panic patients, 154
Remazicon, see flumazenil
requests for services
  in a critical situation, 159
  sources of, 17–18
    for the mentally retarded, 151
research, proposed, 275–76
resolution, in a crisis situation, 165
respect for the patient
  during assessment, 75
  as an ethical principle, 89
responses
  emotional, to disasters, 188
  mobile, to a distressed patient, 69
responsibility
  for hospitalization, 100
  of managed care organizations, 100
  patient's, for participating in a treatment plan, 8–9
  for psychiatric patients in the emergency room, 85
  for seeking crisis treatment, 3
  for a suicidal adolescent, 131–32
restraints
  for agitated retarded patients, 151
  procedure for releasing, 109–10
ReVia, see naltrexone
revolving door syndrome, xiii
Risperdal, see risperidone
risperidone (Risperdal), 265
Robins, L. N., 113

sadness, following losses in natural disasters, 182
safety
  assessing suicidal or homicidal intent by telephone, 62–63
  and confidentiality, legal issues, 93–94
  from dangerous confrontations, in hospitalization, 137
  in dealing with sociopaths, 248
  and need for hospitalization, 31–33

perception of, by a patient in a crisis situation, 165
of personnel, 69–70, 159
  after a crisis is resolved, 166–67
  during communication in a crisis situation, 161
  determining presence of weapons, 6–7, 21
  and political demands, 155
  in a prison setting, 149
  reentering devastated areas, 181
in responding to VIPs, 155
signs of danger, 73
telephone safety checks, 56–57
in working with potentially armed homeless patients, 143
see also law enforcement personnel; security personnel
scheduling, of staff, 42
schizoaffective disorder, 238–39
schizoid personality disorder, 246
schizophrenia, 237–38
  in adolescents, 123–24, 135
  affect in, 208
  involvement of dopamine in, 197
schizophreniform disorder, 238
schizotypal personality disorder, 246–47
school personnel, consulting, in assessing adolescents, 126
security personnel
  assistance from, in approaching violent patients, 108, 109
  in a crisis situation, 164
  emergency room, 83–84
sedation as a side effect
  of antipsychotics, 263
  of benzodiazepines, 266
sedatives, disorders associated with, 231
seizures
  history of, 203–4
  as a side effect
    of antipsychotics, 264
    of clozapine, 265
Serax, see oxazepam
Serentil, see mesoridazine
serotonin, 197
serotonin specific reuptake inhibitors (SSRIs), 197
  side effects of, 270
sertraline (Zoloft), 270
setting limits, see limit setting
severely and persistently mentally ill (SPMI) patients
  deinstitutionalization of, 8

sexual abuse, and defiant or aggressive behavior, 134
sexual dysfunction
  alcohol-induced, 225
  cocaine-induced, 227
  side effect of antipsychotics, 263
sexual relations, between a staff member and a patient, 90
shared psychotic disorder, 239–40
shelters
  for the homeless, interviewing in, 143–44
  in natural disasters, 176–77
side effects of medication
  and age, 138
  antianxiety agents (anxiolytics), 266–67
  anticonvulsants, 271–72
  antidepressants, 267–69
    monoamine oxidase inhibitors, 268–69
    serotonin specific reuptake inhibitors, 270
    tricyclic antidepressants, 267–68
  antipsychotics, 260–64
  atypical antipsychotics, 265
  and compliance, 10
  and delirium, 220
  lithium, 271
  mood stabilizers, 270–71
sign of illness, defined, 38
sleep, involvement of serotonin in, 197
sleep disorders
  alcohol-induced, 225
  sleep terror, 242–43
  sleepwalking, 243
social margin, loss of, by the homeless mentally ill, 142
social phobia, 233
social support system, *see* support system
sociopathic behaviors, consequences for, 147
sociopaths, in a hostage situation, 158
sodium valproate (Depakote), 272
  for depression, with a history of mania, 236
somatization disorder, 234
somatoform disorders, 234–35
space requirements, 53–55
special populations, 119–56
SPMI, *see* severely and persistently mentally ill patients
SSRIs, *see* serotonin specific reuptake inhibitors
standard of proof, for civil commitment, 96
Stelazine, *see* trifluoperazine
stress, secretion of cortisol during, 197

substance abuse
  accompanying depression, 236
  among adolescents, 135–36
  alcohol, defined, 224
  clearing intoxicants from prisoners, 146
  crack cocaine, 27–29
  in a crisis situation, 162, 168–69
  among the homeless, 142–43
  interview questions about, 203
  modeling of, by parents, 135
  motivating patients to accept treatment, 27
  testing for, 214–15
suicidal intent
  assessing by telephone, 62–63
  in cocaine withdrawal, 227
  of an emergency room patient, 205, 210–11
  and intoxication, 215–16
suicide, 113–18
  in adolescents, 130–32
  in adolescents with substance abuse problems, 137
  rate of, for jail inmates, 145
  risk for
    and age, 138
    after natural disasters, 184
supervisors
  aid from, with difficult patients, 64, 154–55
  goals for, 51–52
support groups, for physically abusive patients, 246
supportive listening, after a disaster, 183
support system
  for the crisis team, 41–43
  supervision for clinicians, 43
  connection with, 29
  establishing the nature of in an interview, 202–3
  and hospitalization, 31, 34–35
  importance after a disaster, 188
survivor's guilt, 182
symptom, defined, 38
synaptic cleft, 197
syndrome of inappropriate antidiuretic hormone, 272
systematization of emergency psychiatric services, 39–40
  security policies and procedures, 70–71
systemic lupus erythematosus, psychotic symptoms associated with medication for, 201

tacrine, for elderly patients, 140
Tagamet, *see* cimetidine

Tarasoff v. Regents of University of California, 94
tardive dyskinesia (TD), as a side effect of antipsychotics, 262
TCAs, *see* tricyclic antidepressants
TD, *see* tardive dyskinesia
teambuilding, 50–51
Tegretol, *see* carbamazepine
telephone
    crisis intervention via, 60–66
        the chronic or manipulative caller, 63–64
        general principles, 61
        the truly suicidal caller, 62–63
    initial contact via, 68–70
temporal lobe, 195–96
temporal lobe epilepsy, 195–96
tent cities, delivering services in, 187
therapeutic alliance, *see* treatment alliance
therapist, information from, 71, 126
thiamine
    administering to alcoholics, 216
    deficiency of, 223
thioridazine (Mellaril), 259
    anticholinergic side effects of, 262
    for paranoid personality disorder, 246
thiothixene (Navane), 144–45, 259
Thorazine, *see* chlorpromazine
Tofranil, *see* imipramine
Tourette's disorder, clonidine (Catapres) for, 273
training, for crisis clinicians, 277
translation, by family or staff, for retarded individuals, 151
transportation
    of patients, by emergency medical services or police, 166
    providing to the crisis team, 57
tranylcypromine (Parnate), 268
trazodone (Desyrel), side effects of, 270
treatment alliance, 7, 11, 29, 74–75, 168
    with adolescents, 128
    with agoraphobic patients, 153–54
    establishing by telephone, 61
    as a goal of a mobile visit, 68
    in an interview, 200–204
treatment plan
    for adolescents abused sexually or physically, 134

for chronic telephone callers, 64
for the elderly, 138–39
for suicidal patients, 116–17
tricyclic antidepressants (TCAs), 267–68
    overdose of, 217
trifluoperazine (Stelazine), 259
Trilafon, *see* perphenazine
Tylenol, *see* acetaminophen
Tyson, Shannon, 77, 157, 193, 258

unreasonable search and seizure, 97
urinary tract infection (UTI), delirium caused by, 213–14
UTI, *see* urinary tract infection
utilitarianism, 89

Valium, *see* diazepam
valproic acid (Depakene)
    for adolescents, 134
    for bipolar disorder, 272
venlafaxine (Effexor), high blood pressure as a side effect of, 270
Versed, *see* midazolam
very important persons (VIPs), managing, 154–56
video recording, in a crisis situation, 163
violence, management of, 105–11
VIPs, *see* very important persons

Wellbutrin, *see* bupropion
Wernicke's aphasia, 207, 225
Wernicke's encephalopathy, 216
Wickline v. State of California, 100–101
Wilson v. Blue Cross of California, 100
withdrawal syndrome
    from alcohol, 183–184, 225–26
    from benzodiazepines, 267
    from cocaine, 227
    delirium as part of, 220
    from diazepam, 231
    from opiates, 230

Xanax, *see* alprazolam

Zoloft, *see* sertraline
zolpidem (Ambien), for insomnia, 273